This book is dedicated
to my wife
Janet

SECRET YORK:
Walks within the City Walls

Les Pierce

Published by Sigma Leisure – an imprint of
Sigma Press, 1 South Oak Lane, Wilmslow, Cheshire SK9 6AR, England.

British Library Cataloguing in Publication Data
A CIP record for this book is available from the British Library.

ISBN: 1-85058-447-8

Typesetting and Design by: Sigma Press, Wilmslow, Cheshire.

Illustrations and painting for cover: Jim Park

Illustrations on pages 53 and 87: Zoë Hall

Cover Design: Manchester Free Press

Maps: Paul Eldred

Printed by: Manchester Free Press

Disclaimer: the information in this book is given in good faith and is believed to be correct at the time of publication. No responsibility is accepted by either the author or publisher for errors or omissions, or for any loss or injury howsoever caused.

Foreword

Some years ago, I was a stranger working in York and, during my lunch breaks, made an effort to acquaint myself with the delights of the city. I walked many miles through many streets and, because of those enjoyable excursions, I thought I had discovered the true York.

But in reading Les Pierce's book, I realise how little I had actually learned about York's host of secrets. There is indeed a secret York; it is a York that is part of our history and yet it is a York which has managed to avoid much of the public's attention. It is a York which has revealed itself to a chosen few – and Les Pierce is one of those fortunate people privileged to have gained an intimate knowledge.

For all that is widely known about this beautiful old city, there remains so much which is undiscovered, concealed or forgotten. In this well-planned book, Les Pierce uses his knowledge of York to reveal those secrets and his guidance is complemented by Jim Park's atmospheric drawings and Paul Eldred's intelligent maps.

Within these pages you'll find countless delights – like the potato robbery that never was, the need to exterminate cats in 1604, the fact that the Barbican centre stands on the site of a former cattle market, stories of old inns and an account of York's struggle to gain a university. These pages are packed with intriguing information – and it is information that you can enjoy as you tour the city armed with a copy of *Secret York*.

Nicholas Rhea

(Nicholas Rhea is author of the Constable books from which the ITV series "Heartbeat" is derived.)

Preface

So, why "Secret York"? After all, wherever you go in our wonderful treasure-house of a city, you can read informative plaques which tell you something about what happened, who lived, or what used to be, where you are standing.

I have tried to fill in some of the gaps left by the traditional guide books and give a more personal idea of what kind of people built and shaped the city, how they lived and some of the incredible things that used to, and in some cases, still go on.

However, any book on York can only give a glimpse of the place. There are so many layers, so many hidden corners and so many bits that are vanishing without trace. This guide cannot claim to be exhaustive or comprehensive. There are bound to be omissions but if "Secret York" encourages you to walk around with your eyes open and look up above street level, it will have achieved something.

The Bibliography indicates a number of books and publications which would be of interest to anyone wishing for further reading.

Some parts of the York jigsaw insist on retaining their secrets. For instance, who was the mysterious painter of Castlegate? Why was a city-centre warehouse used as a mortuary? Which city-centre barber shop was the scene of wild orgies even before the Swingin' Sixties and did Glenn Miller really visit York to have his hair cut behind screens? And why does the city have so many cats climbing up the wall?

And just when I thought the book was finished, the York Archaeological Trust and the ARC started a long-running excavation at the rear of Ellerker's Shop on Walmgate. Who's to say what treasures and/or surprises Feoffees' Yard (rhymes with Fifi) will yield? Who can tell whether the next excavation will find another Jorvik?

How to use "Secret York"? It is divided into seven Routes which you can follow into the city centre. Route 7 is the Central Area. Each Route has a map. On some of these, the outlying sections are on a smaller scale than the city sections and are drawn separately. This is simply so that places of interest can be indicated more clearly in relation to each other.

Places mentioned in the text are numbered and you will find the numbers on the Route map. Facing each map is a list of places featured. There is also an alphabetical list of places for each Route.

The Routes are more enjoyably followed on foot, because York is so walkable – most of the Routes should take no more than 45 minutes.

I would like to thank my wife and family for living with me while "Secret York" took shape. I am also grateful to the staff at York Central Reference Library and the Yorkshire Evening Press Library for their patient assistance. I thank Mr. Geoff Knaggs for being a mine of information and a constant source of encouragement. Ravi Cremona did a great job in reading through the manuscript and making many invaluable suggestions.

Finally, "Secret York" would not have looked so good without the unique talents of Jim Park and the timely help of Paul Eldred. Both have exceeded my wildest expectations.

Les Pierce

Contents

Route 1

Entering the City

Route Index

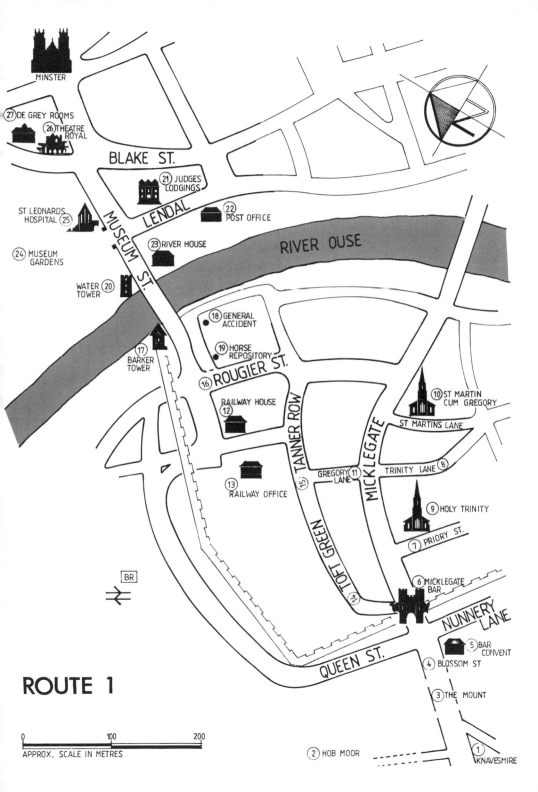

MINSTER

27 DE GREY ROOMS
26 THEATRE ROYAL

BLAKE ST.

21 JUDGES LODGINGS

LENDAL

22 POST OFFICE

ST LEONARDS HOSPITAL 25

23 RIVER HOUSE

RIVER OUSE

24 MUSEUM GARDENS

MUSEUM ST.

WATER TOWER 20

18 GENERAL ACCIDENT

19 HORSE REPOSITORY

17 BARKER TOWER

16 ROUGIER ST.

RAILWAY HOUSE 12

TANNER ROW

10 ST MARTIN CUM GREGORY

ST MARTINS LANE

MICKLEGATE

15 GREGORY LANE

11

TRINITY LANE 8

13 RAILWAY OFFICE

9 HOLY TRINITY

7 PRIORY ST.

TOFT GREEN

6 MICKLEGATE BAR

14

NUNNERY LANE

BR

5 BAR CONVENT

4 BLOSSOM ST

QUEEN ST.

3 THE MOUNT

ROUTE 1

0   100   200

APPROX. SCALE IN METRES

2 HOB MOOR

1 KNAVESMIRE

Alphabetical Index

The Route

This is the traditional route of entry to the city of York and you are in good company – most royal visitors have passed this way, in one way or another. It has certainly been the way to go for devotees of the sport of kings since 1730, when horse-racing started on the Knavesmire [1].

You will probably have noticed the big hotel which dominates the race-course. It used to be called the Chase Hotel. When the present York railway station was being planned, one Englishman and his castle stood in the way. He refused all offers of money and would only budge when the North Eastern Railway company promised to build him a new house. You have just passed it.

Long before that, however, the Knavesmire was the spot where many unfortunates met a sudden death. Until the late fourteenth century it was the monks who had the privilege of carrying out the death penalty – "infantheof" – on criminals caught in the act. This privilege extended over the villages of Bishopthorpe, Bilborough and Monkton. The gallows were situated near a place called Butt Close where the villagers of Dringhouses used to practise archery. Until a few years ago, a pub called "The Butt's Close" kept the association. The romantic connection was lost when the building became a bank.

Then, on 1st March 1379, following a riot by monks, the city bailiffs decided to move into the death business and ordered a new gallows to be built on ground opposite Hob Moor [2]. In those days, before computers and consultation procedures, they didn't hang about, and the gallows were constructed and erected within a week. A rapist, Edward Hewison, met his end before the month was out. They remained in place for over 433 years, their last victim being another rapist, and another Edward – Private Hughes of the 18th Dragoons, in August 1801. They were not removed until 1812.

One sorry tale perfectly illustrates how the story of York can weave in and out of time and pop up when you least expect it. On 3rd October 1696, Arthur Mangey was executed on the Knaves-mire for counterfeiting. He was a member of an old York family and a distinguished goldsmith. He moved to Leeds and made the civic mace for Leeds corporation for which he was paid

£60.11s.6d. on 3rd November 1664. Two years later he was charged with clipping and forgery.

In 1832 some old premises were being demolished in Briggate, the oldest part of Leeds and workmen found a small room concealed, and long forgotten, in the loft. Implements used in coining were recovered, as well as a shilling of 1567.

At Mangey's trial his accomplice and the chief prosecution witness, Norcross, stated that he saw him stamp a piece of mixed metal with the head of Charles II and that the coining took place in a small chamber in the roof of the house.

On 24th February 1993, a late seventeenth century silver trefid spoon bearing the Leeds Assay mark with the letters A.R.E. on the reverse of the bowl and a fleur-de-lys decoration came up for sale in the Malton auction room of Boulton and Cooper. The spoon also bore the maker's mark: A.M. A hush descended over a packed room and the spoon fetched £1,380.

Just opposite the site of the York Tyburn is Hob Moor. Nowadays it is an area of rustic peace and tranquillity but was once a sinister place where food and drink were brought and left by country people so that they didn't need to come too near to the plague-ridden citizens [2].

As you proceed nearer to the city you pass the Mount [3], a genteel area famous for its Quaker Girls' School and large hotels. Its other contribution to a better world is to provide a home for York's premier Big Band. The Modernaires Orchestra regularly rehearses and plays for dancing in the Church Hall of the English Martyrs, Dalton Terrace, as they have done since just after World War II.

Can you imagine a hot air balloon hovering high above the Mount? Such things are a common sight nowadays and you may even be able to see one as you read this. Imagine the view you would have from this balloon – the whole of York would be laid out beneath your gaze – as pretty as a picture.

Such a picture was made by Nathaniel Whittock in 1856 but he didn't use a balloon. He relied instead on detailed observations at ground level and it is remarkable how little has changed. You can buy a splendid book featuring a reproduction of the print from York City Art Gallery (See Route 6). Whittock had already done bird's-eye views of Oxford, Melbourne and Hull, plus three of London. He wrote the world's first manual of photography in 1839.

In the thirteenth century, it was the site of the Chapel of St James, where members of the Guild of the Hospital of St John of Jerusalem who had been unfortunate enough to be hanged could be brought for a Christian burial. This happened to one such member, John Elenstreng, in 1280 but then he was found to be alive. A King's pardon followed promptly and we don't know any more about him.

Much later, it was the scene of even greater turmoil when the Parliamentarians set up a gun battery to pound the city during the Civil War.

If the Mount conjures up thoughts of war let Blossom Street [4] soothe the troubled breast. The name is derived from "Ploxwangate" – Ploughman's Street. A Romano-British burial site was excavated here in 1990. One of the tombs contained an adolescent wearing hobnail boots.

Just between the cinema and the Windmill Public House on the corner another burial was explored – to reveal a nineteenth century greyhound.

On the corner of Blossom Street across from Micklegate Bar [6] stands the Bar Convent [5], home of two of the best-kept secrets in York. When the Convent was founded, Catholicism was just about tolerated as long as it kept a very low profile. Therefore when a chapel was built within the Convent it had to be done in secret so that none of it was visible from the outside.

The other secret was a painting, given to the Convent in the 1870s and long believed to be by the tutor of the seventeenth century French artist Eugène le Sueur. Then, the picture, a crucifixion scene, was exhibited in Leeds City Art Gallery and an expert recognised its true worth. It was a rare example of Eugène's work. When the Convent was facing closure in 1994 through lack of funds, it was decided to sell the painting. The auction exceeded all hopes and Le Sueur's secret masterpiece fetched almost four hundred thousand pounds – no sweat! It was bought on behalf of the National Gallery

It is a relief to arrive at the City Walls at last but just outside, on the corner, is the imposing Punch Bowl Hotel. We think of Political Correctness as a recent obsession but almost 200 years ago, even drinking habits came under close scrutiny. The Tories preferred claret, sack and canary wines – the flavours of the past. On the other hand, the Whigs wanted progress and change. What could be more fashionable than punch – the yuppie tipple of Georgian England? So the chances are that today's Punch Bowl Hotel was yesterday's hotbed of reform – at least until closing-time.

Passing through Micklegate Bar, you can read the informative notice for yourself. Spot the Shakespeare connection! The Micklegate Run is one notorious feature of life in the city. Exuberance has a long history in this area. There was a riot in Micklegate on 31st December 1546. Perhaps that is why the Bar provided accommodation for the local constabulary. The last person to be born in the Bar was Philip Walter Burgess – on 9th August 1908. His father was a policeman.

It is here that York is proclaimed as capital of the Yorkshire Ridings on 1st August each year.

You would probably be surprised at how many monasteries and convents there are still in York today but that number is insignificant compared to the Middle Ages. You end up wondering how such a compact city centre could find room for lay people when so much of its space was taken up by the religious orders and their great houses.

One such was the Benedictine Priory of the Holy Trinity. You will have to wait for Route 6 to see anything of it but for now only the names remain in Priory Street [7] and Trinity Lane [8]. Priory Street runs through the site of the thirteenth century gateway which was demolished last century to make way for Victorian houses. The "modern" street carries on the religious tradition by accommodating huge places of worship for various faiths from Baptists to United Reform. The York Directory of 1816 tells us that there was a Temporary House for the Friendless and Fallen at 7, Trinity Lane.

Standing back from the bustle of Micklegate is Holy Trinity Church. It was not always so aloof, having a hay-loft tucked in between the tower and the nave until 1897. A slaughter-house built as a lean-to was not pulled down until 1903 [9].

In medieval times the first Thursday after Trinity Sunday brought the Festival of Corpus Christi and with it the Mystery Plays. These plays were put on by the 92 separate trade associations or gilds within the city and everyone took part, from the Lord Mayor, councillors and clergy to the ordinary people. There were

55 tableaux with between five and six hundred performers and 120 torchbearers. They combined to tell the story of Christianity in a simple direct way that was moving emotionally as well as literally. Each play was performed on a cart which was dragged from place to place.

The last complete performance was in 1569 and the streets of York had to wait until 1994 for a repeat. About 700 local people re-created the first complete street performance of the Mystery Plays for 400 years. The carts were all hand-pulled and songs were plain-sung in the original Latin. Actors ranged from a donkey, through children, to a Parish Priest. The Ark was constructed by a boat-builder from Los Angeles. Even the weather was perfect and the whole event was a magical blend of past and present which encapsulated the secret of York's continuing popularity.

Apart from this authentic re-creation, the plays are regularly put on for the York Festival. They have usually taken place in the Museum Gardens, using the Abbey ruins as a back-drop. Actresses Mary Ure and Dame Judi Dench both attended The Mount School and made their public debuts in the Mystery Plays.

In the old days the first play – "The Creation" – began at Trinity Priory Gateway and by the time the first cart reached Pavement, another twelve were being played simultaneously. In 1397 Richard II came to the spot to see the plays for himself.

Just where the street turns to go down towards the river you will notice a very dignified house on the left which looks fit for a Lord Mayor – and so it was during the eighteenth century. Dark secrets lurk behind its imposing front door. It was very probably a home for cock fights which were held every morning of Race Week.

As you walk down Micklegate past these elegant town houses and before you digress by way of Gregory Lane [11] you could not feel further away from the country and yet two hundred years ago the country would have come to you. In the eighteenth century the main trade in York was butter. The product came of course from a wide area around about. An army of dairymaids would milk nine cows each for £9 a year and the butter would be brought in to the Butter Market in St Martin's Churchyard [10]. A Butter Stand had been there since the seventeenth century and the butter had to be of a high standard for the London market.

Salted butter could keep for at least a year and was shipped by brigantine from York to Hull and then by coastal vessels to the capital. In 1787 a labouring family with five children would eat half a pound of butter a week. This, with bread, was a staple diet. On the other hand, a middle-class family in London with four children and two maids would get through a pound of the stuff in a day. At 9d. (about 4p) a pound that was a lot of bread.

In the early nineteenth century, however, improved farming techniques meant that the Vale of York was producing richer butter which was creamier but didn't keep so well. This coincided with the spread of cheaper Irish butter which was starting to become flavour of the month with the London merchants. By 1820 the butter trade in York had melted away and in 1828 the Butter Stand was demolished.

So if you now digress along Gregory Lane you will find yourself on Toft Green [14], once the site of a Dominican Friary. It was also known as Pageant Green, because of its connection with the Mystery Plays. Back in 1814 it was the site of the House of Correction and before that there was a cattle market for fat beasts every Friday. Now it houses a well-known night-spot. No comment!

In case you're wondering about the name of Gregory Lane, it is all that remains of the Church of St Gregory, which was a casualty in 1547. It was amalgamated with St Martin's, which is now called St Martin-cum-Gregory. If you branched off along St Martin's Lane, it would be more a case of "Come Dancing" than "cum Gregory", since you would end up on Route 2, but more of that later.

Walk down the dismal road, just as Charles Dickens would have done as he left York's first Railway Station on his way to visit his brother who worked round the corner in an office which is now a hotel. But, as you return, don't expect the station-master to delay the train for your arrival. He wouldn't have done it for the great writer either. Nor will a porter provide a pair of foot-warmers for you if the weather is chilly, as he would do for Joseph Rowntree as he set off on his weekly day-out to Scarborough.

The huge red brick and stone building which stands behind graceful railings was purpose-built as railway headquarters [12]. It towers opposite another elegant edifice, now West Office, which was originally the Station Hotel [13] when it was adjacent to York's first station. Following a flying half-hour visit by Queen Victoria on 14th September 1854 it became the Royal Station Hotel. She stopped for lunch en route for Balmoral. Was this the first example of fast food on the Inter City?

As you pass by the iron gates, remember that this is not really a street. Until recently, a Railway Policeman used to stand on duty once a year and charge a penny toll, to maintain the Railway's rights of passage.

Then, as now, the Royal Family was always in the news. Their every move was of public interest. Royal watchers would have had to be pretty determined to find out about this flying visit, however. The "Yorkshire Gazette" of 16th September 1854 was its usual self but readers had first to wade through reports of the Ellerton-on-Swale Autumnal Vegetable Show, the Cholera epidemic at West Hartlepool and a breakdown on the Great Western Railway. Eventually, after a blow-by-blow account of the Cutlers' Feast in Sheffield, their patience was rewarded on Page 8.

The Queen had a punishing schedule. She had left Osborne on the Wednesday and spent the night at Buckingham House. On Thursday she left King's Cross on the dot at 8am and was to arrive in York at 12.45pm. The paper published the times of her passing through every station on the way. The platform at York Station was covered with a very rich tapestry carpet supplied by G. and H. Brown of High Ousegate.

Her Majesty alighted at 12.44pm and a sumptuous luncheon was served to the Royal party. A splendid luncheon was reserved for her attendants. She remained in the Station Hotel (which was henceforth called the Royal Station Hotel) thirty minutes precisely and the whole journey from London to Edinburgh took 10 hours 45 minutes.

The hotel landlord then allowed inquisitive members of the public to pass through the suite of apartments used by the honoured visitors. Having satisfied their curiosity, readers of the Gazette were allowed to catch up on the really important matters of the day like the meeting of the Eskdale and District Horticultural Society, the St Leger and the Cesarewitch Stakes.

At the foot of Tanner Row [15], don't blink or you might miss

York's central bus station [16]. The bulk of General Accident (Part I) completely obliterates the fact that once a whole community lived on the site, housed in Colton's Hospital. The tiny low building was even then in the shadow of the great comb factory of Thomas Rougier. The Rougiers left France around 1686 and landed at Liverpool. After many enterprises they settled in York and around 1794 started a horn factory. This was a great success – they supplied combs to the Royal Family – until 1931 when they went out of business.

Bear right and walk towards the River. Just before Lendal Bridge you will notice an odd little round building standing half in the water, half on land. This is the Barker Tower [17]. Oak bark was an essential ingredient in the leather tanning process.

Occasionally the tower is more in the water than out – perhaps befitting its former use as a mortuary for those unlucky enough to drown in the treacherous Ouse.

You cannot have avoided noticing the vast stone-clad building just before you crossed Lendal Bridge. This is the main office of General Accident Insurance Company [18]. It stands on the spot where Rowntrees had their first chocolate factory before moving out to Switzerland via Haxby Road.

Joseph Rowntree went there to help his brother with his Cocoa Works in 1862. It was an old iron foundry and employed a dozen men and a donkey. One of their star products was "Homoeopathic Cocoa" with arrowroot but it was only when a Frenchman called Claude Gaget showed them how to make Crystallized Gum Pastilles in 1879 that the business took off. Before the end of the century they had moved out to the new factory and in 1906 started one of the world's first pension schemes for over 4,000 employees.

The oriental-looking archways standing forlornly next to the pub on Tanner's Moat are all that remain of one of York's most splendid oddities – the Horse Repository [19]. Established in 1826, one of its owners used to live in the old Queen's Hotel on Micklegate. It was a huge multi-storey building and horses would climb a spiral ramp to reach their stables. It obviously stood much higher than the present arches and was resplendent with the words "Botterill's Horse Repository" in large Victorian lettering. The facility catered for a better class of horse. Whereas most would make do with an inn yard, the select few would find luxury accommodation and be cossetted within its brown and white glazed brick walls.

During the flood of 1947, the tarred oak briquettes which formed the floor floated up and the gates had to be hastily closed to prevent them disappearing downstream. It was demolished in the Sixties to make room for a different kind of horse power.

Across the river stands a more craggy-looking tower which was also used as a mortuary in 1879 and has an even more interesting past. After 1682 it stood quite a lot taller and was used as a Water Tower [20]. Half the city was supplied on Monday, Wednesday and Friday, while the other half received their liquid on Tuesday, Thursday and Saturday. We don't know what they used on Sunday but at Assizes and during Race Week, all citizens benefitted every day. They would do anything to impress the tourists, even in those days. The Waterworks used to have a suite of rooms containing plunge, warm, slipper, shower, vapour and medicated baths.

The rather attractive tree growing in front of the tower is a weeping elm, grown from a cutting brought from Napoleon's grave on St Helena. The Napoleon connection was visible until recently outside a sweet-shop in Lendal. A life-size wooden effigy of the Emperor used to stand on the pavement. The pace of modern life was too much for the old chap, apparently, and he had to be moved indoors.

The Judges' Lodging [21] stands on the site of St Wilfrid's Church which also failed to keep up with the pace of things back in 1547. Even the Post Office has a grand history, being built on the site of a Friary which existed between 1268 and 1539 [22].

As you crossed the river you will have noticed another substantial edifice with a boat yard directly beneath it. This is River House [23], possibly the North's poshest Bed and Breakfast. It was built before the motor age so that the landed gentry could doss down after living it up in the Assembly Rooms.

In those days, bridge-building was still a risky business. On 27th September 1861 the final girder was being lowered into place on the Lendal Bridge when it slipped and brought the whole structure crashing down, killing five workmen. A new design was chosen, based on Westminster Bridge and the girders were lifted out of the water and used to build the first Valley Bridge at Scarborough.

Many people who visit York enjoy a walk in the Museum

Gardens [24] and admire the antics of the peacocks and squirrels. Last century you had to pay a penny for the privilege but now all are free to view the atmospheric ruins of St Mary's Abbey.

Most visitors walk straight past the entrance of the gardens in their eagerness to get from Station to Minster and back again, and then completely ignore the ruins of the hospital of St Leonard's Priory [25] which stand next to York City Library. Not so long ago, the hospital – once the largest in the North of England – was the library, or at least, the Information Bureau.

The Priory, founded by William the Conqueror, and the Abbey were so close that their walls abutted.

Way back in the fifteenth century there lived in York a man called Jucundus. He lived so well and had such an ample form that he might have been called "Rotundus". After one exceptionally lavish banquet in honour of a new Lord Mayor he woke up feeling so wretched that he vowed henceforth to eat only bread and vegetables and to drink only water. He would also sleep but six hours out of the twenty-four.

Such a régime could only be found in one kind of establishment and since Health Farms had not yet been invented our friend opted for the brand of self-denial practised at St Leonard's.

With the passing of time and much water, Jucundus lost his merry, well-proportioned air and became comparatively thin and rather dispirited. Again he made a vow – one binge a year and then twelve months of beans and cabbage, fasting and misery. Unfortunately this vow coincided with York Fair. With its dancing dogs, spice stalls and drinking booths, this was a really serious opportunity to let your hair down, even if you were a monk. So, while his more disciplined brothers were still asleep, Jucundus marched off, with the porter's keys and a crown he had taken from his money box.

All might have been well if only Jucundus had known where to draw the line, but around midnight it was not so much a matter of where, as which one. Having been so good for so long our friend found it all too easy to give in to excess.

Early next morning, the monks arose and were called to find him reclining in a medieval version of a swing-boat. Catching sight of his confrères, Jucundus was capable only of giving out a mighty belch. The force of the eructation caused him to tumble out of the boat and, completely overcome with wine, he was wheeled home in a barrow. This was the easiest way of conveying the prone figure, and as they trundled through the narrow streets some of the monks were heard singing: "He ain't heavy, he's my brother."

His case was at once brought before the Priory Chapter; but there could be no leniency towards a man who had been caught napping in a swing-boat, and who could only offer a burp in his defence. They sentenced him to be walled up alive in a niche of the Priory cellar, and that without delay. As he was helped, or if truth be told, rolled down the cellar stairs his utterances made no more sense than they had in the swing-boat.

In only a few minutes, zealous monks mixed the mortar and brought bricks to wall up Jucundus in his living grave. There's no doubt that not many things clear the mind better than being walled up in a cellar and no sooner was the work complete than the unfortunate friar realised his predicament. He kicked and battled with such force that the wall behind him gave way and he rolled backwards into the cellars of the Abbey of St Mary.

Sobered by his exertions, he mounted the stairs and found himself among the brethren of the Benedictine Order – an order so severe that they were only allowed to speak on Easter Day. Thus it was that no-one asked Jucundus how or why he came to be there, but merely accepted him as a new recruit.

Twelve months and a day passed and the monk in charge of the cellar died. By a happy quirk of fate, Jucundus, who had been a model of sobriety, was invited by the Abbot to fill the vacancy. He gladly accepted and eagerly commenced his duties. As soon as his comrades were asleep, he repaired to the cellar to renew acquaintance with other long-lost friends. Come the dawn and Jucundus was nowhere to be found. After a long and fruitless search, the monks, who could wait no longer for their breakfast, headed for the cellar. There the new guardian of the spirits was to be observed, flat on his back beneath a large barrel of red wine lately brought by the Abbot from Gascony.

To the Benedictines, thirsty for beer after their early morning labours, all the culprit could offer by way of explanation was a loud belch which echoed round the vaulted cellar like rumbling thunder. A Chapter of the order was held on the spot and, after excommunication by bell, book and candle, it was decreed that the guilty brother should be walled up alive on the scene of his crime.

So, in that very cellar, a convenient recess was found – the identical one out of which the offender had rolled a year and a day before. He was bricked and mortared just as efficiently as before, offering wind as his only resistance.

By one of those amazing coincidences with which our history is bedevilled, the cellarer of St Leonard's had just then descended to his wine-vault to prepare for his comrades' dinner. Little wonder that the prisoner's bellowing burps alarmed him. He hastened his brothers to the very place, where they stood as if transfixed by a holy apparition – and distinctly recognised the asyllabic eruptions which issued almost supernaturally from the cold stones of the cellar. It could be no other than the long-lost Jucundus. It was a miracle! Hands tore down the wall even more eagerly than they had built it up and with excited voice they shouted:

"Jucundus, our Prior! Saint Jucundus, our Head and Father!"

And on the shoulders of his erstwhile brethren, the errant monk was borne joyfully to the seat of the recently deceased Prior.

At the time of the Dissolution, the Priory of St Leonard's was worth £500 11s 1d, compared with the Abbey of St Mary's, which brought £2,085 1s 5d into King Henry's greedy coffers. We do not know the state of their wine cellar in 1540 but we may assume that with a man like Jucundus at their head, the last years of monastic life were merry ones, at least for the monks of St Leonard's.

Continue along Museum Street and then turn left at the traffic lights and you will soon be at the Theatre Royal [26]. The site has had a variety of uses. Starting out as the Hospital of St Peter it later became the Hospital of St Leonard. The Theatre Club bar has a vaulted ceiling which is almost all that remains, apart from the 15' deep well which is under the stage. This may have made life difficult in the intervening years when the site was a tennis court. We will meet another relic of the theatre's past on Route 3.

Opposite: The Theatre Royal

The Theatre Royal has had a long and varied history. D.W. Griffith's epic film, "Birth of a Nation", was shown here in November 1916. In 1992 it staged the Mystery Plays for the first time and has featured most of the "greats", from Berwick Kaler to Charlton Heston.

These few relics of the hospital are a poor memorial to the good works that were done in its past. In 1293 it cared for 229 men and women patients. At the gates, 232 loaves and 256 herrings were given away every week. On Sundays, 33 dinners were given out and washed down with 14 gallons of beer. Perhaps the winos and down-and-outs who congregate in the Museum Gardens are waiting for a return to the good old days.

In addition, 8 dinners were prepared for lepers and just so that no-one felt left out, each prisoner in the Castle received a Sunday loaf. Twenty-six boys were cared for in the orphanage.

Next to the Theatre Royal are the De Grey Rooms [27]. Built last century as a social centre for officers, it now houses the City's main tourist office. Upstairs, the elegant accommodation still echoes to music of a degenerate nature but it was surely in its prime during and just after the War when it throbbed to the beat of the Big Bands. One of the more memorable was led by a certain Johnny Sutton and featured a third trumpet player called John Prendergast. One day he produced one of his own compositions: "Lady de Grey". Next, the great Stan Kenton played one of his pieces during a concert at the Rialto and, before you could say "Rock 'n' Roll", he was on a plane to America and became world-renowned as John Barry. We shall meet him again on Route 3.

Route 2

Riverside Tales

Route Index

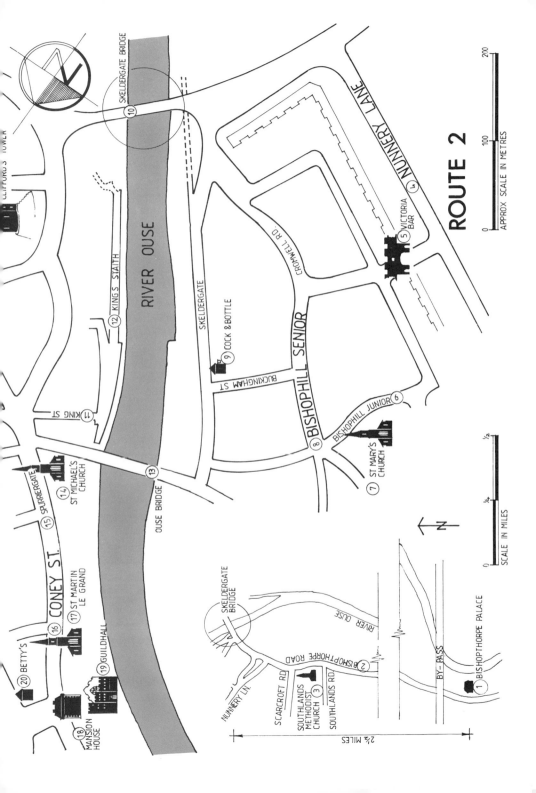

ROUTE 2

APPROX SCALE IN METRES
0   100   200

SCALE IN MILES
0   ¼   ½

N

2½ MILES

RIVER OUSE

KING'S STAITH

SKELDERGATE

CROMWELL RD

BUCKINGHAM ST

BISHOPHILL SENIOR

BISHOPHILL JUNIOR

NUNNERY LANE

CONEY ST.

SPURRIERGATE

SKELDERGATE BRIDGE

OUSE BRIDGE

KING ST

CLIFFORD'S TOWER

SKELDERGATE BRIDGE

BISHOPTHORPE ROAD

RIVER OUSE

NUNNERY LN

SCARCROFT RD

SOUTHLANDS RD

BY-PASS

1 BISHOPTHORPE PALACE
2 BISHOPTHORPE ROAD
3 SOUTHLANDS METHODIST CHURCH
4 NUNNERY LANE
5 VICTORIA BAR
6 BISHOPHILL JUNIOR
7 ST MARY'S CHURCH
8 BISHOPHILL SENIOR
9 COCK & BOTTLE
10
11 KING ST
12 KING'S STAITH
13 OUSE BRIDGE
14 ST MICHAEL'S CHURCH
15 SPURRIERGATE
16 BETTY'S
17 ST MARTIN LE GRAND
18 MANSION HOUSE
19 GUILDHALL
20 BETTY'S

Alphabetical Index

The Route

This route into the city starts with a glance in the direction of the peaceful village of Bishopthorpe. Nestling on a bend in the river Ouse is the Archbishop's Palace [1], a glorious hotchpotch of architectural styles. Largely built with stone from the earlier Archbishop's residence at Cawood Castle, one can think of no finer place to enjoy the calm of a summer day than its grassy waterside terrace.

One such fine day earlier this century, the Archbishop was entertaining a newly-elected Labour Prime Minister to tea. "Nice company you're keeping these days," called a passing bargee. Before the Primate could show his indignation the boatman shouted: "It was the Prime Minister I had in mind!"

In 1312 the warden of Galtres Forest, Hugh de Neville, had to provide wood and charcoal for the King's visit – a trifling amount of 100 oaks. No wonder there aren't too many forests around York nowadays.

Things really started to hot up in 1405, however, when Archbishop Scroope collected a large force in the same forest and marched against King Henry IV. Their protest was short-lived – they were betrayed and the leaders immediately conveyed to Pontefract Castle. That was always a bad sign and didn't bode well for career prospects. The King ordered them to be transferred to the Archbishop's Palace. He didn't bother with formalities like evidence or a trial. You might say that he was unscrupulous but in fact he merely wanted to be "Scroope-less". So he instructed a Judge to pronounce the death sentence. The Judge must have had a speech impediment so the King asked William Fulthorpe to pronounce it, which he did without too much difficulty.

The unfortunate Archbishop was promptly put onto a horse of little value and made to sit facing backwards and without a saddle. From there he was taken to a mound just off the York Road, or Bishopthorpe Road [2] as it is now called, somewhere between Southlands Road and Scarcroft Road, probably where the South-lands Methodist Church [3] stands today. He asked the executioner to give him five strokes – in token of the five wounds of Christ – and died on Monday 8th June, 1405. As far as Archbishop Scroope was concerned, the Southlands really did give birth to the blues. As you pass by this distinctive building with its twin pyramid towers and semi-circular apse, reflect on the perils of being a Top Person five hundred years ago.

The bustling little shopping street provides an interesting interlude before you reach the city walls which run along Nunnery Lane [4]. Walking along them you pass a homely little pub, the Edward VII, home-town local of Yorkshire hero, Henry Wharton. Somewhere along this stretch of wall is a real part of Secret York. At the end of 1991 it was announced that radar was to be used to survey the city walls in order to pin-point areas in need of restoration. By the following July they had discovered a hidden chamber under a known seventeenth century chamber at Bitchdaughter Tower, at the junction of Baile Hill and Newton Terrace. In fact the chambers are so secret that, although they know they're there, they haven't yet worked out a way to get into them.

Standing next to Victoria Bar [5], a recently-made passage through the walls, is the Moat Hotel. It looks so neat and welcoming now but it was originally built as a hospital.

Through Victoria Bar you are faced with a virtual warren of Victorian terraces. Bear left and follow Lower Priory Street round past the large chapel on the corner of Priory Street. Next to the church of St Mary's [7] on Bishophill Junior [6] stands a decrepit-looking little hall with an immaculate blue and gold painted sign – The McPherson School of Dancing. For many years now, the proprietors, Dennis and Rita Cole, as well as many of their students, have had the feeling that they were not alone in the building.

It all started back in the Sixties. First there was the sound of coins being counted in the lobby. Rita heard it from the other end of the hall and it got louder as she approached and continued even when she stood in the waiting area. The sound of heavy coins being flicked off a table and then slammed down was unmistakable.

Her mother heard it on a separate occasion but neither woman said anything until husband Dennis and some students heard the rattle of wire coat-hangers, also in the lobby. When they went to investigate there was just one swinging, even though it was midsummer and there were no coats hanging. No-one had been seen or heard coming into the school either.

Opposite: The McPherson School of Dancing

Then Rita had another brush with the unknown when a sudden musty smell and a forceful rush of cold air pushed her up the steps from the cellar when she had been sweeping up.

At a Christmas party night, youngsters put their soft drinks money onto a table on the edge of the dance floor and then saw one of the coins leap onto the floor.

The only alarming occurrence was when a friend was taking their classes while they were away on holiday. Rita's mother was roused from her slumbers by police with the news that the dance school's front doors were wide open and all lights on. The man and his wife had just locked up at the back and then saw a book leap off a packed shelf on the platform and clear the record-player to land on the floor. They were hurrying to the exit when a cigarette packet lying between them and the door suddenly flew up into the balloon-net hanging from the ceiling. That was enough for the stand-ins; they didn't stop till they got back to Hull.

The experiences continue to the present day. Rita, Dennis and their students have come to expect the unexpected and no-one feels threatened. So is there an explanation?

A few years ago a young student came to York from Sheffield and joined the classes. She had not heard of the "phenomena". She was in the habit of having a private lesson in the afternoon, going home for tea and returning for an evening class. On one occasion she came back and asked Rita who the old lady was. Rita assured her that no old lady had been there but the girl insisted that she had seen an elderly lady in the lobby as she was leaving the hall. She gave a detailed description: blue-grey hair, smart navy-blue suit with a bow ribbon on her blouse.

Rita asked if she would recognise the lady if she saw her again and brought out a large black and white photograph taken at Grosvenor House, London. It was taken at the Imperial Congress of Teachers of Ballroom Dancing around 1949, complete with Victor Sylvester and master of ceremonies. The young student had no hesitation in picking out the lady sitting at the front table in the centre of the photograph. It was Mary McPherson, who had started the Dance School and sold it to Rita and Dennis. Rita remembers her standing in the lobby and saying: "I'll never leave this place."

Resisting the temptation to walk down St Martin's Lane, turn right and go towards Skeldergate Bridge via Bishophill Senior [8] and Cromwell Road and then down towards the river and Skeldergate. The Cock and Bottle public house [9] on the corner of Albion Street was originally a garden shed used by the Duke of Buckingham for chemical experiments. It stood in the grounds of Buckingham House. The only remains now are the street names – Buckingham Street, Court and Terrace. The rather handsome building now converted into apartments that we noticed opposite St Mary's Church is virtually all that remains of the Buckingham Works. Thomas Cooke had his factory here and made high precision optical instruments which went everywhere from the Royal Observatory to Everest and the South Pole. Since the firm moved out to Haxby Road their equipment has been used by NASA to analyse samples of Moon rock. Between 1802 and 1807, the City Gaol was built at the end of Cromwell Road and had its own scaffold which was occasionally used for felons who had committed offences within the city boundaries. Thus in 1820 William Brown, alias Morley Stubbs, was found guilty of robbing John Armstrong on New Walk, near Blue Bridge on the evening of 23rd November. He was subsequently hanged within sight of the scene of his crime. The prison was demolished prior to the building of Skeldergate Bridge in 1880 [10].

In the old days, if you were on Skeldergate you were going places. During the thirteenth and fourteenth centuries York traded direct with the Baltic, the Netherlands and Bordeaux. Last century you could catch a steamer daily to London, Hull and even Rotherham.

You could catch a steamer of a different kind on the other side of the river. Way back in 1856 the Yorkshire Gazette carried an advert for Peruvian Guano, Rape Nuts and Manure specially prepared for Autumn Wheat. The only address given was Henry Richardson, Manure Works, York, but if you had been walking along the King's Staith then, you would have had a pretty shrewd idea where the business was carried on. A later edition of the York Trade Directory tells us that Richardson and Dennis of King Street [11] were seed crushers, chemical manure and mustard manufacturers. Obviously there was plenty of brass in that pile of muck.

As you cross the bridge and walk along the river towards the town centre, imagine the scene on 16th July 1631, as the Aldermen, Sheriff and 24 Chamberlains held their annual Fishing Day and between them caught 41 salmon – enough to have one each and give the rest to the poor.

In fact the Ouse used to contain chub, bream, barbel, pike, trout and royal sturgeon. Porpoises regularly followed the salmon and in 1685 a specimen 10 feet long was captured on Clifton Ings. A bottle-nosed dolphin was seen at Cawood in 1828 and two seals made an appearance at Naburn in 1892. A white whale followed in 1905 while in January 1909, someone managed to spot an otter near Ouse Bridge.

Once a year, the King's Staith [12] contrives to re-create something approaching the hustle and bustle of former times. On one late winter day you might imagine yourself in a distant land.

Log fires are burning and potent aromas mingle with harsh wood smoke. A tall man is gnawing what looks like an animal's jawbone and is exchanging remarks with others in an unfamiliar tongue. Women in long dark embroidered dresses are busy stirring the burnished metal cooking pots and suddenly a shout goes up as a wooden boat speeds past, its team of oarsmen working and looking as one in identical blue and white patterned sweaters. The lilt of an accordion forms a sound-track.

No, this isn't some Norwegian Fjord, but York during the annual Viking Festival, when one Saturday morning the waterfront is invaded by a new model army of Norsemen and women whose only weapons seem to be unlimited charm and endless offers of food and drink. They light their log fires on portable stone hearths and set up their cauldrons to produce fish soup, prawn broth or mussels in white wine.

Yes, that man is chewing a sheep's jawbone and anyone can try a portion of sheep's head – they're ready-smoked and then boiled and served with a helping of mashed turnip, or could it be Swede? The man is in fact quite a celebrity, a fiddler, but no ordinary fiddler. His instrument is the Hardanger fiddle, a dragon-headed specimen inlaid with black and white hardwoods and complete with drone so that it provides its own eery accompaniment. Its tuning is unique yet sounds strangely familiar – the open strings inspired Grieg when he wrote his Peer Gynt Suite.

Then there are the boats – solidly made of best timber – and at least two have intricately carved dragon prows. The dragon head is held fast by an ingeniously placed dowel and can be speedily removed when the boat takes to the high seas or is air-borne.

Present-day Vikings they may be, but mugs they are not, and all have day-jobs, so how else did you think they would get the boats to England? Watching one crew tackle their packed lunch – a whole leg of reindeer, washed down with swigs from a brimming horn of beer – it is easy to imagine how their forefathers might have sculled up that same river all those centuries ago. There's plenty to tempt the palate: seal-meat with seaweed mayonnaise, various cured meats and assorted sausage. Should you still feel peckish, over at another stand they'll cut you a slice of smoked salmon and, while you're waiting, pull you a measure of traditional old ale. It's amazing how hungry you get watching the rowers in action.

While all this consumption is going on, the Norwegians, who seem to outnumber everyone else, stand around chatting to each other, renewing acquaintances or explaining the many crafts being demonstrated and giving an insight into their way of life. They seem perfectly at home. One chap is busily working on the construction of his own wooden boat, just as he would any Saturday morning.

When they cut you a slice of cured lamb, you notice that the knife is hand-made with a uniquely decorated handle. Their clothes are all traditional but definitely functional – while everyone else is shivering in anoraks and scarves they're out on the river with just a jersey between them and the icy February wind. The sight of so many longships and even shortships powered by oar and sail gives just a hint of how busy the river must have been when it was the commercial heart of the city.

There have been several Ouse Bridges [13]. The first wooden one was already ancient when Archbishop William Fitzherbert arrived in York in 1153. So many turned out to meet him that the structure gave way, but none died. William was instantly promoted to Saint. It didn't do him much good as he died three weeks later of a fever.

A stone replacement was built in 1235 and stood for well over 300 years. Then, following heavy frosts, snows and floods, the two centre arches collapsed and twelve houses and twelve people were lost. The next bridge stood for almost another 300 years until the present version was built in 1820. It was a toll bridge for nine years. The first "free" load to cross it was timber for the Minster following the fire caused by Jonathan Martin. Today's Ouse Bridge is a far cry from its predecessor. Apart from the fact that it was built in two stages – you can see the join running lengthways underneath – it is a fairly innocuous structure. The old Ouse Bridge was certainly not a place for the faint-hearted. It housed the York Kydcote, or Prison, and in the time of Henry VIII, four City Sheriff's Officers received £2 13s. 4d. for keeping three prisoners and hanging up their quarters after execution. They were also allowed to keep the prisoners' clothes. A blacksmith was paid 3s. (15p) for setting on and taking off the fetters from any prisoners brought there.

One such was Margaret Clitheroe, who lived in the Shambles (Route 5). She was found guilty of hiding a Jesuit priest and in 1586 was brought to the cell which was underneath the main gaol and often flooded to the height of 16" above floor level. Her sentence was to be pressed to death by a door on which was placed 800lbs of iron.

At the bottom end of the of the wage structure, a widow, Agnes Grethede, was paid 2s. a year to clean the "pyssing howes on Ouse Bridge", according to the York Civic Record of 9th December 1544.

The old bridge also accommodated a council chamber and a chapel. The debtor's prison was demolished in 1724. In 1541 King Henry VIII came to visit the city – an event which caused more fear than joy, because the city had recently supported the failed Pilgrimage of Grace against the King. Its leader, Robert Aske, had been hung in July 1537 at Pavement (Route 5) on a special scaffold 13 feet high.

So, prior to the visit, much planning went into ways of ingratiating and boot-licking for the Merry Monarch. There was to be a musical greeting on the roof of St William's Chapel on the bridge. Houses were to be decorated and the streets were to be cleaned of all rubbish. Included perhaps in this urban cleansing programme was the banishing of beggars from the city streets, or at least the tidying-up of the same. The York Civic Records tell us that in readiness for the King's visit a "Master Beggar" was to be appointed for each ward. The other beggars would wear a badge and could only beg on Sunday and Friday – and then only when the "Master Beggar" was present.

The corporation was to provide cloth for four special gowns to be made up for the Master Beggars with a badge on the sleeve. They were to be provided with birch rods "to execute ther offyce after the best maner that can be devised".

Anyway, as you clamber up the stone steps onto the new Ouse Bridge, don't worry: the streets are now cleaned regularly as a matter of course, whether you are a royal visitor or not. However, although in August 1583 the corporation ordered that no Master Beggars should be appointed henceforth, their descendants are still with us.

If you turn right at the top of the steps and then cross at the traffic lights, you will find yourself outside St Michael's Church [14] at the start of Spurriergate [15].

Nowadays schools, hospitals and churches hold fairs – or even fayres – when they need to raise funds. The Archbishop of York used to hold an annual Fair on the Feast of St Peter or Lammas. For three days the city was under his jurisdiction. The bell of St Michael's Church was rung at 3pm on 31st July. The sheriffs would then surrender their white wands of office to the Primate in their court on Ouse Bridge. This act of waiving their wands enabled the Archbishop to receive a toll for all horses, cows and sheep coming in, and for every one sold, on leaving the Fair.

He also pocketed 12d. (5p) for every pack or basket brought in for sale on horse-back and then took the same amount from the buyers as they left. At the end of the Fair, at 3pm on 2nd August, the bell of St Michael's was rung again and the sheriffs were re-united with their wands. Now that's how to run a fayre and make a profit. The only consolation was that a dinner was provided in the taverns at the beginning and end of the Fair.

A few hundred years later, there were still money-making opportunities in the city. The "Yorkshire Gazette" of 28th October 1856 carried a tempting advertisement: how to make £1000 per annum for £1. All you had to do was to send a SAE to Thomas Gray Esq at 87, Chancery Lane, London.

Hurry along and you're soon on Coney Street [16]. Somewhere along here, in 1607, a servant was murdered. His master, Stephen Dobson, was subsequently executed on 3rd April.

A plaque at either end of the British Home Stores site is all that remains of the Black Swan Inn. Further down Coney Street, on the other side, just past the ruins of St Martin-le-Grand [17], is another plaque to commemorate another great inn, the George. The only visible evidence is a single column standing by the side passage-way. One of its more illustrious guests was Sir John Vanbrugh, who stayed there while supervising the building of Castle Howard. The previous dwelling of Charles Howard, Henderskelfe Castle, had been destroyed by fire in 1693, only ten years after being modernised. In fact William Talman, who had just been involved in another great pile at Chatsworth, was supposed to design the new home for the third Earl of Carlisle. Then Sir John, a well-known soldier, playwright and co-member of the Kit Kat Club, took one look at the plans and exclaimed that he could do much better. He sketched out his ideas and got the job on the spot. Not bad for his first attempt! Work started in 1700 and was still not finished when he died in 1726.

One of Yorkshire's greatest sons, John Metcalf of Knaresborough was a another regular patron later in the same century. One foggy night, another customer new to the area was wondering anxiously how he was going to get to Harrogate, twenty miles away. Jack Metcalf casually mentioned that he was going most of the way himself and would show him the way. In due course the men mounted their horses and only weeks later when the stranger returned to the inn did he find out that his guide was indeed Blind Jack. This amazing man's exploits as horse-rider, musician, trans-port entrepreneur and road-builder deserve a whole book to them-selves but one example will suffice here.

The White Swan plaques tell us that the coach journey from York to London took four days. In 1740 Jack was in the capital on business and an acquaintance, Colonel Liddell, invited him to join him in his coach for the long ride back up North. Our hero declined, declaring that he would be quicker on his own two legs. A bet was made that the coach would reach Harrogate first – within eight days. No prizes for guessing who won, but Blind Jack was in Wetherby by the end of day six and claimed his ten guineas by a comfortable margin.

Where New Street meets Coney Street stands a handsome stone building with a bright red coat of arms on the corner. Maybe the motto means that banking is a bit of a "boar". Its greatest asset is now unfortunately its biggest drawback. The magnificent domed ceiling with its richly painted vegetable embellishments no longer finds favour with today's architects who need to use every cubic centimetre of space. The building must have been one of Yorkshire's prettiest banks.

Across Coney Street stands perhaps the saddest but certainly one of the most uplifting buildings in the city. Following Churchill's policy of bringing fire and destruction to Germany, Hitler retaliated by ordering the Luftwaffe to destroy certain cities in England. These were chosen, not on strategic grounds, but according to their rating in the Baedeker tourist guides. Following Exeter and Bath, York was obviously a prime choice, being then even more than now, a virtually complete medieval city.

On the night of 29th April 1942, with a full moon, between 40 and 70 German bombers flew over the city and caused significant damage to the station and almost destroyed the church of St Martin-le-Grand [17]. About 80 people lost their lives that night. Many houses were destroyed, as well as Rowntree's warehouse and the Guildhall which faced each other across the Ouse. The railway stables were burnt out. The miracle was how the Minster survived. On such a night it could scarcely have provided a bigger target. Perhaps a greater power intervened to put off the thunderbolt for a few years.

The heart of St Martin's lives on, leaner and possibly fitter than before. Certainly its interior is a model of simplicity and acoustic perfection. The amazing window was put into store at the outbreak of war and was therefore ready to be reinstated when the reconstruction was complete.

Just opposite St Martin's was the Leopard Inn. From here the last Mail Coach to London departed in 1842. Nearby was York's first Turkish bath.

Carrying on past the Mansion House [18], you could easily miss the passageway leading to Guildhall. If the Minster survived that raid, the other main casualty was the height of irony. The Guildhall [19] was nearing completion of a three-year restoration programme to deal with death-watch beetle. Now it was a burnt-out shell and the whole process had to begin all over again.

In 1476, a Wine Assize was held there to fix the price of wine. Gascony red imported through Hull cost £6 per tun – 252 gallons.

Other red or white wine could be sold at 8d. per gallon – just over 3p in today's currency. These prices were low compared to 1462 when red wine was extortionately priced at between 10d. and a shilling (5p). White was a shilling and sweet wine could fetch 1/2d. You could buy a moorcock for 2½d., a rabbit for 3½d. The upper classes would pay 1s. for a capon or a heron, 1/8 (one shilling and eight old pence) for a pheasant and 3s. for a peacock. If you like fish, you would have loved these prices: salmon at 1s., pike at 3s., Lamprey, the only fish to carry a health warning, cost 3/4 (three shillings and four old pence). The Assize of Wine is occasionally resurrected as a charity stunt, with Lord Mayor, Sheriffs and Councillors descending on city centre hostelries and assessing their liquid assets.

Today, the Guildhall may look picturesque but it houses a dynamic City Council which still takes a lead in the life of the city. It gave its citizens a Charter long before Central Government got round to the idea and it has made York probably the most bicycle-friendly city in the country.

Just across from the Guildhall stands a very genteel tea-room – Betty's [20]. It is hard to imagine a more prim and proper establishment, yet during World War II the downstairs bar was known as "The Briefing Room" or "The Dive". It was the favourite haunt of thousands of Bomber crews and other service personnel of every rank and nationality stationed around Yorkshire and beyond.

During the revelry which would take place before or after missions to Cologne, Hamburg or Berlin the young men might be invited by the landlord's wife to use her diamond engagement ring to scratch a name, a date or a message into the surface of the big mirror behind the bar.

Today, the mirror stands in a corridor opposite the gents' toilet but it is surrounded by photographs and other memorabilia. It is a moving experience to read the 568 names – many of them Canadians or Americans who were stationed at bases all around York. Indeed the cafe and its mirror are probably more famous on the other side of the Atlantic. One transatlantic widow came over recently and was searching for her husband's name on the glass. After many minutes she gave up and was about to leave when she turned round to look at the photographs on the wall opposite. There was her husband, pictured with the rest of his crew as they prepared their aircraft for its next mission.

Route 3

Banquets and Battles

Route Index

Number on Map	*Place*
1	Cawood
2	Riccall
3	Battle of Fulford
4	Fulford Village
5	Water Fulford Hall
6	Fulford Cross
7	Cemetery
8	Ambrose Street
9	Fulford Church
10	Hartoft Street
11	Theatre Arches
12	Blue Bridge Lane
13	Mecca Bingo
14	Mason's Arms
15	Castle Mill
16	Crown Court
17	St George's Field
18	Clifford's Tower
19	Eye of York
20	Castlegate
21	Coppergate Square
22	Piccadilly
23	Merchantgate
24	Fossbridge
25	Walmgate
26	Ellerker's
27	Walmgate Bar
28	George Street
29	Fishergate Bar
30	St George's Churchyard

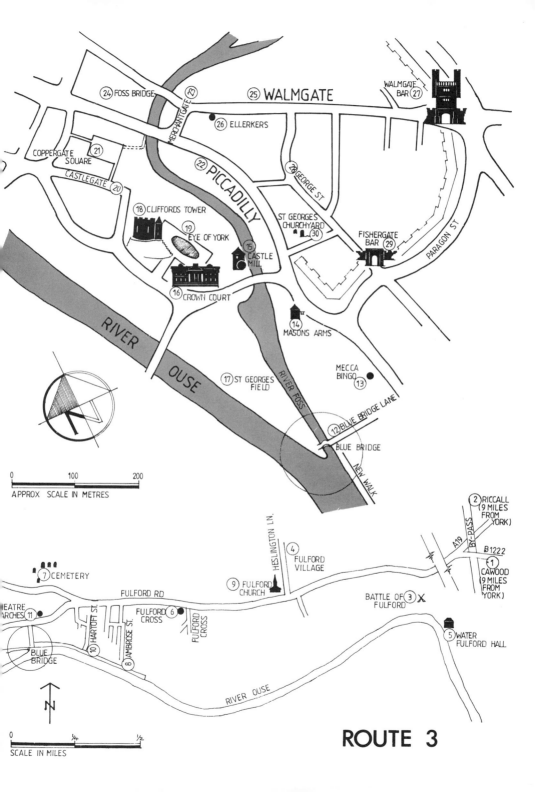

Alphabetical Index

The Route

This route could be said to have its roots way back to the south of the city in the sleepy villages of Cawood [1] and Riccall [2]. These havens of peace and tranquillity provide a gentle initiation into the ways of the world.

If you passed through Riccall, it is worth noting that in the twelfth century, its annual value to the Crown was 30 shillings, whereas Ripon brought in £7 10s.

On 4th June 1465, George Neville was enthroned in York Minster. During the Installation banquet in the Archbishop's castle at Cawood (of which only the gate-house remains – the rest having been carted off to build the Archbishop's Palace at Bishopthorpe) 2,000 people sat down to a light buffet comprising:

104 oxen; 6 wild bulls; 1,000 sheep; 304 calves; 2,000 pigs; 304 small pigs; 500 stags; 4,000 rabbits;

4,000 pigeons; 2,000 chickens; 2,000 geese; 1,000 capons;

1,200 quail; 400 plovers; 200 pheasants; 400 herons;

400 swans; 104 peacocks; 608 pike and bream; 12 porpoises and seals; unspecified numbers of salmon, sturgeon, conger eel, trout and lobsters.

The whole was doubtless washed down by hundreds of barrels of wine and beer.

When the King came to York 13 years later, he was met by the Lord Mayor and Aldermen. £35 was spent on gifts for the royal visitor: demain bread; sponge bread; 12 cygnets; 12 pike and 2 barrels of red Gascony wine.

What a feast!

It could have been worse. When King John visited York on 25th March 1200, the citizens were fined £100 for not turning out to meet him.

The crowds may not turn out to meet you now but in the winter months you may notice that the area to the left of the road, in other words between road and river, is liable to flood. You would not be too surprised to learn that the village you are approaching was originally called Water Fulford but you may not have realised that here took place the last Norse victory on English soil – the Battle of Fulford [3].

Things got a little confusing in 1066, partly because there were at least two Harolds: Harold Godwinson, King of England and Harold, also known as Harald, Hardrada, King of Norway. Harold's brother Tostig was also involved but was not on the same side.

So the scene is set. Harald Hardrada together with Tostig and the Earl of Northumbria sailed up the Ouse, disembarked at Riccall and marched toward York. On Wednesday 20th September 1066, the invaders were confronted by the men of Jorvik. It was not a good day for the locals. According to the Icelandic Saga there were so many dead in the deep water-filled ditch that the Norsemen were able to walk across it without getting their feet wet. By the Sunday, York was in the hands of the outsiders and Harald Hardrada claimed 150 hostages.

On Monday 25th September Harald and Tostig had gone for a stroll to Tadcaster but had to hurry over to Stamford Bridge where Harold Godwinson, King of England, was waiting. For them it was indeed a bridge too far. Retribution was waiting in the swirling waters of the Derwent. Harald and Tostig were both slain.

There was no time for complacency, however, as William the Bastard had just arrived fresh from France and Harold's own date with destiny was only a long march away at Hastings on 14th October. Morcar, the Earl of Northumbria, came out of things better than most – he ended up owning Fulford and by the time of the Domesday Book in 1087 it was worth 16 shillings.

As you pass through the present village [4] you will appreciate that it has always had pretensions, even before the golf club was established. The Yearly Account Roll for St Mary's Abbey, 1528-29, reveals that a tenement in Fulford was let for 30 shillings per annum. A similar property in Bootham was a steal at twenty.

The present village is a combination of the two ancient villages: Gate Fulford and Water Fulford. The latter was part of a gift of land from William the Bastard to Count Alan of Brittany in 1078.

It is a complete coincidence that Fulford's only delicacy was the Fulford Biscuit – a water biscuit of course. It was developed by the Leng family late last century. Unfortunately, when George Leng died, the recipe was lost for ever.

In 1896 it was hoped to impose a speed limit of 10 mph on motor cars on Main Street. A horse and water-cart were to be provided to keep the dust down. Such a slow life-style was not to the liking of all Fulford residents. One of them, Richard Atcherley, raced for the Schneider Trophy and held the world air speed record at 322 mph in the 1930s when he was 25.

You may notice at least one dwelling bearing the name "Turpin Cottage" or something similar. Just about every old house along Main Street claims that the notorious highwayman slept there, rested his horse on the patio or simply broke in on the way to a bigger job.

As befits an ancient village, Fulford has its fair share of traditions. One of these involved Beating the Bounds – an old method of ensuring that boundaries were maintained and ownership of lands kept secure. It was no idle ritual but a real act of corporate will which involved the vicar, churchwardens, the parish clerk, the sextons, the choir and the parishioners, not to mention real beating!

They would set out on the Long Perambulation and partake of bread and ale – Perambulation Ale. The route would go along the river and the men would carry wands (for beating), a pitcher (for smashing), and a cock (read on). When they reached Water Fulford Hall [5], the old manor house which is best seen from the river, they would enter the porch and smash the pot near the boundary stone. Then they would follow the river to another stone just opposite the Archbishop's Palace.

The cock would then be released and a chase would ensue. Whoever caught the fowl had to behead it over the stone – but was then allowed to keep it. Could this have been the origin of "getting the bird"?

Finally the whole party would wend its weary way to an inn near St Martin's on Micklegate, where dinner would be enjoyed. Since this repast could cost £14 – a huge sum – it is not surprising that the Lord of the Manor discouraged the tradition. He didn't like the way it ate into his profits from the sale of butter – 80,000 firkins sold annually at the Butter Stand (see Route 1). So the last Beating took place in 1863, although occasional mini-beatings have been revived in 1992-93. You will be relieved to know that there was no cruelty either to pottery or poultry, but the Perambulation Ale tasted as good as ever.

Of course when the representatives of the City did their version of beating the bounds it was on a much more splendid scale. For a start they would proceed on horseback. On Riding Day, which could be on any day between Martinmas and Christmas, the Sheriffs would tour the city accompanied by the City Waits, the municipal musicians, kitted out in scarlet livery and silver badges. Things could go wrong, however, as on any day out. In 1537 there was a riot for some reason. The custom of Sheriff's Riding has been revived in recent years. It takes place on St Thomas' Day.

Just opposite the present-day garrison you pass a narrow lane called Fulford Cross and then you will notice that the low wall along the pavement has to make a dog-leg turn to accommodate a stumpy stone column. This is all that remains of Fulford Cross [6].

When Henry VIII visited the city on 15th September 1541, he upset the plans of the corporation by not arriving by the traditional royal route – Micklegate (See Route 1). Instead he came, like you, via Fulford. To show who was the boss after the recently failed coup – the Pilgrimage of Grace – he made the entire corporation and 120 ordinary citizens kneel at Fulford Cross and read out "a proposition of submission" which began:

"Most mighty and victorious Prince . . . "

They then had to admit that:

"We, your humble subjects have grievously, heinously and traitourously offended"

and continued through several pages of grovelling on the theme that: "Whereby your Grace having the lives, lands and goods of us wretches at your will and pleasure – we have been repentant from the bottom of our stomach . . . "

How could he refuse to pardon the city? Especially since they had gone to the trouble of building him a new palace just for his stay, which lasted all of 12 days.

Although Fulford traditionally extended as far as the city walls, the area between where the road forks into Cemetery Road is now known as Fishergate. The cemetery [7] is nowadays a tourist attraction in its own right, with wild-life walks and guided tours. It was opened in 1836 by a private company.

This part of York has a very theatrical flavour. Fulford itself was the home of many pop groups in the Swingin' Sixties – the best known being Gerry B. and the Rockafellas. Their front-man became even more famous as Dustin Gee, the television comedian who died tragically young in 1986. He started life as Gerald Harrison in Ambrose Street [8] which you have just passed but would not have noticed because it lies in a maze of streets off the main road. Working with Harry Stammers, a famous stained glass artist, he obviously fancied seeing his own name in lights. His funeral filled St Oswald's Church [9], which we have also just passed. Among the mourners were stars of "Coronation Street" and the Krankies. Surviving members of the Rockafellas and other local pop musicians of that era still meet up for reunion gigs in aid of charity.

Just before you reached Fishergate you will have passed another maze of little Victorian streets lying between the A19 and the river. Again you would not have noticed because it lies off the main road and is only indicated by a small sign. In one of these, Hartoft Street [10], was born one of the great British comics – Frankie Howerd – in 1922. Titter ye not, missus!

In Fishergate itself there is an almost surreal sight. Just opposite the Light Horseman public house stands what looks like a row of medieva_ stone arches with a modern block of flats inserted in it [11]. These are all that remain of the arches which the Victorians put up outside the Theatre Royal to give it an olde worlde look back in 1835.

If you turn down Blue Bridge Lane [12] you are following the border of St Andrew's Priory and you will end up on the New Walk which was created in 1734 so that elegant members of society could strut their stuff down by the riverside. Nowadays all strata of society have to strut very carefully in order not to step in the stuff left by our canine companions.

Another explanation for the name New Walk is that it is another way of saying "Newarke", as opposed to "Aldwarke". We shall meet Aldwark, or "old works" on Route 4. The Newarke refers to the "new works" which were across the river on Baile Hill – all that remains of the latest in early Norman civil defence structures.

It was near the Blue Bridge – so called because it was originally, and still is, painted blue – that William Brown alias Morley Stubbs committed the robbery that led to his execution in 1820.

A pair of Crimea cannon used to stand by the bridge. It is raised at least once a week to allow a barge full of paper to reach the offices of the Yorkshire Evening Press which lie a little further along the River Foss.

If, however, you carry on along the main road you cannot fail to notice the enormous former cinema just before the Novotel. This was once a Mecca for fans of Big Band music. Local impresario Xavier Prendergast booked all the great American names to come and entertain the populace – a real tonic in Post-War York. He used to live in the building now known as the York Pavilion Hotel, which you just passed on Fulford Main Street. Jazz enthusiasts still recall seeing legends like Lionel Hampton and Stan Kenton at the Rialto.

Then his son gave up playing second trumpet in local outfits and after starting his own group, the John Barry Seven, went over to Hollywood to become a big noise in the movies. He is far better known as John Barry and his Oscar-winning film credits include "Midnight Cowboy", "Zulu", "Born Free" and "Dances with Wolves". The building is now a Mecca for fans of Bingo [13].

Just across the road stands one of York's two convents. The Nunnery of the Sisters of St Vincent finally closed in 1972.

It is hard to imagine that, until a few years ago, the area to the left was occupied by an enormous glassworks. A little further on and a neat pub fairly creaking with coats of arms faces the corner of the city walls. The Mason's Arms [14] has almost as many shields as John Barry has Oscars and although it desperately tries to look old, was only built this century. It houses several fragments from York Castle gate-house which was demolished in the Thirties, including some very fine panelling and the fireplace from the courtroom.

Opposite: The Mason's Arms

Crossing Castle Bridge, you are in the shadow of all that is left of York Castle Walls. On the banks of the Foss stands an old water mill looking as if it had been there for ever. In fact it has only been there since Dr. Kirk, the founder of the Castle Museum, brought it there from Raindale, just north of Pickering. It was donated in 1935, but not removed and rebuilt until 1966. That particular area was always known as Castle Mills from medieval times when there were many wind mills, so it is not really an alien transplant [15].

Where the road turns into Tower Street you see the back of the Crown Court [16] built in 1727. It was from a window to the right that the condemned felon was taken out onto the scaffold before an appreciative crowd gathered across the road on St George's Field [17]. If you look carefully where the railings meet the pavement there is a stone marking the boundary between City and County. From here you would have had a pretty good view of the New Drop. In 1729 a warm-up act was provided in the form of a Ducking Stool. Nowadays the whole area forms part of a flood defence system, otherwise known by its technical acronym: B.H.I.T. or Big Hole In T'ground. There is also a S.H.I.T. or Small Hole In T'ground, otherwise known as a public toilet. The whole, if not the hole, is surrounded by a car park, a sad end to what was once York's main place of popular entertainment.

Joking apart, the whole scheme took over ten years to complete and cost over £3 million. A hi-tech sensor system will trigger off a series of gates to divert flood waters and prevent sewage overflow into the River Foss. A quarter of York residents – 25,000 – should now be able to sleep peacefully in their beds without fear of that wet feeling. During excavation of the Big Hole, workmen discovered remains of a 12th century Chapel of the Knights Templar. St George's Field was also the site of one of York's first swimming pools. Anyone trying to swim now would only be able to go through the motions.

Nowadays the remains of the Castle look quaint, especially on November 5th when they form the centre-piece of a firework display second to none and the one occasion in the year which seems to bring the whole of York together.

Until 1934, however, the whole area was surrounded by forbidding gritstone walls. Entry was through a fortified gateway opposite Clifford Street. In Victorian times a popular Sunday walk would take in the public space around Clifford's Tower and include a look at the Prison Governor's deer which had a free run about the place.

Even earlier in 1727, Samuel Waud bought the land which included the tower and enjoyed having the mother of all follies as part of his garden – just the thing for pastoral picnics. Between 1826 and 1934 a semi-circular building, the Felons' Prison, stood between the mound and the Female Prison.

Long before these additions and subtractions, York Castle simply included what we now call Clifford's Tower [18] and the area that now contains the Museum and Crown Court. That section was surrounded not only by a high wall but a moat as well, which lapped around the base of the mound. The two sections were linked by a drawbridge.

The castle was the physical embodiment of the King's presence in York. It cost Henry II £15 to build the original wooden keep in 1172. In the fourteenth century the Royal Mint had 12 furnaces constantly at work. The Castle's other main use was as a gaol and on average 30 prisoners per annum died a "natural death" within its confines. Between 1370 and 1879, 564 met an unnatural end.

Some time in the mid eighteenth century William Thompson, a felon, suddenly and unaccountably disappeared after supposedly escaping from the Castle. On 8th July 1780 some workmen were clearing away rubbish behind the courthouse which straddles the line of the original defence walls of the Castle. They found a human skeleton laid out about a metre from the wall with the leg bones enclosed in double irons. It is probable that Thompson had reached the top of the Old Courthouse using a ladder and had then fallen to his death. He had lain there ever since, hidden by nettles and high weeds.

In 1761, 121 French prisoners cut away the bars of their windows. Twenty escaped over the walls and although six were recaptured, 14 were never heard of again. It is obviously a pure coincidence that one of the oldest standing buildings within sight of the Castle today houses a French restaurant: Chez François.

One of the more bizarre episodes concerns John Bartendale, a piper. He was hanged on 27th March 1634 "but insufficiently" in the words of Captain A. W. Twyford, Governor of York Castle.

After three quarters of an hour he was cut down and buried near the gallows. Shortly afterwards a servant of Lord Hesselwood came riding along and saw the earth heave. He promptly dismounted and dug up the lucky chap who was taken to the Castle, pardoned and became an ostler.

All these grisly events occurred within sight and sound of the green oval known as the Eye of York [19], or what was the Castle Yard. In 1989 excavations revealed a tunnel running from the Eye of York into the basement of the Crown Court. It was probably used to convey prisoners directly into court.

Elections used to take place here before the electoral reforms of 1832. We find it a bit of a chore to go along to our local polling station every once in a while to do something which takes a matter of seconds. In those days an election could take over a fortnight.

Consider the parliamentary election of Knights of the Shire in October 1597. Only Freeholders of 40 shillings per annum were eligible to vote and they converged on York from all over the county.

People gathered on the Eye of York and divided according to their preference. The counters used to make notches on sticks for every score of voters. Then one side accused the other of including: "citizens and inhabitants of York, women and children and other strangers not having lawful voices."

Not surprisingly such a system was open to abuse and had to change eventually. This didn't prevent 29 elections from being held in the seventeenth century alone.

In the eighteenth century, 28 such affairs took place and votes were recorded at temporary booths erected on the spot. In 1807 one election lasted 15 days. Twenty-three thousand freeholders travelled to York and all the inns and taverns were full to capacity. William Wilberforce, the anti-slavery campaigner, and Lord Milton of Wentworth were elected but the Honourable Henry Lascelles of Harewood lost. The contest cost both noble houses over £200,000. The last such election took place in 1831.

If you have had enough of politics you should head for Castlegate [20], site of that French restaurant, but once much more famous for the Blue Boar Inn.

This is where Dick Turpin's body was taken after his execution. He was buried and then promptly dug up by surgeons. He was finally laid to rest in ... Well, you'll just have to wait and see. Castlegate was once 50 yards longer and extended right up to the walls of the Castle. There was a stone which marked the boundary between City and County, just like the one we saw earlier. In 1422 the High Sheriff arrested a woman in a house on the city side and put her in the Castle. The Lord Mayor intervened and compelled her to be returned.

Resist the temptation (for now anyway) to join the queue for the Jorvik Viking Centre in Coppergate Square [21] even if a band is playing. When Cravens the sweetmakers left their factory in Coppergate in 1966, it was first planned to use the building for a restaurant and dance-hall, or at least a coffee bar. Instead, cut through one of the big stores in order to reach Piccadilly [22]. Then use Merchantgate [23], which was created at the turn of the century for a tram route, to reach Fossgate and the cobbled surface of Fossbridge [24].

Henry I, son of William the Bastard, restored the privilege of "infantheof" to the Archbishop of York and so the Archiepiscopal scaffold stood at Foss Bridge, so that the Primate could exercise his power of "furca et fossa" and punish men by hanging and women by drowning. The holy man also claimed legal title to a toll of every third penny paid at the fish market held on or near the bridge.

Turn back at the bridge and you are on Walmgate [25], now quite a run-down area. This is an improvement on last century when it was an extremely run-down area with some of the worst slums in Europe, according to Joseph Rowntree. In the really bad old days one of the few free distractions was to watch the carts conveying condemned men to execution at Green Dykes – further out of town off Hull Road. Once a woman had her leg broken in the six thousand strong crowd and a young man suffered a broken thigh.

One of the oldest established businesses in Walmgate, and probably in York, is Ellerker's [26], the purveyors of high-class kit for man and beast. The firm started trading in 1795. Then they dealt in ropes and tarpaulins. The yard behind was once a street leading down to the river, which is now Piccadilly. About seventeen houses stood in Feoffees' Yard until the tram shed was built across it.

Now the York Archaeological Trust have started to excavate there and visitors can see a real "dig", as it progresses from the surface down through the layers of earth and time. Indeed, anyone wishing to "have a go" at being an archaeologist is invited to call at the ARC (Route 5) for details.

It is often said that Walmgate's Irish population was a result of railway building in the last century. In fact most of the Irish came over in force after the terrible potato famine in 1846.

They were attracted by hopes of agricultural employment but in reality found poverty to equal the miseries back in the Emerald Isle. Some, of course, did find work in the chicory fields around York, including one gang which walked out to Tollerton in 1852 with instructions to dig up a crop of chicory. The farmer happily took himself off to Knaresborough Fair. What is remarkable is not that they dug up a neighbouring four acres of teasels, but that they were paid for their labours.

It was a hard life as they had to walk many miles out to the villages and then back at the end of the day. Unfortunately this was also seasonal work and couldn't sustain a growing immigrant population. They lived in the most atrocious conditions in Walmgate. At the time, the area had at least 17 pubs. Almost every one had a yard in which would be crammed houses, pigsties and slaughterhouses. Last century, there were 94 private slaughter-houses in the city. Since the vast majority of the butchers worked in the Shambles, most of the animals had to be killed in Walmgate.

One of the most infamous was Butcher's Yard, where over 50 people occupied three lodging houses and a row of cottages. They shared a single privy.

By 1871 there were over sixteen thousand Irish in Walmgate, almost half the city's total. They lived side by side with bone-merchants, fish-bone dealers and gut scrapers, not to mention a huge dung-heap behind St Margaret's Church.

In 1850 James Smith commented that the River Foss was "a great open cesspool" – open to half the city's sewers. The area was easy prey to Typhus Fever.

Not surprisingly tempers flared occasionally. The police declared that it was unsafe to go down on Sunday night unless in a company of five or six. Between 1840 and 1875 there were 40 cases of Irish disturbances involving between 20 and 400 people.

On one occasion, a man called O'Donnell was arrested after assaulting the landlord of the Fat Ox public house. He escaped into Long Close Lane and the officer found between three and four hundred Irish fighting among themselves with a variety of weapons. On at least one occasion the police were found to have been over-violent themselves in their dealings with the Sons of Erin.

The period of Irish occupation was not without moments of humour or light relief. In 1849, an Irishman was accused of indecent exposure but had merely been trying to wash his clothes at Castle Mills Bridge. Once, a certain Joseph Lyon was found guilty of stealing a pair of sugar tongs from the Prison Governor's house. He happened to be in jail at the time.

Joseph Rowntree was not too obsessed with making chocolate to ignore the suffering of his fellow men just behind the family shop on Pavement. He had been to Ireland as a boy and seen the famine at first-hand. Perhaps this was to motivate his influential study into Poverty at the turn of this century, when he noted that some buildings in Hungate were worse than London slums. His objective research led to improvements then and the Rowntree Foundation continues to inform and prick the public conscience to this day.

Back in the last century the place was a hive of industry. The first Ordnance Survey map of 1852 shows that there were at least two iron foundries, a bleach yard, stone yard, skin yard and two timber yards. By the river stood a Steam Corn Mill driven by a 20 horse-power engine. There was also a tannery, a brewery and with so many Irish immigrants, not surprisingly, a Linen Manufactory. At the Fossbridge end of Walmgate was a regular pig market and if you look carefully at the bridge and the old almshouse next to it you will notice iron rings which remain from when the beasts had to be tethered.

With at least 17 pubs in the district it was fitting that one of them should have been called the Ham and Barrel. The most famous of them, the King William Hotel can still be seen, but not in Walmgate. Now the frontage is in the Castle Museum.

The cattle market was a fortnightly affair until the new market was built outside the walls in 1827.

In 1327, prior to the War against the Scots, King Edward II came to York, together with soldiers loyal to Sir John Beaumont of Hainault. They lodged in Walmgate and on Trinity Sunday the King held court near the Castle, in the house of the Friars Minor. This was at the Franciscan Friary by the River Ouse. A banquet and ball followed. In the midst of the revels, a brawl broke out between Sir John's men and some archers from Lincolnshire. The fighting was so serious that 300 were killed and 80 archers ended up being buried under one stone in St Clement's churchyard in Fossgate. The Essex men were sent home in disgrace but one can't help thinking that if they were so obstreperous against their own side, they would have been a real asset against the Scots.

When you read some accounts of life in the Walmgate of old it wasn't much better even at the beginning of this century. Still, one of its sons ended up being Chief Inspector of Police in York.

The church of St Clement's was one of fifteen York churches that were condemned as redundant in 1547 and almost entirely demolished. They live on in the subconscious of the city streets and just as there used to be a pub for every day of the year, there must have once been almost as many religious buildings. You certainly get the feeling that almost every building in York was at one time or another a church, a monastery or an inn.

St Clement's was not alone, as there were three others in Walmgate: St Peter-le-Willows, St George at Beanhills and All Saints. All were snuffed out in 1547.

Now you are within sight of Walmgate Bar [27], the only gateway in York to retain its barbican, and which housed a family until 1959. One of its residents recalled watching lorries with high loads getting stuck beneath the gateway. They had to stop and let the air out of the tyres in order to continue. Turn right into George Street [28] and follow the gently curving terrace till you come at last to St George's Church. The Roman Catholic church was built to cater for the sudden influx of Irish who came to escape famine last century.

Before you lies the petite Fishergate Bar [29] and a short cut to the Barbican Centre. Now you see it but for 300 years you wouldn't have. In 1489 a tax was levied for a war against Brittany. This was very unpopular in the North as they hadn't yet started burning our sheep. One of the main protestors, a man called John Chambres, was hanged on a special gibbet on Clifford's Tower with his fellow lobbyists neatly arranged below him. In the riot which nearly always followed such matters, some buildings were set alight. As a punishment for the people at this end of the city, Fishergate Bar was walled up so they would have further to come with their carts.

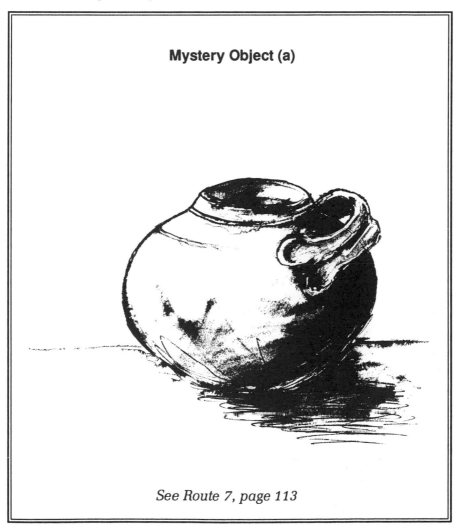

Mystery Object (a)

See Route 7, page 113

It was only opened up again in 1827 when the new cattle market was built. Just round the walls stands the tall Fishergate Tower. You have to remember that when it was built, the River Foss lapped at its base and Piccadilly was in fact the river bed. When the road foundations were being prepared, swan mussels were found embedded in the soil – some up to 6" in length. The Postern gateway at the side of the tower was added so that people didn't have to keep getting their feet wet when they came into the city to market.

In the graveyard [30] opposite St George's church you will find one enormous stone, not quite big enough to accommodate 80 archers, but quite sufficient to provide the last resting-place for the villain Dick Turpin.

Route 4

Following
the Foss

Route Index

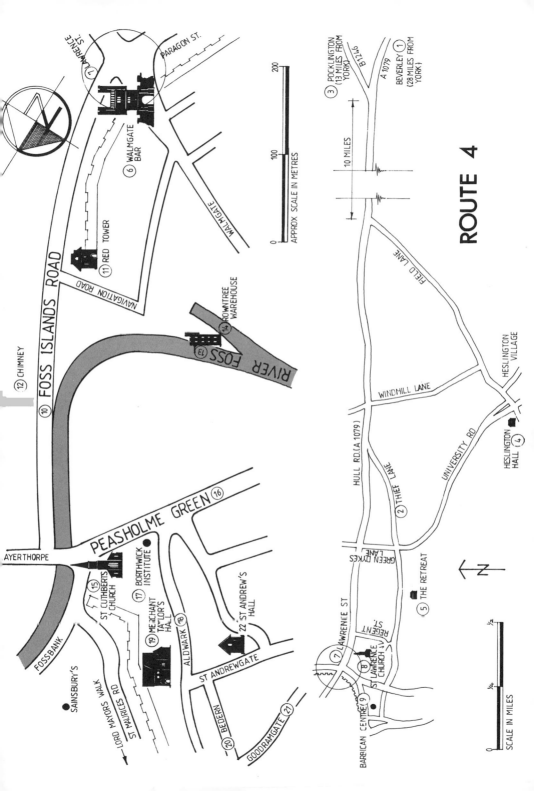

ROUTE 4

Alphabetical Index

The Route

As you approach York from afar, spare a thought for others who made the same journey long ago. Hopefully you will enjoy your stay more than they did.

In 1676 Leonard Gaskill and Peter Rook came all the way from Beverley [1] and ended up being the last two victims to hang on the gallows of St Leonard's on 1st May. Their crime was sheep stealing and they met their end at Garrow Hill or Green Dykes on Hull Road – near what is now known as Thief Lane [2].

A few years earlier in 1649, one Isabella Billington was hanged and also burnt for crucifying her mother at Pocklington [3]. To make things worse she subsequently offered a calf and a cock as a burnt sacrifice. Her husband was hanged on the same occasion for no other reason than being her husband and therefore accountable for her actions.

So, having survived your journey via those twin hot-beds of crime, Beverley and Pocklington, you will be glad to glimpse a wonderful building – Heslington Hall [4] standing in very tranquil surroundings. Now it is the headquarters of the University of York but has a chequered history. Tradition has that it was built as a suitable residence for Queen Elizabeth I in anticipation of a visit which never materialised. It was home to the Yarbrugh family in the eighteenth century. They specialised in being fairly illiterate, very rich and extremely obsessed with horse racing. One of them had the splendid name of Yarbrugh Yarbrugh. Another, Charles, was a prominent early member of the Ancient Society of York Florists. When his garden was robbed, he offered a reward of ten guineas for information leading to the discovery of the thieves. During World War II it was the Headquarters of 64 Group Bomber Command and it finally became the nucleus of the University of York in 1962.

Between here and the city walls the most remarkable feature is the Retreat Hospital [5]. Built near the site of a Civil War gun battery, Lamel Hill, it was the Quakers' answer to the traditional lunatic asylum. (See Route 6) Instead of locking people with mental health problems away in squalid surroundings and laughing at them, you gave them civilised surroundings, plenty of good food and interesting things to do. Incredibly they put this vision into action 150 years ago.

Meanwhile we are now at Walmgate Bar [6], having probably passed by one of York's several monasteries on Lawrence Street [7] without even noticing. In the grounds of St Lawrence Church [8] is the tower from the old church of St Lawrence which used to be on Walmgate. This is the only one of York's gates to have kept its massively fortified barbican. In 1570, a watch was posted here: "so that no suspect person of Rotherham or Selby resort unto this city".

Until the 1960s, the cattle market operated nearby on the site now occupied by the Barbican Centre and Pool [9]. Irish cattle were brought by rail to the Foss Islands Goods Station and drovers would conduct them to the pens which stood by the Bar Walls.

Nearby, archaeologists have recently found evidence of a leper hospital. Illness was never far away in this very poor part of the city. During the Plague of 1604 all dogs and cats had to be destroyed. The exterminating officer received 2d. (a bit less than 1p) for each cat that he killed and was allowed to keep the skin. When the Plague re-appeared in 1631, a man called Luke was publicly whipped for dancing and playing the fiddle outside Walmgate Bar where the disease was most prevalent.

As you travel along Foss Islands Road [10] you will notice that the walls suddenly come to a halt at a red-brick tower [11]. This was quite deliberate because hundreds of years ago all this area was under water as part of the King's Fish Pond and as such, a constant source of bickering by the Corporation as to who owned what and who should pay what and to whom. There must be more references to the Royal Fishery in the York Civic Records than to any other single matter.

Now the area has all been drained and, in hot summers, there doesn't even seem to be enough water to fill what is left of the River Foss. The tall chimney was built at the turn of the century along with a refuse incineration plant [12]. At 177 ft, it is only 20 ft short of York Minster and when it was recently repaired and restored, the job took a year. It may appear somewhat blotchy – thanks to camouflage paint applied in World War I to foil the Zeppelins.

York suffered greatly at the hands of the Luftwaffe, as was seen on Route 2. The losses during World War I were on a lesser scale but created havoc all the same. One night in May 1916, a Zeppelin dropped 18 bombs and killed nine people.

One man was killed in St Saviour's Place (See Route 5) after a night at the cinema. During a later Zeppelin raid the following September, one woman died of shock and six sick horses also succumbed to the terror from the sky. Barnitt's of Colliergate quickly brought out the "Zeppalarm" which sold at 7/6 (about 37p) and went like hot cakes. It was fitted to the gas bracket and rang a bell if the gas was lowered.

The city was full of anti-German feeling and the Rowntree Company and family were a constant target for those who found the Quaker love of peace at odds with the national mood. If only those armchair critics had known the facts. Lawrence Rowntree had wasted no time in joining the Friends' Ambulance Unit which was helping the Belgians in the Ypres area. On 15th September 1916, tanks were used for the first time and one of the most famous of these was known as Crème de Menthe. After it had successfully attacked a sugar factory, the driver stepped out, only to be hit by shrapnel. It was none other than Lawrence Rowntree. He was sent home for treatment but returned to the front as an artillery officer and was killed at Passchendaele.

The folks back home would have queued to see films of the Battle of the Somme at the Electric Theatre on Fossgate. The industrial buildings around here stand on the site of a huge goods station built last century to bring cattle to market. A line also ran off to the Rowntree Works and another cargo was tar. Although all vestiges have now gone, a good part of the network of tracks enjoys a new lease of life, forming the basis of York's Cycle Tracks.

Visitors to York could be forgiven for thinking that the city had only one river. Entering by Routes 1 or 2, they cross Lendal, Ouse and Skeldergate Bridges and can't fail to be impressed by the variety of ways of enjoying the Ouse – boats of every size from kayak to floating restaurant.

The unassuming Foss [13] has its own story to tell but it takes some teasing out. Hard to believe that it was once of vital importance and even saved the city from great peril more than once. There is evidence that the Romans used it for some sort of industrial purpose. Well, they would have done, wouldn't they? Massive stone blocks found near Fossbridge still have to be explained.

All was quiet on the waterfront for the next thousand years. The Danes ruled York from 876 to 954 and the death of Eric Bloodaxe. They couldn't bear to let go and even came back to capture the castle in 1069. This so infuriated William the Bastard that he re-took the city and completely devastated the whole of Northern England to teach them a lesson. In fact, he ought to be called William the Fat Bastard. By the time he died, he was said to resemble a pregnant woman.

Attempts to force his body into a stone sarcophagus in the church of St Stephen at Caen in Normandy ended in it bursting and filling the place with a foul stench. "Tripes à la mode de Caen" will never taste quite the same again.

He decided to rebuild the castle. We see it now in the form of Clifford's Tower. Another bright idea was to dam up the waters of the Foss to create a Fishpond. His representative, the Sheriff, lived in the castle and had to pay the keepers of the Fishpond.

In 1312, two keepers were paid 2d. per day but by 1454, one man received 6d. a day. Only the keeper was allowed to have a boat on the water. This tradition lives on today, but now the boat is provided by Sainsbury's.

The other difficult thing to imagine is that the city walls were not built as the world's biggest flower bed. They were meant to be defensive and had a moat running right round. This moat was fed by the Foss and the water power was harnessed by many water mills strategically placed around the walls.

The only problem was that the fish-garths, or traps made with stakes and entwined osier, didn't exactly help the flow of the river and caused endless friction between the various sets of monks who owned the mills and the local fishermen.

Nowadays the flow isn't helped by silting, the dumping of rubbish and a string of long hot summers. But at least things have improved since the early eighteenth century when the eminent historian Francis Drake said that it was "in summer time little better than a stinking morass."

By comparison it is now teeming with fish, with gudgeon, chub, dace, roach and bleak, to name but a few. To name a few more, it gives a home to stickleback, pike, perch and even trout. You could also find Miller's Thumb – perhaps a casualty during the fights with the anglers. This incredible fish is also known as Bullhead and is a broad-headed creature which likes to dwell on the river bottom and protects itself with large spines and can change its colour when necessary to blend with the background. Recently it has been filmed guarding its eggs – the eyes could be clearly seen inside the eggs.

The stone loach is also abundant, which is good news because it is a well-known indicator of a fish-friendly environment, being extremely sensitive to pollution. Kingfishers can be seen on the stretch behind Castle Mills but a new pest has reared its far from ugly head. Mink are on the increase, especially on the parts of the river in the centre of town.

Otters were frequent river users until 1924 when the New Earswick weir was removed, causing the water-level to drop.

On 27th May 1777 "The York Courant" announced that a new pleasure-boat, constructed of sheet iron, had just been launched on the river. It was twelve feet long, carried fifteen passengers and could be carried to and from the water by two men. It was the world's first iron ship and portable, too.

On Route 3 we encountered the new flood-relief station on St George's Field. The heart of that problem was caused in 1757 when Naburn Lock was installed. This raised the level of the Ouse and meant that whenever the Ouse flooded, the Foss backed up and flooded all the drains. Still, it only took 200 years to get round to sorting out the problem.

This would have been bad news for swimmers just below Yearsley Bridge near the Rowntree Factory on Haxby Road. In 1859 the Corporation converted a stretch of the river into an open-air swimming bath. This was achieved by the novel method of paving about 100 yards of the river-bed. The Committee proposed the idea in June and it opened in September at a cost of £300 – probably less than your average patio nowadays. Dressing sheds were built on the West Bank and an attendant was provided.

York folk know a good thing when they see one and as no charge was made for this facility, it remained in use from 1859 to 1935. Just in case they enjoyed it too much, the Watch Committee took over the nearby Lock Keeper's Cottage in 1882 as a residence for a Police Constable. He could have it for a shilling a week. In return he had not only to supervise the locks and the bathers, but feed the swans as well.

Sooner or later the River Foss had to earn its keep and most of the King's Fishpond has long since been drained and put to industrial use.

In 1879 the North Eastern Railway opened the Foss Islands Goods Station on reclaimed land. The area housed Electricity and Gas generators and the coal was brought in by barge.

The large red-brick building [14] with the turret which stands seemingly marooned on a bend of the river used to belong to a flour mill. Then Rowntrees took it over in 1937 and it could handle 3,000 tons of cocoa beans a year. After 1967 it contained 130,000 tons of sugar from Czechoslovakia and Holland. It was going to house the Rowntree Chocolate Experience but the Recession melted their enthusiasm.

The central European connection has a long tradition in this part of York. Just across the river in Hungate, Leetham's introduced the Hungarian Roller Method in 1880 and their establishment was known as the Anglo-Hungarian Flour Mill. It went the way of the Carmelite Friary before it.

Now that so much of the industry that huddled round the Foss basin has evaporated, the only heavy vessel to use the river is the one that brings newsprint to the offices of the Yorkshire Evening Press.

In years gone by, York had several newspapers which regaled the local readership with news from abroad as well as titbits from nearer home. One solid publication was the Yorkshire Gazette – guaranteed to be full of plum stories. The adverts were good too.

In the middle of the last century, not many advertisers used illustrations but one did, consistently – Ali Ahmed's Treasures of the Desert. This featured an Eastern gentleman extolling the virtues of the said treasures. These were anti-bilious pills which could cure anything from swimming in the head, through constipation, flatulence, diarrhoea and palpitating of the heart to spasms; in fact nervous debility of every kind.

The reports of court cases had a certain flair. In December 1854, there was an Impudent Robbery in which three lads stole a plum cake from the shop of Mr. Craven, confectioner, of Pavement. They owned up and did a fortnight hard labour in the House of Correction.

The following week, readers quaked at news of the Extraordinary Potato Robbery. This was extraordinary because no potatoes were either stolen or found – the felons were merely suspected of contemplating such a robbery.

Nowadays we are accustomed to stories about the wrong kind of leaves, but way back in November 1854, such things were big news, especially in York. A carter, Isaac Kilner, found himself in the dock, charged with removing scrapings from the road leading to Tang Hall.

He claimed not to know that the scrapings were the property of the Corporation and that a certain James Barber purchased them regularly from the City Surveyor.

The scrapings were particularly valuable in mid-autumn as a manure, on account of the large quantity of fallen leaves and Mr. Kilner suggested that it was the leaves he was really after. He protested ignorance of the law and the charge was dismissed.

Some crimes have always been around. In October the same year, a story entitled "Juvenile Depravity" told of two eleven-year-old boys who took improper liberties with a twelve-year-old girl on Walmgate Stray. They were fined 2s.6d. each, with costs and their parents, on the recommendation of the bench, promised to give the lads a severe whipping.

You could follow the Foss and meander into the city centre via the castellated bulk of the old Rowntree's Warehouse which has now been adapted to provide luxury apartments. Or you could turn left over the bridge and arrive at Peasholme Green [16], passing by the ancient church of St Cuthbert's [15] which is enjoying a new lease of life with a growing congregation. Constantine the Great was proclaimed Emperor here in 306 AD The Black Swan Inn looks calmly onto the green where between 1576 and 1593 the Lord Mayor and his brethren would enjoy bear-baiting.

The stone building opposite is now the Borthwick Institute [17] but was until 1946 the home of the Blue Coat Boys. These boys from very poor backgrounds were fed and educated back to something like a useful expectation of life. The records show that more than a few were already beyond any help and died before the regime of regular food and hard work could benefit them. Today the treatment of these lads seems harsh but it was fair and gave them a good start. One at least, became Lord Mayor of York. Rhodes Brown, who founded Brown's store in St Sampson's Square (See Route 7) was a Blue Coat Boy. The building was then known as St Anthony's Hall and was one of the three places officially designated for the lodging of the poor. Before that it was used for wool-spinning and then as an arms store.

When the Blue Coat Boys were finally shown the door, the building became the home for the ecclesiastical archives of the North of England. This was to provide the heart of postgraduate research in the new University of York. The old dormitory became a fully equipped laboratory for the conservation and preservation of documents. There they work minor miracles, converting something that looks like a soggy lettuce into an immaculate parchment.

Continue along Aldwark [18] with its dwellings which must be among the most desirable in the city and listen out for a cock crowing. At "The Sign of the Cock" was one of York's many cock-pits where fights were held every morning of Race Week. Walking hereabouts reminds you that although so much of old York remains, countless layers of the past have had to be swept away just to keep up with modern life. It used to be said that York had a pub for every day of the year. This is not quite true nowadays, but must have been not too long ago. In fact, by the turn of the century almost as many pubs had disappeared as exist today.

Many fascinating names have gone, including the Three Jolly Butchers from Church Street and the Barefoot which was enticingly situated on Micklegate, not to mention the Hand and Whip in Castlegate. Vegetables were a good source of inspiration, with the Artichoke, also on Micklegate. York had at least two Barleycorns, one in Coppergate and another in Bedern.

Anyone suffering from depression should have avoided the Black Dog in High Ousegate, but would have been all right in the Jolly Bacchus. There was an inn on Ouse Bridge and even a bar within a bar. In 1516 you could have frequented The George within Bootham Bar.

Opposite: The Rowntree Warehouse

Certain houses had a bad name. The Reindeer on Thursday Market (See Route 7) hoped to change for the better when it became the Hand and Heart last century. Things didn't quite work out, however, because it was constantly in the news for being an unruly house. In 1854 it was the scene of "Mock Concerts". Punters were allowed in for 2d. They hoped for a glass of ale and some "entertainment" but they usually had to make do with a punch-up.

Some inn-names would now be considered to be in very bad taste, especially the Gallows House on Tadcaster Road. The Fighting Cocks in Walmgate and the Whale Fishery in Carmelite Street would also have had an image problem nowadays. However, the Lottery in St Nicholas Place off Hull Road would now have been in the height of fashion – pity it closed last century.

The Merchant Taylors' Hall [19] stands well back from the road and next to it, the caretaker's dwelling. It was established in 1452 as an almshouse and rebuilt in 1730 to house four poor brothers or sisters. The neighbours must have liked a quiet life even then, because the inmates had to live peaceably and without brawling. They had to go to church twice on Sundays and were "not to let any children come in to play or make any dirt." Any breach in this code of conduct meant instant expulsion.

One of the oddest things about York is the number of street names consisting of one word. We've already met Pavement and Bootham and no end of "-gates".

Perhaps the most obscure of these is Bedern [20]. It doesn't help much when you learn that it derives from an Anglo-Saxon word meaning "house of prayer". As you meander through a delightful residential area with its individual dwellings and lush gardens it doesn't seem obvious that this was once a communal residence for the College of the Vicars-Choral.

In our busy secular world we are so used to being organised, governed and kept in line by government officials of all kinds. It is hard to imagine life in the Middle Ages, when much of life was organised by the Church. And a great number of the Top People happened to be in York.

The Cathedral was almost another seat of local government. The Dean, Treasurer, Precentor and Chancellor were at the very top of the ladder, along with 32 other canons – literally the "big guns" of the church administration. These canons had to be away a lot looking after their estates to make sure the money kept coming in. That meant that they needed a deputy to sing in the choir during the many daily services in the Minster. So they employed a "vice-chorister" or, as they would say, a "vicar-choral" just to do the "voice-over" while they were on the road doing the merchandising.

In 1396 Richard II gave permission for a bridge to be built over Goodramgate [21] so that the Vicars-Choral could pass to and from services without being molested by unruly citizens and even highwaymen.

By 1500, however, there were only 20 vicars and they ceased to have their meals together. The whole place was becoming more and more run down and in 1644 St Peter's School moved into parts of the college complex when their own premises were damaged during the Siege of York.

In 1647 a petition went before Parliament to establish a Northern University in York and use the College site and its Hall. So the current University of York must have had one of the longest gestation periods in the country – over 300 years from conception to reality.

The inhabitants of York and the Northern parts of England were at pains to let Parliament know that it was about time they realised that the two existing universities of Oxbridge alone could no longer continue to uphold the Glory of Europe.

They pointed to the lack of scholars which led to a preponderance of illiterate men. They acknowledged that Northerners had a reputation for being rude and almost barbarous – because they were not as close to universities as the lucky Southerners who constantly basked in their Light and Influence. It was claimed that a Northern University would help to dispel the Popery, Superstition and Ignorance abounding north of Watford.

They earnestly underlined the advantages of York – its healthy situation, the cheapness of food and fuel – and indicated a ready-made site – the College of the Vicars Choral with its proximity to the Minster Library.

The following year another Petition was presented which emphasised that the city now had a printer. Unfortunately, Parliament was then preoccupied with other matters such as the execution of Charles I and war with the Scots. Further attempts were made in the early nineteenth century but Durham won the race in 1832.

The University of York recently purchased a manuscript copy of the Petition at Sotheby's for £1,500. They have a facsimile on display at Heslington Hall but the original document is kept at the Borthwick Institute.

In the intervening years things went from bad to worse and after 1840 the whole site was a slum, no doubt due to overcrowding. The Irish population which came over to escape the famine went from seven in 1841 to 374 in 1851.

The last hundred years of the Bedern saw a steady decline. In 1893, the Hall and other buildings were sold off for £294.10s., becoming first a bakery and then a pork butcher's. Thank goodness the City of York stepped in and stopped the rot by getting the Hall and two other buildings restored. One of these is St Andrew's Hall [22]. It is the only one of the churches condemned in 1547 which is still standing.

The rest was bulldozed to make way for the splendidly imaginative housing seen today. The Hall was brought back to life by the builders and in the process revealed many forgotten features. It is now the spiritual home of the Gild of Freemen, the Gild of Building and the Company of Cordwainers.

Things were not always so cosy between Guilds, especially where the Cordwainers were concerned. In 1490, the shoe-makers and weavers were in dispute because the former had not carried torches in the Corpus Christi procession. This was a serious matter and they refused to pay the fine imposed by the Lord Mayor. The quarrel dragged on for almost a year and the King was eventually involved. He wrote a stiff letter ordering the craftsmen to settle their differences and live at peace.

Route 5

Foul Deeds and Just Rewards

Route Index

Number on Map	*Place*
1	Sheriff Hutton
2	Heworth
3	The Groves
4	Penley's Grove Street
5	Clarence Street
6	Haxby Road
7	Wigginton Road
8	Union Terrace
9	Lord Mayor's Walk
10	Gillygate
11	Monk Bar
12	St Maurice's Churchyard
13	Ice House
14	Hospital
15	Monkgate
16	Bay Horse
17	Goodramgate
18	King's Square
19	Shambles
20	Pavement
21	St Crux Church Hall
22	St Saviourgate
23	ARC
24	Colliergate
25	Stonebow
26	Carmelite Friary
27	Hungate
28	Whip-ma-Whop-ma-gate
29	Golden Fleece
30	Herbert House

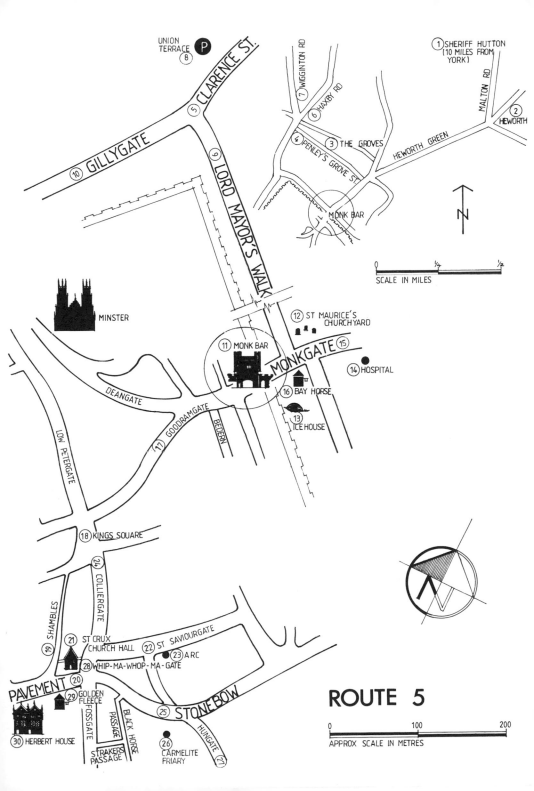

ROUTE 5

Alphabetical Index

The Route

If you follow this route you could pass Sheriff Hutton [1] – the village, not the man. We last heard of it on Route 1 in connection with Edward Hewison. He was a 20-year-old soldier in the Earl of Northumberland's Light Horse and the first man to be hanged on the Knavesmire. He had raped a maid-servant belonging to the castle whose sheer size is a constant surprise to visitors – the castle, not the maid-servant, you understand. Afterwards his body was gibbeted in a field in Sheriff Hutton Road.

After such a beginning this route is not for the faint-hearted. It is a sorry tale of ghastly deeds and even worse endings. So here goes:

The "village" of Heworth [2] is now much sought-after for its peaceful atmosphere but has seen more than its fair share of gore over the years. The body of Robert Aske, the unsuccessful leader of the doomed Pilgrimage of Grace ended up on Heworth Moor but we shall find out more at the end of our journey.

If the eerie calm of village life is too much to bear, it may be a relief to enter the bustling warren of "The Groves" [3]. These streets were built in the last century as a solution to the over-crowding of the teeming tenements elsewhere in the city. The houses look pretty alike from the outside as they stand in rows of solid Victorian uniformity.

In fact they were individually designed to provide quite varied accommodation for all strata of nineteenth century society. Some houses were destined for people with servants, some for skilled manual workers, others for professional people and so on. They must have seemed the ultimate in luxury when they came on the market and were eagerly snapped up by purchasers who were maybe unaware that they were being socially engineered to form well-balanced neighbourhoods with a good mix of classes and incomes.

"The Groves" were originally called Payne Leas Crofts – hence the present street named "Penley's Grove Street" [4]. Before all this harmony was imposed, things occasionally got out of hand. On 12th January 1674, George Aislaby fought a duel with Jonathan Jennings. The reason for the unpleasantness is as unfathomable as the result, for if you read two history books you will probably find two versions of both. It may have been something as trivial as how one treated his or the other's sister-in-law. What is not disputed is that Aislaby lived at the Treasurer's House, a stone's throw away over the bar walls on Route 7. Now that is another possible minefield of mis-information. When the last Treasurer resigned his post in 1547, he gave as his reason: no treasure.

The building is well worth a visit, however, the more so if you like to look for spectral phenomena. In 1954, a local plumber, Harry Martindale, was working in the cellar. He was amazed to see a whole Roman Legion suddenly marching through the wall. His amazement was compounded because they appeared to be cut off at the knees.

Much later it was realised that the floor of the cellar had been raised by about a foot since Roman times and therefore the soldiers had, in fact, been on the level, albeit their level.

Whichever way you turn you will probably come out on Haxby Road [6] or Clarence Street [5]. The innocent looking children's playground on the corner of Wigginton [7] and Haxby Roads was once the location of both the Horse Fair and the gallows of the Dean and Chapter of York. The site was marked by a stone cross. The Fabric Rolls in York Minster show that in 1693, £5 5s.10d. (about £5.29) was expended "for re-building the gallows in the Horse-faire and the stocks in the Minster yard".

Followers of Rugby League will always remember Clarence Street as the home of the game in York. Nowadays the black and yellow men play at Ryedale Stadium.

A car park is a depressing sight at the best of times, but when it takes the place of a ballroom and a skating rink, it seems a double let-down. Not so long ago, people would flock to the Grand Ballroom on Union Terrace [8].

Turning into Lord Mayor's Walk [9] it is hard to imagine that local people would get their milk from a farm which stood on the corner of Gillygate [10] until the turn of the century. Echoes of that rustic past occasionally surface when travelling people bring their horses to graze on the slopes of the Bar Walls, or even on the car park – not a very fruitful occupation, to be sure.

Monk Bar [11] was once a prison for the Freemen of York. Whether it was for them to incarcerate others, or for those freemen who transgressed, is not clear. Directly across the road is a small part of a graveyard – all that remains of St Maurice's Churchyard [12]. One of the stones commemorates a man who was a perpetual overseer. Perhaps he didn't take his Bile Beans.

If you go up on the walls at this point and look across the road from the Ice House [13] below you will spot a tall red-brick building – yet another of York's elegant but redundant hospitals, built in 1850. Its south facing side had cast iron balconies so that patients could enjoy an uninterrupted view of the Gas Works. A lot of water has flowed under the bridge since it was last used for healing purposes, however. It has provided office space for York-shire Water [14] and its other useful function is to hide the garish Sainsbury store.

Just round the corner on Monkgate [15] is the old Grey Coat School for Girls which was the female equivalent of the Blue Coat School last seen on Route 4. Now it is a Health Centre. Let us hope that the staff are a bit more humane than in the old days. At a recent Open Day an elderly lady, a former Grey Coat Girl, suddenly spied her old class-mates gathered round a stern-looking headmis-tress. Apparently the ladies looked, and were, much more fero-cious than their male counterparts.

The yard and stables of the Bay Horse Inn [16] once resounded to the grunts of prize porkers. On 4th November 1856, the York-shire Gazette reported a revival of the Old Ebor Pig Show. After being held in Walmgate, it changed its venue and forty active gentlemen came along to show their interest in the breeding of swine and ended with a convivial dinner provided by Mr. Hornsey the landlord.

Passing through Monk Bar you arrive on Goodramgate [17], a very interesting street with much to look at. In fact the portcullis of Monk Bar is the only one in the city still capable of being lowered. This is only done on special occasions, the last being in 1953, to mark the Coronation of Queen Elizabeth II.

The Gazette regularly carried adverts for a Foreign Photographic Studio at No. 34. All work was guaranteed and Augustus Mahalski undertook Carte de Visite portraits of the highest quality.

Near the far end of Goodramgate is the oldest row of houses in York. Opposite them stands a block which surely won't last as long. This disaster in concrete replaced one of the most popular of the city's dance halls – the Albany. It was only built earlier in the century but incorporated a sprung maple floor. The musicians had to walk under it to reach the stage and could see the great springs bracing themselves for the ordeal to come.

You will eventually be deposited on King's Square [18]. It is hard to imagine that until 1937 there was a church here and its church-yard was used to keep animals before they were slaughtered and taken to the many butchers' shops in the Shambles [19]. Years before that, the congregation had moved round the corner to St Sampson's. Bringing the livestock into the church was perhaps taking the meaning of "flock" too literally. At the turn of the century the vast majority of all the city's butchers worked, as they had always done, in this narrow slit of a street. Now there's no church and no purveyors of flesh either: the only hams are to be found entertaining the tourists.

Jostle your way down the Shambles and before you know it you'll be on the Pavement [20], literally. This short street once led continuously to High Ousegate before chunks were demolished to create Piccadilly and Parliament Street. To make way for progress, sorry, traffic, at least one medieval inn, The Eagle and Child, and another church which was inconsiderate enough to stand in the middle of the road, had to be removed. We will hear of the inn later. The church, St Crux, was blown up in 1887. It was supposed to be unsafe but proved to be of such sturdy construction that dynamite was necessary to bring it down.

Just before you land on the Pavement you could make a left turn along an extremely narrow passage along the side of St Crux church hall [21]. Facing you is the backwater known as St Saviourgate [22]. With its varied buildings it is a relief from the concrete boredom of Stonebow. A great pillared church, a transplanted hospital and staid town houses seem to stand in limbo. A redundant church now houses the Archaeological Resource Centre [23], where ancient and modern rub shoulders in unexpected harmony. Anyone can go in and literally touch the past – real stones and bones, sherds and turds. The most prized relics are indeed fossilised Viking and Anglo-Saxon stools. After such encounters it may be a relief to use the interactive computers.

Opposite: Hospital

This is the power house which drives the preservation of old York. Here they classify many of the finds from digs all over the city. It is at the ARC that the delicate conservation work is carried out. We shall encounter a perfect example on Route 7.

They are so skilled, they can tackle work from near and far. They have even restored a cannon from one of Sir Francis Drake's warships. The rusted mass had been on the seabed for four centuries.

From the Colliergate [24] end of the street, it would be easy to think of the place as nothing more than a taxi rank. It may have had a similar function in the eighteenth century when being a chairman meant a more energetic life-style than running a quango. In 1798 the rates for chairmen were as follows:

"For every fare from any place within the walls of the city, or liberty of St Peter's, or from any place within the walls – to any place without any bar or postern . . . not exceeding half a mile before ten at night – sixpence.

The same after ten – one shilling. Exceeding half a mile, before ten – one shilling. The same after ten – one shilling and sixpence. For waiting and carrying – for the first hour before ten – one shilling (including the fare) . . . "

If you look at the Sedan chair in the Castle Museum and imagine its weight, even without a passenger, you will agree that the chairpersons deserved every penny.

This century saw a return to such traditional values, when a well-known resident of Walmgate (Route 3) called Anthony Foy would convey drunken bodies home in a wheelbarrow for a few pence. Whether he ever came this far is debatable, but he was a worthy successor to the monks we met on Route 1.

The twentieth century looms over the street from the far end in the uninspiring form of the Inland Revenue building.One of the best thing about York is that most of its beauty is so entrenched in its history. The miracle is that so much of it is still here, despite floods, fires, invasions and the internal combustion engine.

It is incredible that you can be immersed in the Shambles one minute and the next be assaulted by the Stonebow [25] – York's answer to Town Planning.What the Luftwaffe tried to do by stealth, the planners did in broad daylight and presumably collected a handsome fee into the bargain. The horrible ensemble of concrete blocks has only one merit. It will not stand for ever and then hopefully will make way for something more worthy of York.

Maybe people said the same thing back in the thirteenth century when, somewhere behind the Telephone Exchange, the Carmelites built their Friary [26]. In 1314 they were given royal permission to have the only other boat on the River Foss in order to bring building materials on site. The King even gave them eight oaks to start them off. We shall never know how it looked – it can't have been any worse than what you see now – but the place was never a haven of peace and quiet even in those days.

In 1358, for example, there was a dispute concerning one Richard Thornton. It was alleged that "within the years of puberty he was ensnared and seduced by the Carmelites and so took the habit." Getting the Abbey Habit had a completely different meaning then, obviously, but since he was under fourteen, the King intervened and took him into his protection.

After such a start, things could only get worse and they did. In 1374, Friar John Wy killed another Friar, John Harald. We don't know why, but in 1386 he was pardoned and reprieved. Just before that, in 1385, a plasterer, John de Driffield, was fined 20 marks for building an oven so badly that it completely collapsed.

Such unsavoury goings-on no doubt left a nasty taste for the people living nearby but that was nothing to what was to come. The nondescript thoroughfare known as Hungate [27] may look uninspiring today but it used to be a refuse dump for the butchers of the Shambles.

In 1409 the parishioners of St John the Baptist complained because their priest could hardly get through the service due to the stench of rotting meat. It was simply offal.

So what do the authorities do when they have a problem? Make it legal, of course. Consequently Hungate was appointed an official dumping ground in 1524. Perhaps anything that was to come could be seen as an improvement. The Carmelites were not about to give in without a struggle. Even they had some standards. In 1573 it was decreed that anyone laying dung against the Friary wall in Hungate should pay 12d. for every load. By the time of the closure, the pay-roll included just the prior, nine friars and three novices.

You can still see the remains of a low stone wall – all that is left of the Friary – if you walk down Black Horse Passage. Any connection with a dung-heap is purely coincidental.

Just round the corner from the Shambles is York's shortest street with probably the longest and most unfathomable name [28]. The plaque gives the scholarly explanation but the goings-on throughout history suggest that the connection with whipping was never far from the truth.

The York Civic Records of 1570 refer to a "little cart of this city which was made for the whipping of vagabonds." It was trundled out to Monk Bridge and probably passed this way.

In 1572 they refer to a trio who were sentenced to be carted about the city on Saturday – market day. Their crime was not original but the punishment possibly was. A mariner had been carrying on with the wife of a cobbler. A widow had allowed them to carry on in her house. All three found themselves on the carpet and then in the cart. The widow appeared with a paper on her head. Her offences were written in great letters.

In 1571 Thomas Brigham, a barber, was found to have been selling cakes of wax mixed with turpentine. The trouble was that he was selling them as pure wax. He was ordered to be set upon a scaffold at Pavement with a paper on his forehead. The message was that he admitted to attempting to swindle the Queen's subjects. He had to endure this from 7am to 1pm – and also had two wax cakes hanging from front and back. It must have been a relief when he was led off to prison.

Of course it was very easy to fall foul of the law in those days. In 1570 it was ordained that at least two people from each household had to come to sermons in the Minster on Sundays and Holy Days. In 1571 taverns were ordered to close on Sundays and later the same year, there was an enquiry into the eating of meat during Lent. Most of the city came out of this with a clean bill of health. The only two transgressions were in Bootham. John Harper, a tailor, was found to have eaten a calf. George Wilson was the butcher who killed the animal.

Finally, in July 1571, there was a Queen's Commission which called for stricter treatment of "lewd persons, vagabonds, sturdy beggars, masterless men and others." Loitering soldiers were also cited as a social evil and suggested remedies were the stocks and plentiful whippings. You can have a lot of fun reading the Civic Records. The old spellings give a clue to the pronunciation at the time. For instance, we now have beggars, but back in the sixteenth century, they also had: offendars, spynnars, prisonars, forynars and travylars, not to mention ropars, tolle gatherars and tannars.

Some early names are not without charm. One of the first Danish Kings of York was Ivar the Boneless, son of Ragnor. No doubt a more manly figure was one of the first English Kings: Edmund Ironside, but even he can't compete with one of the original Essex Men. The Domesday Book mentions a prominent and fecund landowner around Dunmow whose Latin name, Humfrid Aurei Testiculi, is rendered by the translator as Humphrey Goldenbollocks.

With so much evidence of crime and punishment in sixteenth century York it is perhaps ironic that in the same year, a draper's servant, James Sympson of Newcastle, was granted a passport to visit the city "so long as he shall honestly and quietly behave himself."

As we saw on Route 1, York was always a centre for punishing the more serious crimes and had more than its share of venues and methods for carrying out the ultimate chastisement. In 1776, Eliza Bordington was hanged and then her body was taken down and burnt. She had poisoned her husband. Following special pleading by Queen Charlotte, the consort of George III, the punishment of burning women for the crime of "Petty Treason" was abolished in 1789.

A couple of years later, on the night of 9th February 1791, Spence Broughton robbed the mail between Rotherham and Sheffield. He was tried in York and hanged on 24th March 1792. Then he was gibbeted. This was an embellishment on the standard form of execution and some Judges of Assize were rather partial to it. It involved suspending the body in a prominent place near the scene of the crime.

Therefore in this case, Spence was hung in chains on a gibbet near Attercliffe Common, to the south of the road leading from Sheffield to Rotherham – probably not very far from the Sheffield Arena. It had to be not less than 300 yards from the road and was the last gibbet-post erected in Yorkshire. The post remained in position until 1828, complete with the irons, the skull and a few bones and rags still attached. The grisly custom was repealed in 1834.

In the early fourteenth century Andrew de Barclay was condemned for conspiracy with the Scots. It was ordered that he be:

> "hanged, drawn and beheaded; that your heart and bowels and entrails, whence come your traitorous thoughts, be torn out and burnt to ashes, and that the ashes be scattered to the winds; that your body be cut into four quarters . . . "

This was so that one of the quarters could be hanged upon the bridge at York. The others toured the country with stops at major venues in Newcastle, Carlisle and Shrewsbury. The head adorned London Bridge.

Somewhat later, in 1557, Thomas Stafford committed treason against Queen Mary. He went to Dieppe and then for some reason landed at Scarborough, captured the castle and then surrendered. That was his big mistake. His execution and those of his fellow traitors played havoc with municipal finances.

What was really needed was a public-spirited individual to make a grand gesture, as in 1572, when the Lord Mayor said that he would fund the building of the scaffold at Pavement for the execution of the Earl of Northumberland.

Since no such offer was forthcoming, it was grudgingly decided that:

> "the expense of boiling, carving and setting up of the carcases of the late traitors about this city, amounting to 12s.6d. should be paid out of the corporation funds."

The implements used for such delicate work look just like a large carving knife and fork. They are illustrated in old books and were housed in York Castle. They are probably still there.

So much for the great and the good. "The Records of York Castle" by Captain A. W. Twyford FRGS (Late 21st Hussars), Governor H.M. Prison York Castle, tell a sorry tale of crime and punishment for the rest of society. For them life and death were much more routine, but occasionally the crimes and sentences bear the stamp of eccentricity.

For example, Robert Bickerdicke, who met his end in 1586 for Petty Treason: "in that he would not express his opinion as to which side he would take in the event of the King of Spain invading England." He was tried twice for this offence, Judge Rhodes being dissatisfied with the verdict of "Not guilty" returned on his first trial. This could be the first time that sitting on the fence was a capital offence.

We have already met the husband of Isabella Billington (Route 4) who was hanged "because it was his great misfortune to be her husband, from which it was argued that he was answerable for her deeds."

On the same day, Dolly Dilby was hanged for witchcraft. She said that she received 10s. at a time from the devil.

Sometimes there were strange coincidences, as on 9th April 1842, when two men were hanged for wife-murder. Each man was blind in his right eye.

On 7th April 1787, William Bryan swung for stealing 4s.6d., besides 4 farthings and some clothes. The same day, Daniel Goldthorpe suffered for stealing a piece of cloth. His wife had a long argument with the hangman and was eventually given his clothes.

Certain crimes were recurrent but in 1828, three men were the last to be hanged for horse-stealing. The murder of a spouse was very common, with murder of a maid-servant a close runner-up. In 1578, William Henry de Boyle was punished for strangling his maid while his wife and two daughters looked on.

In 1775, a Captain John Bolton was said to have strangled his maid "with a fife", but hanged himself in his cell. We are not told with which musical instrument he accomplished this deed.

The ladies seemed to find original methods and motives for killing their menfolk. In 1671, Ann Pinchbecke brained her husband with an axe, while in 1821, Ann Barber poisoned her husband "of whom she professed to be "stalled" (tired)".

Sometimes a prank could go horribly wrong, as on 17th April 1790, when six young men were hanged "for having, in a spirit of fun, run away with a basket containing food belonging to their chum, who, losing his temper, charged them with stealing, and then felt himself bound to adhere to his charge."

Perhaps York witnessed the first "copy-cat" murder. In 1856, William Dove was hanged for poisoning his wife. He had read reports of another trial where a doctor failed to discover strychnine in a murder victim and unsuccessfully tried the same strategy.

At least two attorneys were hanged for forging wills and in 1753, William Smith was suspended for murdering six relations – an early serial killer, perhaps.

The crimes were sometimes bizarre. William Parkinson murdered "a Scotchman". We are not told whether bagpipes were involved. Charles Normanton was convicted at the age of seventeen, and the height of 4 feet 8 inches., of the murder of a gentleman aged 67. In 1661, two men robbed one Mr. Melrose and cut off his nose in the Forest of Galtres.

Sometimes the justice was almost poetic, as when James Waller, a poacher, was hanged for murdering a gamekeeper. Occasionally the routine crimes created milestones, as when William Jackson murdered his sister and, on 18th August 1874, took part in the first private execution within the Castle Walls.

As far as the records show, only one man ever seems to have been reprieved. That was a man called Attwood in 1682, and he was literally being dragged to his execution when it happened.

This is just about where we came in. Pavement was a favourite spot for executions, among spectators at least. After the failed Pilgrimage of Grace, one of the highest in rank, Lord Hussey, was first "hanged for twenty minutes, then cut down, stripped and laid upon a stage built close to the gallows, where his head was cut off, his body quartered". It reads more like a recipe than an account of an execution.

The same fate was reserved for the Abbots of Jervaulx, Rieveaulx and Fountains as well as the Prior of Burlington. After the execution of the leader, Robert Aske, his body was taken to Master Robert Pyements at the sign of the Eagle and Child and fixed in chains. Next day the sheriff, escorted by troops of light horse and many citizens, retraced our steps back to Heworth Moor. There the corpse was suspended from a 35' high gibbet and left there for twenty years. Going up in the world obviously had a different meaning in those days.

An effigy of Oliver Cromwell was even hung to show how

unpopular he was. He was dressed up in a pink satin suit, hanged and then dumped into a tar barrel along with the gallows and burnt, to the delight of a thousand citizens.

Nowadays, the only thing hanging around is the inn-sign of the Golden Fleece [29]. This pub used to be called the Golden Hart but has a ghost story with a twist that only came to light in 1994. An

Mystery Object (b)

See Route 7, page 113

American tourist sleeping in the hotel awoke to find that she had written the name of a Canadian airman and the name of the pub on a piece of paper by her bedside. Apparently an airman did fall out of a window and through a glass roof to his death during the World War II. The pub was well frequented by allied airmen from the many local airfields.

One theory is that the ghost is homesick and has gone back across the Atlantic with the lady tourist. Furthermore, if the lady can find time to go over the border into Canada, the ghost will probably feel at home at last and stop making a nuisance of himself.

A couple of doors away, next to the Herbert House [30], was the grocery opened by Joseph Rowntree's father, Joseph. It was here that the younger Joseph served his apprenticeship along with another young man with a sweet tooth – George Cadbury. Behind the shop, in Lady Peckitt's Yard, young Joseph started the Adult School with his brother and taught reading and writing every Sunday morning till he was almost sixty years old. The shop was still functioning as Rowntrees of Scarborough until well after the war.

Route 6

Only Wolves and Horses

Route Index

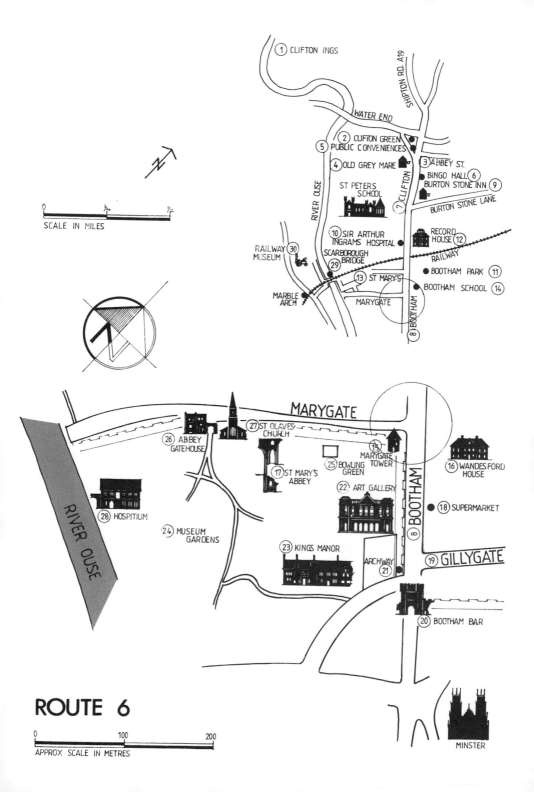

① CLIFTON INGS

SHIPTON RD. A19

WATER END

② CLIFTON GREEN
⑤ PUBLIC CONVENIENCES
③ ABBEY ST.
④ OLD GREY MARE
BINGO HALL ⑥
BURTON STONE INN ⑨
ST PETERS SCHOOL
⑦ CLIFTON
BURTON STONE LANE
RIVER OUSE
⑩ SIR ARTHUR INGRAMS HOSPITAL
RECORD HOUSE ⑫
RAILWAY MUSEUM ㉚
SCARBOROUGH BRIDGE
㉙
RAILWAY
BOOTHAM PARK ⑪
⑬ ST MARYS
BOOTHAM SCHOOL ⑭
MARBLE ARCH
MARYGATE
⑧ BOOTHAM

SCALE IN MILES

0   ¼   ½

N

MARYGATE

㉗ ST OLAVES CHURCH
㉖ ABBEY GATEHOUSE
⑮ MARYGATE TOWER
㉕ BOWLING GREEN
⑯ WANDESFORD HOUSE
⑰ ST MARY'S ABBEY
㉒ ART GALLERY
㉘ HOSPITIUM
BOOTHAM
⑱ SUPERMARKET
RIVER OUSE
㉔ MUSEUM GARDENS
㉓ KINGS MANOR
ARCHWAY ㉑
⑲ GILLYGATE
⑳ BOOTHAM BAR

ROUTE 6

0   100   200

APPROX SCALE IN METRES

MINSTER

Alphabetical Index

The Route

Approaching York from the north, it is hard to imagine that less than a thousand years ago, you would have been terrified of wolves which also roamed the dense Forest of Galtres. No-one would have dared to venture out without a guide. Not even this book would have been much use then. Anyone letting loose a dog in the King's Forest would have been fined 3 shillings (15p) – a small fortune.

By the sixteenth century, malt merchants had consumed all the woods within 20 miles of York for timber to burn in their malt-kilns. The last tree of the Forest was apparently taken down in the Summer of 1948. It stood near Clifton Green [2] at the north side of Abbey Street [3].

All this clearing of forests meant that by then there was sufficient clear space on Clifton Ings [1] for horse-racing to take place. The winning horse would have a silver bell placed on its headgear. The bell was to be returned to the Lord Mayor after twelve months but in the meantime the owner could bring any other horse to run against it for the bell. The wager was always the magic sum of 6s. 8d. – about 33p.

Horse-racing on the Ings lasted 200 years so that it could be said that the first race there was the 1530 and the last the 1730. Racing would nowadays be a risky affair unless it involved sea-horses. The area is liable to flood in a very spectacular fashion, which is why the Ings don't stage the Ebor any more. The final meeting lasted five days. Because of severe flooding, the Wednesday race had to be postponed until Saturday. So a safer environment had to be found – among the hangers-on at the Knavesmire.

Things went from strength to strength and in August 1804, the world's first woman jockey took to the turf. Twenty-two-year-old Alicia Meynell rode side-saddle and led for the first three miles but eventually lost and then publicly tore her opponent, Captain William Flint, off a strip for lack of courtesy.

Talking of magnificent specimens, a ten-foot long salmon was captured on Clifton Ings in 1685. In case this sounds a little improbable, remember that even now, fish find themselves in ponds and pools whenever the river floods.

In 1528 an acre of meadow land at Clifton was let for 2 shillings per year. The cost of mowing was 6d. and it cost a further 6d. to cart the hay to St Mary's Abbey. Recall that 12d. is 5p in present-day currency.

Today, the village green evokes such a pleasant rustic atmosphere that you can easily imagine a village pub called "The Maypole" but it is nowhere to be seen. On 30th April 1649 Grace Bland was hanged for burning it down. On that day 23 other people were executed – including Isabella Billington whom we met on Route 4.

A couple of years before that, drinkers would have met two sisters, Elizabeth and Helen Drysdale, who were maids to Dame Robinson. She ran the inn before it burnt down. Next on the site was first the Grey Horse and then the Old Grey Mare [4]. The girls had to go too far and poured oxalic acid into their sweethearts' drinks and ended up on St Leonard's Gallows.

Even the public conveniences [5] at the Bootham end of the green look in keeping with the bucolic village scene. Hard to believe that they are one of the few relics of one of York's twentieth century innovations.

At the beginning of the century York was keen to modernise its transport network and had electric trams linking Acomb, Dringhouses, Fulford and Haxby Road. By 1914, new routes were prepared for motor buses. With the advent of war, petrol was difficult to obtain so the corporation opted for an imaginative solution and became one of only eight towns in Britain to run battery-operated Electrobuses.

On 15th February 1915, two brand-new state-of-the-art electrobuses were delivered, at a cost of £1,172. They could carry 22 passengers each. There were two routes – City to Clifton and City to Heworth.

The present-day conveniences are housed in the booster station which cost £85 to build. The bus fare was 1d. for a 15 minute journey.

Unfortunately, the electrobus had solid tyres which damaged road surfaces. The fact that its two ton chassis had to carry a two-ton battery didn't help either and passengers tended not to like having to dismount so that the vehicle could cross Layerthorpe

Bridge. So York's futuristic experiment came to an end in 1921. The buses were sold for £10 each.

The electrobuses were not the only odd means of transport to be seen in York during the First World War. In 1917 the teeming Leeman Road area was clamouring for a bus service of its own. They would have liked a petrol bus but because of the shortages they had to make do with a gas-powered contraption. The gas bag had to be carried on a trailer, instead of on the roof as was the custom, so that the thing could pass through Marble Arch where Leeman Road goes under the railway.

So after our glimpse back to the future we pass the Clifton Bingo Hall [6] which was obviously built as a luxury cinema and used to incorporate an up-market dance-hall in its hey-day. Much of the land between here and the river was once owned by a certain Guy Fawkes, probably the most famous old boy of St Peter's School. Needless to say, the school's annual bonfire does not feature a Guy. In the past they have burnt effigies of Frankenstein or the Belles of St Trinian's.

Just before Clifton [7] becomes Bootham [8], we pass the Burton Stone Inn [9], which takes its name from the Burton Stone which had the same function as the Hob Moor Stone encountered on Route 1. What you see is said to have formed the base of a cross. Another explanation is that the depressions used to contain vinegar. Townspeople would place money in the vinegar, in order not to pass on the Plague to the country folk who brought provisions to the spot.

The stone is all that remains of Burton Stone Lane's past. It used to be known as Chapel Lane and long gone is Lady Mill which was the site of the Abbot of St Mary's private gallows.

The long row of brick cottages [10] just over the road after the rambling frontage of St Peter's School was built by Sir Arthur Ingram in 1632. They formed a hospital for 10 poor widows. The magnificent doorway was taken from Holy Trinity in Micklegate when it was demolished in 1630 at a cost of 13s. 4d.

This almshouse always had a certain style, inside as well as out. It was one of the few where the inmates wore a uniform. In the seventeenth century this took the form of a heavy gown made up from 5 yards of serge, canvas and a yard of buckram, plus a yard of bone. On each shoulder was a silver cock – the founder's family crest. These were still worn into the last century.

From one old hospital to another: this time the country's oldest asylum still in use – Bootham Park [11]. Certainly it has one of the most beautiful exteriors in the land and it was opened in 1777 and designed by John Carr. Unfortunately the interior failed to match and in the early part of the nineteenth century it was at the heart of a scandal because of brutal treatment, degrading conditions and shady financial dealings. Last century the grounds were the scene of the Grand Yorkshire Gala. This was a three-day holiday which started out as a flower show and grew to include ox-roasting and Hot Air Balloon rides. The Ancient Society of York Florists can go back even further.

The society was founded back in 1700 as the Royal Society of Gardiners in York and became The Society of York Florists in 1768. It has held shows every year since then, even during times of war, thus making it probably the country's, if not the world's, oldest gardening society. Meetings used to take place at Baynes' Coffee House, 89, Low Petergate (Route 7) but nowadays the primulas have given way to pizzas. Membership dwindled in the 1980s but following a transplant from the city centre, the Society enjoys vigorous growth and looks set to thrive for another 225 years at least. Shows and meetings are now held at Kingsway Junior School in Clifton.

The large square hotel standing further down Bootham on the left has a military record. Don't worry about the arrows on the stone gateposts – the Indians don't arrive yet. The building was called Record House [12] and once housed the Pay Department for Northern Command.

Bootham is now a very genteel-looking thoroughfare but used to cater for quite different appetites. Somewhere opposite the end of St Mary's [13], by the entrance to Bootham Park stood Cockpit House. Apart from the fighting cocks, plays were put on there. It was burnt and pulled down by farmers and labourers protesting against the Militia Act of 1757 which compelled the poor to serve in the Militia. After tearing the lists of names from the hands of constables, they drank all they could find and then torched the building. Whether that was how flame-grilled chicken came to be on the menu, we cannot say.

Surely nothing like that ever happened at Bootham School [14], the famous Quaker establishment, even when the Headmaster insisted on teaching normal lessons on Christmas Day, 1849.

Look across the road and you will see a stumpy round tower which seems to be unpeeling itself from within. Marygate Tower [15] stands on the corner of the old Abbey walls and was used to store the records of the Yorkshire monasteries. During the Civil War it was damaged by a mine. In the Borthwick Institute (Route 4) they have a massive old book, an inventory, whose vellum pages still bear the blackened spherical impression of a cannon ball.

So what do you do with a bad crack in a wall or ceiling? Paper over it of course! Or in the case of a medieval stone tower, build a house over the crack. This solution worked perfectly until 1896 when the Yorkshire Philosophical Society decided that it would be a good idea to clear away some of the houses to reveal the grandeur of the walls and make Bootham more attractive. They revealed the crack – still there after all those years.

The tower was originally perfectly circular with an octagonal interior. When it was repaired, the outer wall followed an irregular curve which resulted in the failure to meet up properly. You can see that odd pieces of masonry were used for the repairs. These include pieces of fluted frieze from a large bay window in the King's Manor which was also damaged in the siege.

Whereas Sir Arthur Ingram's legacy stands right on the pavement, Wandesford House [16] is very easy to miss, especially in Spring and Summer when a leafy screen shields it from the passing gaze. Miss Mary Wandesford was the only unmarried daughter of Christopher Wandesford who played truant from school in order to go and watch the Battle of Marston Moor. He must have gone on to do well as his daughter was able to leave enough money to build a house where ten poor Gentlewomen could live at peace and "retire from the hurry and noise of the world". When no suitable house could be found, a plot of land was bought from William Wilberforce of Hull in 1739. It cost £233 10s. The building was finished in 1743 and the carpenters' bill was £542 0s. 8d. – a good investment as their stairs, doors and windows are still as sound as ever.

As we have already seen, the street catered for all tastes but it is hard to imagine it being more varied than it is now. Shopping has always inflamed the passions. Back in the thirteenth century the Abbott of St Mary's claimed a toll from the market held on Bootham – at the Booths which stood up against his boundary. Then an enquiry said he had no right to any tolls. In the violent affray which ensued, several monks were killed and houses were burned. This was as good a reason as any to call in the builders and up went the walls.

In the eighteenth century, when the Abbey [17] was in ruins, much of its stone was recycled. It went to rebuild the County Gaol which we visited on Route 3. It also helped rebuild Ouse Bridge and repaired Beverley Minster.

Today Bootham has pubs, churches, hospitals, schools, clothes shops and most with an individual flavour. Even the neighbour-hood supermarket [18] hides a classy past. Only a few years ago, the sober doorway, planted solidly between grocery and off-li-cence, gave access to York's one and only roulette room.

In the Sixties, while the youngsters were rocking with Gerry B., a select few of their elders were enjoying the real high life. Behind an anonymous door was a stairway to happiness. York's own Jet Set could unwind at the Society Club and enjoy "Catering without Compromise", conjured up by a real French chef.

In the past, York knew Eric Bloodaxe and George Hudson, the Railway King. In the Sixties, Doctor Beeching wielded a different kind of axe and made the nation's railways tremble in fright. The good doctor, however, liked nothing better, whenever he passed through the city, than to drop his luggage at the Royal Station Hotel and instruct his chauffeur to head for Bootham and a spot of dinner.

Apart from the delicacies for the palate were nibbles for the pocket, with gaming by Crockfords. Whether the doctor played "chemin de fer" is not on record. Anyway, the Society Club prospered for twenty years and had the double distinction of bringing to York the two "R's": roulette and ratatouille. Nowadays the most exciting thing is watching the tourists playing Russian roulette at the Gillygate [19] traffic lights. But life was not always so calm and well ordered.

In April 1487 an ex-mayor of York was murdered while on watch at Bootham Bar [20]. Now you merely risk being trampled by the lines of tourists disgorging from the nearby coach-park. While you contemplate life, try to spot the medieval rôtisserie at the base of the steps up to the Bar Walls.

As you stand with your back to the wall, notice the square tower and the distressed-looking archway [21] which apparently crumbles into the roadway.

When you eventually make it across the road towards the City Art Gallery [22] you will read the plaque which tells that the gateway was made for Princess Margaret in 1503. In fact the gateway was made in 1497 for her father, Henry VII, so that he could go to the Minster while staying as a guest of the Abbot of St Mary's – the Bishop of Carlisle. Yet another royal visit which left a lasting impression on the city's architectural heritage.

Even this pales into insignificance compared with the preparations for Henry's visit. Quite apart from building him a palace, he and his queen were given a gold cup filled with gold.

In an obvious bid to sweeten him up following the city's revolt, (mentioned on Route 3) he was also presented with six gallons of fine hippocras – a blend of white wine and claret – not to mention one dozen comfits, one dozen biscuits and six great fat pykes.

The real delights were one bushel of filberts, a quantity of grain ginger, six loaves of fine sugar and two other intriguing items: one dozen marmellado and some fine sucketts. However, at the head of the list of goodies, as always, was Mayne Bread.

This was presented to important visitors between 1445 and 1662. It was a rich bread, baked by Mayne Bakers in the city and nowhere else. A decree of 1595 stipulated that the bread be baked every Friday morning. Any bread unsold by 5pm had to be sent to the Lord Mayor, Aldermen and Sheriffs who would buy it all up.

By Queen Elizabeth's reign, spiced cake had become more fashionable but for the curious, on the next page is the recipe, as featured in a Yorkshire W.I. recipe book. The bread was last baked in 1951 for the York Festival.

Mayne Bread

Ingredients

12 oz plain flour
8 oz sugar
3 egg yolks
2 egg whites
½ oz yeast
two teaspoons of rose water
one good teaspoon of Coriander seed
one good teaspoon of Carraway seed
one third cup warm milk and water (as for making bread)

Method

Mix together the flour, sugar, coriander and carraway seeds. Add to the three yolks the rose water in one basin. In another basin beat the two whites of egg until stiff. In a third basin put the yeast, warm milk and water.

The whole of the contents of the three basins to be then mixed with the dry ingredients and put to rise in a warm place for approximately twenty minutes. After which, roll out, cut into shape and allow to rise in a warm place again for ten minutes.

Bake in a moderate oven for 10 – 15 minutes, or until golden brown.

We have already heard about the palace built for Henry VIII's visit. There are occasional exhibitions in the cellar of the West Range and it is possible that here are the foundations of the palace built between the Manor and the river. The buildings now known as the King's Manor [23] form a wonderful oasis of calm and freshness, so close to the daily hell of Gillygate's traffic chaos.

Some of the windows are framed in terra-cotta – probably the earliest use of the material in England. The only comparable example is to be found at the Norfolk rectory of Great Snoring, but you would have to be up early to see that.

The buildings have housed the abbot's residence, a council chamber, a ladies' boarding school, a school for the blind, not to mention its function as a royal residence. A more recent occupier is the Goethe Institut – a mecca for all interested in German culture, with its cornucopia of films, books, videos, magazines, audio tapes – Alles in Ordnung, in fact.

In 1541, authorisation was given for payment of 9s. to a hermit who lived there. From 1560 to 1641 it was the seat of the Council of the North. On 31st October 1628, at 10am, a gust of wind blew down seven chimney shafts. The eldest son of the Vice-President of the Council – Sir Edward Osborne – was in his study being taught by a French tutor. When the rubble was cleared, the son was found dead. The French tutor escaped.

Whether he was involved with the carving of the royal coat of arms which adorns the main doorway is not on record, but the "N" of "MON DROIT" is definitely dyslexic.

Apart from the dangers of flying masonry, it was well worth being President of the Council. In 1572, the City welcomed the new incumbent – the Earl of Huntingdon. He was presented with a ton of Gascony wine and four dozen Mayne Bread. The Aldermen lined up to meet him in crimson apparel.

The whole group of buildings is now kept in pristine condition. The cleaning bill must be considerable. Even when Henry and Katherine Howard came, it cost £8. 10s. 2d. to cleanse the place in readiness.

If you back out of King's Manor and pass through the Museum Gardens [24] without seeing a peacock or a squirrel, you will have created some sort of a record. Peeking through the ruined arches of the Abbey you may just make out the bowling green [25]. Just before dawn one day in May 1684, John William Nevison committed a robbery in Gad's Hill, London. He was seen and so jumped on his mare. Fifteen hours later, round about sunset, he rode into York. Sunrise was 4am that day, sunset 7pm. He arrived at the green behind the remains of the abbey where the Lord Mayor was enjoying a game of bowls. Nevison sought him out and engaged him in conversation, thus establishing a cast-iron alibi. The London witnesses swore to have recognised him, but the Judge and Jury chose not to believe them. Swift Nick, as Charles II called him, was acquitted.

Surely this was a highwayman with a heart, who richly deserved the reputation so wrongly attributed to the later rascal Turpin. His only sin was to be a Yorkshireman.

Nevison was born in Pontefract in 1639 and had all the makings of a folk-hero, a real-life Robin Hood. He was once in a village inn and heard of a poor farmer who had been put out of house and home by the bailiff. The culprit was dining at the inn and had the proceeds of the sale about his person. Nevison pretended to take no heed and retired to bed but then lay in wait and relieved the bailiff of his burden. Next day the farmer received the money and, as far as we know, lived happily ever after.

There is even a place near Pontefract called Nevison's Leap where the road passes through a cutting in the high ground. Our hero was apparently being pursued and coaxed his mount to leap over the road to escape capture. Unfortunately he came to the same end as Turpin, being executed at York on May 14th 1685. He was found guilty of a small robbery at an inn near Sandal. During his imprisonment at York Castle he wore leg-irons weighing 28lbs.

Leave the Museum Gardens via the gate-house [26]. Standing by the gorgeous Church of St Olave [27], it looks the picture of tranquillity.

Between the gate-house and the western end of the church is a space. Lacking a roof it hard to imagine that this was once the chapel of St Mary at the Gate.

At the time of the Abbey it was both courthouse above and prison below. By the nineteenth century it became first the Brown Cow, then the Bay Horse inn and was finally converted into a house in 1840. The pub was moved further down and stood against the walls but was condemned as being insanitary in 1894 and ended up across the road. There used to be 10 pubs of that name in York – now there are only five. Nowadays all that can be said about the lodge is that the inner hall has a short flight of stairs with bulbous balusters.

The large half-timbered building standing in the Gardens by the river is the Hospitium [28] where guests and visitors to the Abbey were entertained. Nowadays the regular craft fairs perform a similar function, dispensing tea and biscuits rather than the mead and roast meats of yore.

Just to prove that it can move with the times, it recently gave floor-space to an inflatable Planetarium – one of the few ever seen in Britain.

Opposite: Abbey Gate House

The tranquil scene is still capable of the odd surprise. One day it might be a brass band, another day you might hear a group of medieval musicians, complete with authentic instruments. In 1994, a Wigwam was erected and a Sioux and an Apache Indian burned a bouquet of sage to inaugurate a Festival of North American Native Culture organised by the ARC (see Route 5).

The spot has been used to make a bigger bang than all the others put together. York is a Royal Saluting Station. The city was granted the honour in 1971, its 1900th Anniversary. It is one of only 12 such stations. The others are either military bases or national capitals. Consequently, on the Anniversary of the Coronation of Queen Elizabeth II, at midday, three guns were each fired seven times at 15 second intervals.

Between the Hospitium and the river, on the site of an old herb garden, was created York's first outdoor swimming baths. They were built in 1837 and last used in 1922 but not demolished until 1969.

When you reach the river you can either turn left for the city centre or go right and cross Scarborough Railway Bridge [29] for a short cut to the National Railway Museum [30] via the Marble Arch mentioned at the beginning of this Route. You will probably see more red bicycles than you ever dreamed of. Not quite on the Peking scale, but impressive nonetheless. York is justly renowned as Britain's foremost cycling city. In Summer it even boasts a Rickshaw service.

Route 7

Central York:
from Minster to
Splash Palace

Route Index

Number on Map	*Place*
1	Minster
2	Minster Library
3	Deanery
4	Treasurer's House
5	St William's College
6	Goodramgate
7	Deangate
8	Stoneyard
9	Minster School
10	Minster Gates
11	Stonegate
12	Coffee Yard
13	Barley Hall
14	Grape Lane
15	Swinegate
16	St Sampson's Square
17	St Sampson's Church
18	Finkle Street
19	Church Street
20	Low Petergate
21	Mad Alice Lane
22	Little Stonegate
23	Punch Bowl
24	Blake Street
25	Assembly Rooms
26	St Helen's Square
27	Davygate
28	Parliament Street
29	Splash Palace

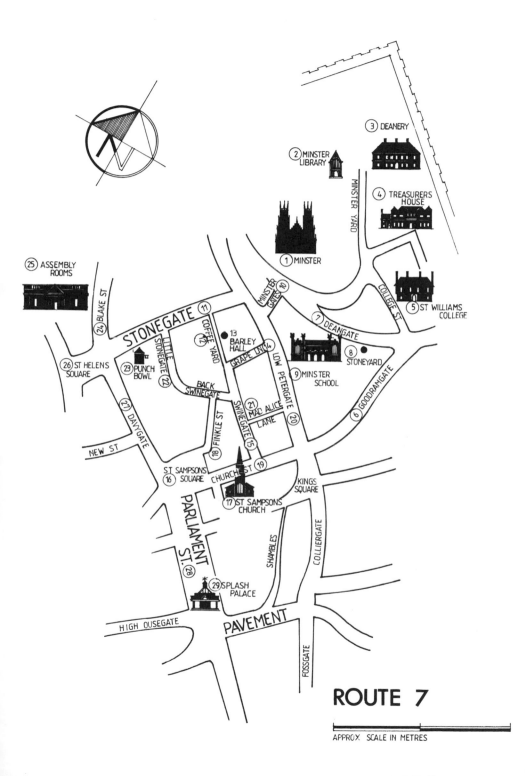

ROUTE 7

APPROX. SCALE IN METRES

Alphabetical Index

The Route

The centre of York has to be the Minster [1]. It is the spiritual heart of Yorkshire and not just because of the design of the huge West window. It dominates not only the city but the countryside for miles. It contains so much history, beauty and art that nothing short of an encyclopaedia could start to do it justice. But if you're wondering:

"What is a Minster anyway?"

Don't worry, it just means a place which "ministers" to an area. It's another word for "cathedral".

No living person can claim to have seen all the Minster because, at any given moment, some part of it is sheathed in scaffolding. Almost every day, a different section is covered up, while another is being revealed. You will always discover something new in the interior or the external façade even if, like me, you walk past it every day.

Whatever the astronomical cost of simply maintaining the fabric, and we are urged to put at least £1 in the box, imagine that in 1399, when there were 29 masons working on the building, they were paid 6d. a day. Carpenters earned 5½d whereas labourers received 4d. each weekday. The exchange rate from old to new money is 12d. = 5p and 20s. = £1. The year's expenditure on building was £430 17s. ½d. I wonder who put in the ½d?

In 1405 the artist-glazier working on the East window was paid 4s. per week.

In 1415 there were 35 masons and the annual bill was £529 6s. 5d.

By 1470 there were only 21 masons and the building budget was down to £235.

Between 1485 and 1504 the average expenditure on interior work at the Minster was £256.

On 31st October 1382, two men had a sword-fight in the Minster and were made to walk before the procession with weapon in one hand and a two-pound candle in the other.

In the sixteenth century it was ordered that at least two people from each household had to come to sermons in the Minster on Sundays and Holy Days.

All these facts are enough to give anyone a thirst and in the reign of Elizabeth I, you wouldn't have had far to go for a drink. Next to the Chapel of St Sepulchre – nowadays the Minster Library [2] – stood a public house known as "The Hole in the Wall". In fact the pub was built onto the chapel when it was purchased by a man called Webster.

Before that the chapel contained a prison – Peter Prison. In 1570 a man called Thomas Wilson, alias Mountain, killed the Abbot of St Mary's and then stabbed the Archbishop of York in the interval between sentence and execution.

When the pub was being demolished in 1816, workmen found a chamber several feet below ground level, approached by a flight of stone steps. Along the walls were the rusting remains of iron staples. Against the wall was a strong oak frame – looking suspiciously like a set of stocks – which extended the whole length of the chamber, over 35' long, 9' wide and 9' high. The present "Hole in the Wall" pub round the corner in High Petergate is of much more recent vintage.

If the Archbishop's Palace (Route 2) is the most idyllic residence outside the city walls, the New Deanery [3] must be the front-runner within. It was built in 1939 to replace the Old Deanery Mark II which stood between 1831 and 1938. Its most memorable feature must have been the bathroom. Water poured from a pipe which had passed twenty times through the kitchen range and could fill a large bath to 100° in three minutes flat.

The whole of Minster Close resembles a Christmas Card, even without snow. The delightful Treasurer's House [4] and St William's College [5] are all as old as they seem and it is a pleasure to walk along College Street, once one of York's most select shopping streets.

By the time you reach Goodramgate [6], you have to pretend that the road isn't there. A hundred years ago the only way through was via the passageway hinted at next to the National Trust Shop. The houses were demolished in 1901 to create the thoroughfare known as Deangate [7]. The change was not without controversy, however. Initially the authorities were going to demolish the old gateway which led onto Goodramgate. When the workmen arrived to carry out their task, they found that Mr. Frank Green, the wealthy owner of the Treasurer's House and St William's College, had chained himself to the oak pillars.

He thereupon produced an alternative plan which spared the archway and involved the demolition of the old Turk's Head Inn and a blacksmith's shop. He also pledged to pay for the preservation and upkeep of the archway.

Next door but one to the Cross Keys pub is the Stoneyard [8] where the ancient skills are still used to keep the Minster's fabric up to scratch.

The Minster School [9] is in fact one of the oldest in the country, having been founded by Paulinus in AD 627 to provide boy choristers for the Minster. The present buildings were only built last century.

The picturesque alley called Minster Gates [10] is all that remains of the High Minster Gates which once guarded the Minster Close. They were part of Peter Prison and the court-house of the Dean and Chapter. The most famous inmate was Jonathan Martin, the arsonist, who was examined here by magistrates of the Liberty of St Peter's following his attempt to burn down the Minster in 1829. His younger brother John was an artist whose visionary prints of biblical and mythical scenes are at last receiving due acclaim.

There were four Liberties in York: the City, St Peter's, the King's and St Mary's. Each had its own court-house, prison and gallows. An offender could escape his pursuers if he managed to step into another Liberty. We have already heard of one such episode on Route 3 and there was another case when the King's bailiff hanged a man from St Mary's. The abbot had the body buried in his garden, whereupon the royal bailiff had the corpse dug up, chained and re-hung, just to prove a point.

If you escape via Minster Gates into the crush of Stonegate [11] you will come under the scrutiny of the Red Devil at the end of Coffee Yard [12]. This is a reminder that this street was for many years a centre of printing.

The printing press came to York in the reign of Henry VII with Frederick Freez, a Dutchman. The corporation ordered him to dwell at "The Bull" in Coney Street and charged him £3 annual rent. Later his son and wife were burnt at the stake for heresy. There's gratitude for you!

However if you would prefer a happier story, here goes. Hugo Goes, son of a printer from Antwerp, set up his press in Stonegate around 1500 and as far as we know, prospered.

These narrow old streets now look so quaint and are full of shops selling articles which, though pleasant, we could well do without. In times past, however, these same streets were literally hives of industry.

In 1328, during the reign of Edward III, there were 180 different trades and professions in York. Two hundred years later, in the time of Henry II, the tradespeople included goldsmiths, drapers, fishmongers, skinners, tanners, ironmongers, walkers, weavers and glovers.

One of the oldest surviving trades is that of surgeon. In 1348, William de Bolton, surgeon of York, was called to Bamborough to remove an arrow from a wounded man. Let us hope the man was wearing his silk undershirt. This would have made the task easier as the surgeon would have pulled on the material, bringing the offending arrow-head with it. Staying with the oldest profession, it is worth noting that York took a lead in Women's Rights years before it became PC. The Civic Records show that in 1572, a lady surgeon, Isabel Warwick, was allowed to work in the city.

Nearer to the present, in the early nineteenth century, there were 99 clockmakers in the city. One of the most prolific, Henry Hindley, lived round the corner on Petergate. Most English towns would have had one or two such craftsmen, but for some reason York was in third place, behind London and Liverpool.

Turning into Coffee Yard [12] you are nearing one of York's best-kept secrets, Barley Hall [13]. Until the 1980s, most people using the short-cut between Stonegate and Grape Lane [14] were totally unaware of what was lying dormant around and over them as they negotiated the dark dusty passageway. The crust of ages covered the tunnel halfway along and the dilapidated plumber's yard looked no more exciting than any other old disused brick building.

But behind the brick lay the skeleton of a medieval house, lived in over 500 years ago by the family of Alderman Snawsell, a wealthy goldsmith and former Lord Mayor of York. Indeed the house was not new when he started renting the disused hospice from Nostell Priory.

Now the grime and grot have been stripped away, the rotting timbers replaced, and York Archaeological Trust are breathing life into the place by re-creating the sumptuous hangings and fine furniture.

Almost all aspects of life are represented within this faithfully restored old edifice. During excavations on the Bedern site a strange pot was discovered. It was round, squat and had an opening at the top, as well as a handle set horizontally on one side. Could it have been some sort of scientific vessel? The colour of the glaze led some experts to suggest that it may well have been used by an alchemist in his experiments to make gold. After much archaeological research and deliberation over its possible use, the solution was much more down to earth. The pot was, in fact, a urinal [Mystery Object (a) – see page 53]. The shape was especially popular in the North of England in the late fourteenth century. The size and shape must make it the original Portaloo.

Urinals of this type were referred to in a document of 1345 when Edward III bought 110 of them at one penny each. He obviously had to show that he was the greatest peer in the land. Standing next to the Urinal is a Dripping Tray [Mystery Object (b) – see page 87]. No, it wasn't for use by medieval incontinents, but was very effective for collecting the juices from a roast joint. Both reproductions were made for Barley Hall by local potter, Zoë Hall. Even if she could be persuaded to make any more of the rather attractive pots she could not promise to hold the price at fourteenth century levels.

Emerging from Coffee Yard into Grape Lane [14] you may not believe that pigs can fly but they are certainly all around you. This is Swinegate [15] and wherever you turn you will spot pigs – on the ground, on the walls, in the bricks. This is a very recent development and as ever in York, when you dig down you find buried treasure. In this case it was neither gold nor precious jewels, but a set of waxed tablets wrapped in a leather cover with a tooled oak-leaf design. Each tablet is made of boxwood with a wax coating and is not quite as big as a raffle ticket. The wax surfaces have writing inscribed on them – probably poetry from the late fourteenth century. The account of how the wax tablets were cleaned, stabilised and preserved reads like a thriller. Using the latest in high technology equipment, skilled technicians juggled improvisation and scientific principles, knowing that one false move could cause five hundred years of history to melt into oblivion.

Nowadays, St Sampson's Square [16] is a plain, empty space, rather like an artist's canvas. It stands ready to accommodate anything from Punch and Judy to religious zealots; Morrismen to charity stalls. Since 1393 it was known as Thursday Market and was always the place to pick up a bargain. You could get four loaves for an (old) penny. Beer, well-brewed and strong was 1d. a gallon, while a carcase of choice beef was yours for £1 0s. 4d. – real cash and carry prices. The less discerning could make do with an unspecified Scotch beast at 12s. a carcase, while anyone who merely needed a snack could have a fat goose for 4d. For those not familiar with pre-decimal currency, 12d. is equal to 5p and there were twenty shillings (20s.) to £1.

By 1528, quantities had become more dainty, while prices had increased substantially. A leg or shoulder of veal was 3d. but you could still buy honey in bulk quite cheaply – 7 gallons for 15d. Fish was very popular and there was a good variety, with turbot at 4d. and small pike at 12d. Twenty-five eels cost 4d. while 60 roaches were 15d. If you wanted meat on the hoof, you could purchase a horse for ten or twelve shillings and a bridle was thrown in for 9d.

The Siege of York brought scarcity and hardship and prices rocketed. In 1643, mutton was hard to swallow at 16s. a quarter, while pork rose to 7s. a stone. Eggs were an incredible 3d. each. Once things settled down, other commodities came on the market. During the Commonwealth years 1654-1660, marriage became a purely civil affair so the banns were published in open market. Eventually such matters were restored to the church and St Sampson's [17] looks on benignly once more, even though it is now a centre for the elderly. It occasionally hosts barn dances, just to show that it is still young at heart. Its west end looks almost provençal with its glittering statue and sparkling stonework. Surely the scene is more peaceful now than at any time in its history. In 1820 the square had nine inns and Finkle Street [18] was known as "Mucky Peg Lane", whoever she was. The square had a super-charged atmosphere earlier this century, when the Electrobuses from Route 6 used to terminate here at the battery-refreshing station. Sometimes it was more fun to watch than filleting fish.

Continue to Church Street [19]. If Stonegate specialised in books, Church Street was the place to go for girdles. Now turn left. At the intersection with Low Petergate [20], a council refuse cart recently fell through the road surface, rather like someone looking at the prices in Betty's. The problem here was an underground void caused by a nineteenth century brick sewer. When the council decided to completely repair the drains they found that the old sewer cut through a great Roman gateway.

In the eighteenth century, 89, Low Petergate was known as Baynes' Coffee House and hosted the early meetings of the Ancient Society of York Florists. Last century it became Tomlinson's Hotel and on 23rd December 1833 a local draper, George Hudson, held a meeting to discuss the latest thing in transport – the railway. Eventually the railway did come to York and Hudson was chairman of the York and North Midland Railway. He was also an enthusiastic member of the Florists and perhaps it is just a coincidence that the land for York's first station was purchased from the Micklegate Nursery.

The York College for Girls stands on the site of the Talbot Inn.

Nearby, at 46 Low Petergate lived Thomas Gent, the printer, who gave his name to the Coffee House next to Barley Hall. Henry Hindley, the most famous of York clockmakers, also lived here for £7 a year. If you turn sharp left into Mad Alice Lane [21] alongside the famous Pork Butcher's you will find yourself back among the piggies.

On the corner of Swinegate and Back Swinegate you will notice a church with the writing literally on the wall. Carry on along Little Stonegate [22] and you should find yourself back on Stonegate. Don't worry if at first you don't succeed. Try and try and then ask somebody else.

There are in York almost as many pubs bearing the name "Punch Bowl" as there are Bay Horses and we learned of their origins on Route 1. The Punch Bowl [23] on Stonegate was once a haunt of Freemasons and in the course of one of our many wars against the French, it was a lodging for French P.O.W.s who were on parole in 1762. These must have been the ones too inept to escape with those we met on Route 3.

When you reach the end of Stonegate, cast a glance up Blake

Street [24]. There lived a joiner, Joseph Penny who built the first gallows for the Knavesmire site in 1379. See Route 1. It took him less than a week and he charged £10 15s. for materials and labour. They stood for over four hundred years.

It may come as no surprise to learn that sites in Coffee Yard, Stonegate and Blake Street were renowned locations for cock fights which were held every morning of Race Week in the eighteenth century.

The Assembly Rooms [25] are well worth a look if only for the superb chandeliers. When restoration was begun earlier this century all but one of them were smashed. No-one in Britain could reproduce them. Then someone on a visit to Venice chanced upon a glassworks. Enquiries revealed not only the original invoice but the eighteenth century pattern books so the ones you see now are a perfect match. They had been a gift from Lord Burlington, the architect.

Anyway you are now in St Helens Square [26] which used to be known as "Cuckold's Square" – even before Betty's Tea Room opened. In the purge of 1547, St Helen's church was partly demolished but then re-built. In the nineteenth century, sixteen mail coaches departed from the square every day. More recently, Terry's Café and Restaurant was a very up-market spot. The loos were reputedly the most luxurious in the land. The sprung dance floor is still preserved beneath carpets in the first floor bank offices. Only the letters on the wall retain a chocolate connection.

As you head down past the Church of St Helen you will see the plaque about Davygate [27] being the approach to Davy Hall.

This was a township within the City of York and was a separate rating area until 1900, despite having been demolished in 1745. The Hall had been divided into tenements and occupied by shoemakers. Who says that history is a load of old cobblers? Upon its demolition a row of houses was erected. The rest garden just past New Street is on the site of Davy Hall.

It took its name from David the Lardiner who was Clerk of the Royal Kitchen and who, as a sideline, took charge of building the King's Castle in the twelfth century.

Therefore the Hall housed a courthouse, prison and larder which had to be stocked from the King's Forest of Galtres.

Incidentally, don't you get the feeling that everybody who was anybody had a prison in York in the old days? Everbody from the King, the Archbishop, the Abbot of St Mary's, the Prior of St Leonard's to name but a few. They must have been competing to find poor devils to fill them, especially as the population was only a few thousand. It didn't reach 8,000 until the early eighteenth century.

Anyway, David was onto a winner. He was entitled to 5d. (2p) a day from the King's purse and every Saturday in the City in York could take a halfpenny loaf, or the cash equivalent, from every baker; a gallon of ale or ½d from every brewer and a pennyworth of meat or ½d from each butcher. He also had four pennyworth of fish from each cartload sold at Fossbridge. David must have had more fun than your average taxman, but even he couldn't live on bread alone, so he collected fourpence out of every debt settled on behalf of the King. No doubt a merry soul, he also found time to be Alderman of the Minstrels.

Perhaps all this talk of cuckolds, girdles and the like is leading quite properly to the tourist centre of York. Parliament Street [28] was once the main market area before giving itself up to the pursuit of leisure. In the nineteenth century it almost had an elegant glass roof put over it.

York has long had a parliamentary connection. In September 1314, Edward II summoned a parliament to meet in the city. The Commons were paid for their attendance and received 4s. a day, exclusive of travel expenses – probably enough to buy a goodly portion of Scotch beast and several gallons of strong beer.

Four years later, there was another parliament. County representatives picked up 5s. (25p) a day, whereas the borough reps were cheap at 2s. Obviously two-tier government has a long and distinguished history. Things were obviously on the decline, however, for by 1319 when a third parliament was summoned in the city, knights of the shire were having to scrape by on 4s. while the lowly men from the boroughs had to make the best of 1s. 8d. – about 8p. It would have been a matter of using your loaf, having a few pints and if you were lucky, finishing off with a quick goose.

Now the street has been transformed into a lively, almost continental piazza, perfect for strolling, sitting, watching or listening.

With the market, shops and offices near at hand it provides a good space for rest and relaxation.

Just the right spot to let your mind wander over the thousands of odd people and events that have shaped the city and given it such a unique character.

The Civic Records for 1572 tell us of a "very rude and barbarous custom" which was maintained in York and no other town or city in the realm.

On St Thomas day, just before Christmas, two disguised persons, called Yule and Yule's wife, would ride through the streets, apparently in a very indecent manner. Their antics were such as to attract great crowds of people who gazed upon them and in the words of the time "often committed other enormities". We are not enlightened any further, but the trouble was that these proceedings drew the good folk of York away from church.

So in 1572, after a petition by six prominent citizens, it was decided that no disguised persons should ride forth that year. That must have smacked of double standards, particularly as there was a strong suspicion that the disguised persons were, in fact, Sheriff's sergeants.

It is perhaps not too surprising that, with its long history, York has seen it all: from environmentally-friendly Electrobuses to the Citizens' Charter. Long before the world was shocked by Dirty Dancing, the streets of York had seen Rude Riding.

So our journey through time and space is about to come to an end and it has been a long day. You must be bursting, so what better place to finish than one of the city's newest sights. Until the early 1990s, the central conveniences were extremely discreet, being entirely underground. Their presence was only indicated by a restrained sign and some dignified railings.

There's no way you could miss the replacement. The Splash Palace [29] took months to complete and was designed on the artichoke principle, that by the time you finish, you're left with at least twice as much as when you started. Consequently we now have a two-storey building, a clock, several Grecian columns, telephone boxes, a baby-changing area, a notice board – and gentlemen still have to go underground.

Opposite: Splash Palace

One visiting French folk-dancer was convinced that it was a new concert-hall. This was perhaps not so far-fetched. When the real concert-hall – the splendid Barbican Centre – was being built, aerial photographs revealed that it did bear a strong resemblance to a toilet.

Anyway, now that you've got your bearings in our wonderful city, keep your eyes open and enjoy it.

Bibliography

The following are some of the books which the author found most useful:

An Account of the City and County of the City of York, George Benson, published 1911; republished 1968 by S.R. Publishers, York.

Records of York Castle, A.W. Twyford & Maj. Arthur Griffiths, published 1880 by Griffith & Farran, ISBN X 40017 016 7.

Portrait of York, Ronald Willis, published by Robert Hale Ltd. ISBN 0 7090 3468 7.

A York Miscellany, I.P. Pressly, published by A. Brown & Sons. ISBN X 01015 265 2.

York Civic Records: Yorks Archaeological Society (YAYAS).

Nathaniel Whittock's Bird's Eye View of the City of York in the 1850s, Hugh Murray, published 1989 by Friends of York City Art Gallery. ISBN 0 95132 700 3.

A History of Fulford, Joan Pickering & Irene H. Briddon, published 1975. ISBN 0 95047 640 4.

Yorks WI Recipe Book – of unknown date but probably mid-1950s.

Some York Almshouses, Elizabeth Brunskill, published by York Georgian Society, 1960.

The Friends of York Minster: 31st Annual Report, published 1959.

Royal Commission on Historical Monuments (England), Vol V: York, ISBN 0 11700 992 X; Vol IV: City of York, ISBN 0 11700 719 6; Vol III: South-West of the Ouse, ISBN 0 11700 466 9.

A Quaker Business Man, Anne Vernon (Sessions), published 1982. ISBN 0900 657 634.

The Baedeker Blitz, Hitler's Attack on Britain's Historic Cities, Niall Rothnie, published 1992 by Ian Allen Ltd. ISBN 0 71102 038 8.

The York Blitz 1942, Leo Kessler & Eric Taylor, published 1986 (Sessions of York). ISBN 1 85072 009 6.

Poverty and Prejudice: A Study of Irish Immigrants in York, Frances Finnegan, published 1982, Cork University Press. ISBN 0902561 235.

York in the Great War 1914-1918, A.J. Peacock, The York Settlement Trust.

This is York, Charles Brunton Knight (Herald Printing Works)

Archaeology in York: Interim, York Archaeological Trust.

York Historian, Yorkshire Architectural and York Archaeological Society.

The River Foss: its History and Natural History, Michael Fife & Peter Walls (Sessions of York), published 1981, ISBN 0 90065 717 X.

A History of Bedern Hall, York, published 1987, Maxiprint York

York through the Eyes of the Artist, Hugh Murray, Sarah Riddick & Richard Green, published 1990, (York City Art Gallery). ISBN 0 903281 10 4.

"...and Proud of it too." Stories from Walmgate, Walmgate & Friends.

Yorkshire Oddities, Incidents and Strange Events, S. Baring-Gould, published 1987 by Smith Settle). ISBN 1 87007 113 1.

Index

We publish guides to individual towns, plus books on walking and cycling in the great outdoors throughout England and Wales. This is a recent selection:

Yorkshire:

YORKSHIRE: A WALK AROUND MY COUNTY – Tony Whittaker *(£6.95)*
YORKSHIRE DALES WALKING: On The Level – Norman Buckley *(£6.95)*
PUB WALKS IN THE YORKSHIRE DALES – Clive Price *(£6.95)*
PUB WALKS ON THE NORTH YORK MOORS & COAST – Stephen Rickerby *(£6.95)*
PUB WALKS IN THE YORKSHIRE WOLDS – Tony Whittaker *(£6.95)*

Lake District:

THE LAKELAND SUMMITS – Tim Synge *(£7.95)*
100 LAKE DISTRICT HILL WALKS – Gordon Brown *(£7.95)*
LAKELAND ROCKY RAMBLES: Geology beneath your feet – Brian Lynas *(£7.95)*
FULL DAYS ON THE FELLS: Challenging Walks – Adrian Dixon *(£7.95)*
PUB WALKS IN THE LAKE DISTRICT – Neil Coates *(£6.95)*
LAKELAND WALKING, ON THE LEVEL – Norman Buckley *(£6.95)*
MOSTLY DOWNHILL: LEISURELY WALKS, LAKE DISTRICT – Alan Pears *(£6.95)*

Cycling . . .

OFF-BEAT CYCLING IN THE PEAK DISTRICT – Clive Smith *(£6.95)*
MORE OFF-BEAT CYCLING IN THE PEAK DISTRICT – Clive Smith *(£6.95)*
CYCLING IN THE LAKE DISTRICT – John Wood *(£7.95)*
CYCLING IN LINCOLNSHIRE – Penny & Bill Howe *(£7.95)*
CYCLING IN NOTTINGHAMSHIRE – Penny & Bill Howe *(£7.95)*
CYCLING IN STAFFORDSHIRE – Linda Wain *(£7.95)*

- plus many more entertaining and educational books being regularly added to our list. All of our books are available from your local bookshop. In case of difficulty, or to obtain our complete catalogue, please contact:

Sigma Leisure, 1 South Oak Lane, Wilmslow, Cheshire SK9 6AR
Phone: 01625 – 531035   Fax: 01625 – 536800

ACCESS and VISA orders welcome – call our friendly sales staff or use our 24 hour Answerphone service! Most orders are despatched on the day we receive your order – you could be enjoying our books in just a couple of days. Please add £2 p&p to all orders.

golf, erap and other 4-letter words

Randy,
Hope you enjoy this.
Marither

Dear Gary,

From the moment I picked up your book until I laid it down, I was convulsed with laughter. Someday I intend to read it.

Your friend,
ERAP

Gary Lising truly inherited his writing talent from his great great grandfather who wrote *Florante at Laura*. Unfortunately, Florante and Laura did not write him back.

Gary as a humorist and a friend, has never changed. He's still the same today as he was when he was young – a sex maniac!

Seriously, I enjoyed reading Gary's book. Take my advice: Read it, it will surely brighten up your day.

Secretary Edgardo Angara
Department of Agriculture

Gary's book, *Golf, Erap and Other 4-Letter Words* is long overdue, unlike the author who was born prematurely, or so I hear.

Gary has made a career of being humorous, and we do need people of humor like him. Humor, after all, helps us cope with all the trials we face daily. But Gary doesn't really need this book to prove his success as a funnyman. One look at his face and people could literally die laughing.

But back to the book. When I got hold of the manuscript he sent me, I couldn't put it down. Must have been the glue in the brown envelope his masterpiece came in, which has remained un-opened.

Secretary Orlando S. Mercado
Department of National Defense

When Gary Lising asked me to say something nice about *Golf, Erap and Other 4-Letter Words,* I pondered on this for a long time. Four-letter words can be tricky; I must have a HOLE in the head for agreeing. And so I started reading the book. I'm stumped for another four-letter word to describe the book. (Hmmm... DROLL, but that's five letters. GREAT... that's too much even for Gary. ODD... but that would be describing Gary's er... looks?)

Enough with the four-letter thing; this is what I got to say about it: GOOD laughs from MEAN jokes is the mark of a ZANY writer!

Secretary Vicente C. Rivera Jr.
Department of Transportation and Communication

Preface

I never say political jokes because very often they get elected. In the past, we can only poke fun at politicians secretly because of our religion. We are devout cowards. I think times have changed and I honestly believe in press freedom. Thus we can now poke fun at politicians because they play with every aspect of our lives. Making fun at politics somewhat relieves the tension that is now confronting our country.

Here now are the collection of jokes, barbs, insults, definitions and anything connected with golf, Erap and other 4-letter words. Stories that have been told and retold ever since Cory left Mitra, ever since Maceda left Erap, ever since Lito Osmeña left John, ever since the Americans left us. People and events mentioned in this book are real. Only the would-be presidents are fiction. I would like to give my deepest gratitude to Ramon Mitra, Danding Cojuangco, Doy Laurel, Fidel Ramos, Lito and John Osmeña, Miriam Defensor-Santiago, Jovy Salonga, Nene Pimentel, Marcelo Fernan, and Madame Imelda Marcos for bringing laughter in the Philippines. Most especially to our President Joseph "Erap" Estrada.

My very special thanks to Vic Vic Villavicencio, Tito Eduque, Bert Lingad, Ton Portillo, Mari Cacho, Pabling Calma, Louie Campos, Edwin Andrews, Leo Caguioa, Mike Cardenas, Ces Catalan, Nocon, Tony Pastelero, Peny Reloza, Jun Sison, Dante Santos, Mon Tuason, Alex Wong, Butz Aquino, Ernesto Maceda, Bert Romulo, Santanina Rasul, Juan Ponce Enrile, Cristina Ponce Enrile, John Osmeña, Ed Angara, Letty Shahani, Popsy Aquino, Jackie Aquino, Kris Aquino and mother, Tom Achacoso, Manny Sibal, Bonnie Alentajan, Abul Alonto, Poch Borromeo, Rico Tantoco, Nedy Tantoco, Eddie Pineda, Marilou Pineda, Raymond Ang, Mary Rose Jacinto, Crispina Belen, Mayor Jojo Binay, Conchitina & Lani Bernardo, Jun Bautista, Amad & Chari Bagatsing, Gretchen Baretto, Sonny Belmonte, Felix Co, Rey Bautista, Leo Baluyot, Janet Basco, Johnny Revilla, Johnny Manahan, Joe Marie & Mary Ann Chan, Nene Chan, Gene Roldan, Ana Co, Helen Chan, Cito Cruz, Nikki Coseteng, Tingting Cojuangco, Noynoy Aquino, Miriam Defensor Santiago, Philip Cruz, Raffy Rufino, Dr. Felix Salgado, Dr. Cynthia Cuayo Juico, Jullie Yap Daza, Peter Dee, Rene Espinosa, Sonny Eusebio, Motonobu Saito, Kazuyuki Uno, Noel Trinidad, Subas Herrero, Danny Gomez, George Ledesma, Joty Javier, Tony Guidotti, Jody de Asis, Ike Joaquin, Geny Lopez, Angela Luz, Nini Licaros, Julius Limpe, Monry Mapa, Mary Montilibano, Edu Manzano, Maricel Soriano, Vilma Santos, Richard Gomez, Joey Marquez, Nanette Inventor, Tony Marco, Jun Urbano, Leo Martinez, Johnson Go, Oscar Orbos, Allan Bacher, Jovy Cruz, Dong Puno, Sonny Jaworski, Mon Fernandez, Dante Silverio, Ed Ocampo, Chito Loyzaga, Noli de Castro, Loren Legarda, Gov. Leviste, Lally Laurel, Ben Roa, Alice Reyes, Carol Rivera, Vic Advincula, Eugene Manalstas, Jun Jun Osmeña, Titus Pardo, Gemma Araneta, Fernando Poe, Jr., Dan Dia, Joe

Velez, Ernie Salas, Toto Samonte, Doy Laurel, Joey Lina, John B & Loudette Banzon, Toto Zaide, Larry Cruz, Dody Agcaoili, Nonie Atabug, Nelia Seril, Mon de la Rosa, Boogie Rodrigo, Apo Hiking Society, Lito Delara, Chito Halos, Bob Hecks, Roger Begre, Henry Sy, Jaime Zobel, Danny Olivares, Joan Orendain, Frido Ong, Father Panfilo, Ipe Pelino, Vic Puyat, Rico Puno, Baby Boy Poblador, Manito Deleon, Arben Santos, Jackie Regala, Ben Ramos, Gatas Santos, Tessie Santos, Eddie Boy Santos, Chini Santos, Boy Santiago, Ricky Soler, Rene Sevilla, Ding Tanjuatco, Gary Valenciano, Bobby Vilar, Tess Valte, Mike Cerqueda, Freddie Webb, Gen. Renato De Villa, Alay sa Kawal, Gigi Zulueta, Santi Dumalo, Tony Rufino, Vince Carlos, Herman Gamboa, Tito Santos, Jun Narvaez, Relly Reyes, Jun Alvendia, Ramon Montano, Alexander Aguirre, Gen. Alfredo Lim, Gen. Biazon, and Gen. Electric, Roman Santos, Rolly Estrella, Mr. Pedrosa, Bel Cunanan, Gen. Thelmo Cunanan, Tito, Vic & Joey, Ed Ocampo, Bobby Littaua, Hector Calma, Alvin Patrimonio, Jojo Lastimosa, Norman Black, Nono Ibazeta, Boy Guevara, John Gokongwei, Albert Villalon, Ernie Magboo, Boy Reyno, Angelique Lazo, Bobong Velez, Nini & Abe Licaros, Janice & Gellie de Belen, Mitch Valdez, Cherie Gil, Peque Gallaga, Carmi Martin, Nova Villa, Tootsie Marco, Butch Valdez, Dondo Lim, Rey Marquez, Charlie Favis, Benjie Paras, Ronnie Magsanoc, and Vice President Gloria Macapagal-Arroyo, thank you all and the rest of my friends whom I failed to mention. *Maraming-maraming salamat po.*

My very special gratitude to:

MARIS and BUGSY—the wind beneath my wings. For being the cause of my happiness and merriment;

JUN and MENCHU LOPEZ—for their friendship which is a treasure to us;

BERT and SYLVIA LINA—for the honor of being part of their family;

RJ and FRANNIE JACINTO—for their unselfish support of my endeavors;

JOE MARI and MARYANN CHAN—for just being there;

NINANG CRISTINA PONCE ENRILE—for being one of the reasons why our country is beautiful;

MIRIAM DEFENSOR-SANTIAGO—for showing us the meaning of guts;

MADAME IMELDA MARCOS—for no matter what they say, I will always believe in her;

CARDINAL SIN—for converting me into the Muslim faith;

JOVY SALONGA—for teaching me that age does not matter if your matter does not age;

DICK GORDON—for he's a jolly good fellow;

JUN URBANO—for being my mentor;

DANDING COJUANGCO—for showing us that we can overcome;

BOSKI TAGAYSAY—for his unwavering support;

The four little big men—ALBERT LINA, ATO MAGADIA, JUN LOPEZ and DONNIES ALAS—for being giants in their fields of endeavor, thus serving as inspiration to their peers;

SHEILA LINA—the mega star of the future;

SYLVIA LINA—for her powerful 5 to 1 vote;

OUR POLITICIANS—for making the Philippines the center of comedy in the entire world;

SEC. VICENTE RIVERA—for coming in my life

POCH BORROMEO—for supporting us through thick and thin

JUN-JUN OSMEÑA—for the benefit of his friendship

ATO and VICKY MAGADIA—for their unwavering support

VICE PRESIDENT GLORIA MACAPAGAL-ARROYO—our future president

About Myself

My name is GARY LISING. If you think I am ugly now, you should have seen me when I was a baby. I am the only baby born inside out.

I was such an ugly baby that when I was born, the doctor held my feet up, took one look at me... and slapped my mother.

Actually, I was part of a twin. My parents were so poor, they had to make a decision. My father said to my mother one evening that they could afford only one baby. They agreed to keep the beautiful baby and drown the ugly one... that's when I first learned how to swim.

My father was so excited at my birth... instead of asking, "Is it a boy or a girl?" He asked, "Am I a father or a mother?"

I was named after my father... they call me Papa.

I was so surprised at my birth that. I couldn't speak for a year and a half.

My poor mother was apologizing to everybody for giving birth to me. Then my father got the itch again and persuaded my mother to try and improve mother nature's work... his being horny is beside the point. She gave birth to my sister... when the priest was about to baptize her, the priest said "What's the boy's name?" And my father said, "It's a girl... you're holding my thumb!"

I grew up to be a "Wonder Boy"... everybody would look at me and wonder.

So many people say that I am very intelligent. Maybe it's because of the many years I spent in school... I spent seven years in kindergarten alone... I wanted to master it!

Then I was accelerated to Grade One after seven short years. I spent three years in Grade One where my father taught me the Fine Art of Honesty. He paid ₱10,000 to the principal and the principal was so touched by the honesty of the money given him that he accelerated me to Grade Six. The rest is history — I repeated myself.

Isms

COMMUNISM: If you have two cows, you give both cows to the government and then the government sells you some of the milk.

SOCIALISM: If you have two cows, you give both cows to the government and then the government gives you some of the milk.

NAZISM: If you have two cows, the government shoots you and takes both cows.

FASCISM: If you have two cows, you kill both of them and give the government half of the milk.

NEW IDEALISM: If you have two cows, you kill one, milk the other and pour the milk down the drain.

CAPITALISM: If you have two cows, you sell one cow and buy a bull.

PHILIPPINISM: If you have two cows, the government will milk you forever.

GARYISM: If you have two cows, you make love to one cow and commit marital infidelity with the other.

A Politician According to Cardinal Lising

The Politician is my shepherd,
I shall not want.
He maketh me to lie down on an empty stomach
He leadeth me to believe in his promises
He disturbeth my soul.
Ye do I walk through the valley of the shadows of depression and recession,
I anticipate no recovery
For he's with me.
He prepareth a reduction in my salary even in the presence of my enemy.
He annointeth my small income with great losses.
My expenses runneth over.
Surely unemployment and poverty shall follow me for the rest of my life.
And I shall dwell in this mortgaged house forever.

The Beauty and the Beast

J.V. with his four caddies

Politically Speaking

EDDIE RAMOS: I kiss only babies that are old enough to vote.

JOVY SALONGA: There are 3 things a man will know when he's getting old: one is loss of memory, the other two, I forgot.

ERAP ESTRADA: I am glad the Bases are out. Who wants to play baseball anyway?

MIRIAM DEFENSOR-SANTIAGO: Balls are not exclusively for men.

DANDING COJUANGCO: I am the future. If you will forget my past, I will give you a present.

NENE PIMENTEL: Like Mitra I was born free—my father is a Doctor.

MARGARITA HOLMES: Politics is like sex. You don't have to be good to enjoy it.

JUAN PONCE ENRILE: When we are flat on our backs, there is no way to look but up.

DOY LAUREL: When I was born, the doctor went up to my mother and said, "Congratulations, Mrs. Laurel, it's a DOY!"

Political Interview

(Enter Gary)

INT.	:	Good evening, Sir, we are very proud to have you with us tonight.
GARY	:	I know that.
INT.	:	Now that you have been elected, how should we address you?
GARY	:	Same address.
INT.	:	No, I mean how should we call you?
GARY	:	Oh, the same telephone number.
INT.	:	Sir, is Erap Manzano your real name?
GARY	:	No, my real name is Erapio Mongpuetmo Manzano.
INT.	:	Erapio Mongpuetmo Manzano?
GARY	:	Yes, Mongpuetmo is my mother's family name. Her first name is Paquita.
INT.	:	Sir, do you believe that there was cheating in the elections?
GARY	:	Yes, definitely, but it was very honest.
INT.	:	You practically won in all parts of the Philippines. In what areas in the country did you lose?
GARY	:	Only one place. In the Namfrel.
INT.	:	Do you have supporters?

15

GARY	:	Yes, I'm wearing them now.
INT.	:	Do you have a political machine?
GARY	:	Yes, all my bodyguards have machine guns.
INT.	:	What is your stand on the abortion bill?
GARY	:	The abortion bill? I will pay it at once.
INT.	:	What do you think of agrarian reform?
GARY	:	Agrarian Reform? Who is he?
INT.	:	Sir, who is your choice to be Speaker of the House?
GARY	:	I think the speaker should be a woman.
INT.	:	Why?
GARY	:	Because a woman has two mouths, but seriously, women generally speaking are generally speaking.
INT.	:	Do you have any plans?
GARY	:	Plans? Well, I have orchids, bonsai and a few vegetables.
INT.	:	I read in your curriculum vitae that you were once a student of the Ateneo.
GARY	:	Of course, can you not detect it in my accent?
INT.	:	Yes, the accent is definitely Ateneo. In Ateneo, did you study the Liturgy?
GARY	:	Liturgy? Of course, not only the Liturgy but also the letters A B C and the rest of the alphabet.
INT.	:	Do you know Manglapus?
GARY	:	Manglapus? Yes, I know him. He is one of my supporters together with Mang Ambo, Mang Pedro and Mang Lucas.
INT.	:	What will happen to Tolentino now?
GARY	:	Tolentino has been appointed Vice-President by Pimentel.
INT.	:	Pimentel will not do that.
GARY	:	I did not say Nene Pimentel appointed him, I said Pepe Pimentel appointed him.
INT.	:	I heard one of your hardworking supporters is also a movie actor.
GARY	:	Yes, Amay Bisaya. He supported me in Ilocos.
INT.	:	Do you have any plans to be President?
GARY	:	No plans.
INT.	:	Why?
GARY	:	Because I want to be king.
INT.	:	Do you have any parting words to our audience?
GARY	:	Yes, strong your courage because in the long of time you will.

This year, my new year's resolution is to help the homeless. There's only one thing wrong with this project. It's very hard to locate them, they don't have any address.

Most of the Army Doctors are First Lieutenants or better except one who's a Private First Class, ever since he gave a certain General a thermometer and told him what to do with it.

A call girl was arrested outside Camp Aguinaldo — for contributing to the delinquency of a Major.

A veterinarian friend of mine was so embarrassed when they caught him having sex with one of his patients.

QUESTION : What do electric trains and a woman's breasts have in common?
ANSWER : They are both intended for children but it's the fathers who play with them.

What are appetizers? Things you nibble on until you lose your appetite.

A Senator I know has ESP — Extremely Small Penis.

What does spaghetti and women have in common? They both wiggle when you eat them.

What did one ball say to the other ball? What are we hanging around here for? We didn't do the shooting.

Jungle Lore: How do Lions make love?
Answer: Same as Rotarians.

Boski Tagaysay read all about the bad effects of smoking so he gave up reading.

Commercial Ad — after trying camels, nine out of ten men switched to women.

When you look around in a men's room, you will know that men are not created equal.

Whenever the Chief Justice goes to the bathroom, he makes an honorable discharge.

What is the favorite fruit of candidates not endorsed by the President? Sour grapes.

Do you know what a Protestant is? It is a place where you buy prots.

Two Senators, members of the negotiating panel for the bases went to the U.S. After a few days they rented a car and went for a ride. They were bumped on the rear by a big black man. One senator went up to the man and said that he will sue him. The black man said, "F...k you." The senator went back to the car and told his colleague, "I think he wants to negotiate."

How did Magic Johnson get AIDS? He got it by playing with Larry's bird.

All green card holders are from La Salle.

A diehard campaigner was asked, "If you have a million pesos, will you give it for his campaign?" "Yes," he said, without hesitation. "If you have a big house will you sell it to contribute to his campaign?" "Yes," he said. "If you have a big land holding will you also donate it to him?" "Yes," he said. "If you have a carabao will you do the same?" "No," he said. "Why not?" "Because," he said, "I have a carabao."

More than just casinos
PAGCOR helps create income opportunities in depressed areas.

There is more to the Philippine Amusement and Gaming Corporation than just casinos, than just affording gaming and leisure activities. Among the many roles it plays and the many tasks it performs, PAGCOR helps fund livelihood projects to make life a little better for people in depressed communities.

In the last six years, at least 82 livelihood projects were financed by the President's Social Fund, to which a big portion of casino income goes. These have given hundreds of families, whose lives are among the millions PAGCOR has touched, not only a source of themselves to become useful and productive citizens. Because, in more ways than one, PAGCOR matters. And PAGCOR cares.

Philippine Amusement & Gaming Corporation
Responding through Responsible Gaming

(Overheard)

REPORTER   :   Mr. Senator, do you believe in synchronized elections?
SENATOR   :   Of course, as long as they are not at the same time.

⚑

A Mayor we know was all for improvements. The first thing he did was to have a paved road built. It ran the whole length of his property.

⚑

You have to hand it to our politicians — they are going to get it anyway.

⚑

Many of our politicians admit that they are self-made men. I am glad they took the responsibility off the rest of us.

⚑

A politician in Metro Manila began his campaign speech this way: "My opponent has been stealing from you for six years. Give me a chance."

⚑

Senator Juan Flavier is so short— whenever it rains, he's the last to know.

⚑

Latest news: With six cemeteries still to be heard from, the election is too close to call.

Until I was 13 years old, I thought girls were just soft boys.

Golfer Mari Cacho was bragging — "I missed a hole in one by only 8 strokes."

A contractor wanted to give an official of the Public Works a small token of appreciation. The contractor asked the official if he would mind having a Mercedes Benz. The official got mad. "I can't accept a bribe," he said. The contractor said if it would be all right if he sold him the Benz.

"How much?" the official asked.

"One hundred pesos," said the contractor. "In that case," the official said, "I'll take two."

A bad smell enveloped Metro Manila, I thought Smoky Mountain erupted.

Ronnie, Rudy and Erap decided to go and see Lydia de Vega run in the SEA Games. They went to the wrong gate and was told by the guard that the particular gate was only for athletes. Ronnie picked up a manhole cover and told the guard that he was a discus thrower. The guard let him in. Rudy also got a long bamboo pole and told him he was a javelin thrower. The guard likewise let him in. Erap had to think fast. So he got a chicken coop wire and went in. The guard stopped him and said, "What sports are you in?" Erap showing the guard the chicken coop wire said, "Fencing."

The Philippines is the inventor of Fast Foods. Every time the people want food, the government tells us to fast.

The flag icon ♭

A nurse walks into a doctor's office. She says, "Doc, what are you doing?" He says, "I'm writing a prescription." She says, "But you're writing with your thermometer." He says, "My God, some assholes got my pen."

What do you call a guy with no arms, no legs and a 12-inch penis? Partially handicapped.

The Philippines has just discovered two drugs that prevent AIDS. The generic names are SAGATRIN and TIRAMID.
SAGATRIN — magpasagasa ka na lang sa tren
TIRAMID — tirahin mo na lang ang maid

What is big and pink and floats in the ocean? Moby's Dick.

What do you call a zipper in Spain? Spanish fly.

Golf is a game where the ball lies poorly and the players well.
— Major General Rolando Vinluan

The AFP is now accepting gays in the Army. A gay friend of mine went to apply. The recruiting officer asked him a few questions. "Can you kill a man?" he asked. My gay friend said, "Yes, but it will take weeks and weeks."

New fad in town: Self-service massage parlor.

A cab driver picks up a nun. He looks in the rearview mirror and says, "You know Sister, I've always fantasized about being with a nun." She says, "Are you Catholic?" He says, "Yes, I am." She says "pull over!" He pulls over. She gets in the front seat and she gives him the best blow job he's ever had. When she gets done, he feels a little guilty and he says to her, "Sister, I am not really a Catholic." She says, "Really? Well, my name is Pitoy and I'm on my way to a costume party."

A senator was asked about his sex life. "Almost every night," he said. "What do you mean?" "Monday night – almost, Tuesday night – almost, Wednesday night – almost, the rest of the week, I rest."

Plurality vote is not legal — fat persons cannot vote twice.

Did you ever notice that when we can finally afford to buy a small car we buy a bigger one?

Golfer Jun Jun Osmeña beats traffic lights to save seconds and waits patiently for hours on the first tee.

DRUNKEN ADVICE: He who drinks, gets drunk. He who gets drunk, falls asleep. He who falls asleep does not sin. He who does not sin goes to heaven. So let's all drink and go to Heaven.

A Senator's wife answered the phone and talked for half an hour. Her husband asked why she talked only for half an hour. She said it was just a wrong number.

A Congressman feeling the pinch of today's economy told his wife that they should cut expenses. "If you could only cook well, we could let the cook go," he said. His wife replied, "Yes, and if you could only make love better, we could get rid of the driver."

Did you know that Cardinal Sin is the Fourteenth in a family of sixteen? His parents made a lot of Sins.

There is a Topless Restaurant located at the Ayala Center. All the waiters are bald.

The reason a man's hair turns gray quicker than his whiskers is because it has a 20-year start.

I know a politician who had everything a man could want — money, home, and the love of a beautiful woman — and then one morning his wife walked in.

I visited the Manila Zoo and the people refused to let me out. They thought I was trying to escape.

A Justice of the Supreme Court was late for his appointment with his barber and was not given a haircut. "Justice Delayed is Justice Denied."

Unemployed school teachers have no class.

An American tourist ordered breakfast at the Pen Lobby and was given dried fish and eggs. "What kind of fish is that?" the American asked. "Daeng, sir," replied the waiter. "DAENG? I think its DEAD ALREADY!" exclaimed the American tourist.

In a separate incident, a Japanese tourist was arrested for mashing a Filipina. When questioned by the police on why he did it, the Japanese said "I RUB HER."

Congratulations are in order for the AFP. They have captured more than 1,200 suspected reds. All were released because of lack of evidence.

27

The King and I

Torres, Gomez, Casas and Lising:
The Four Golfers of the Apocalypse

China also has its own version of the Sparrows. They are called the Peking Ducks.

My editor asked me to cover the eclipse — I couldn't write anything about it because it was too dark.

It's bad luck to have thirteen people seated at a table, especially if you're paying the check.

There is a new vanishing cream deodorant — you vanish and the people wonder where the odor is coming from.

There is a fine difference between love and passion: Love is blind, Passion is cock-eyed.

Reports say, the Marcoses have AIDS — Acquired International Deposits in Switzerland.

I've discovered a way to avoid paying Income Tax: don't work.

An Executive I know always deducts his gambling losses as a medical expense because according to him, gambling is a sickness.

If you resist temptation, it may never come again.

A Philippine plane had its first successful test flight. With the success of the test flight, the inventor of the RP-made plane is bent on inventing a spaceship that can land on the sun. I asked him how he can accomplish this test without burning the spaceship. "I will only make it fly at night," he replied.

Our Senate and Congress have a "Conscience Bloc." They block their conscience.

Middle age is when a girl you smile at thinks you are one of her father's friends.

Just when we think we can make both ends meet, someone comes along and moves the ends.

Religion is a form of fire escape.

Our doctor of laws can't seem to find a cure for our government.

QUESTION: Who is the man who wore a white turban and then rode a pig?
ANSWER: Lawrence of Poland.

How to avoid falling hair: Step out of the way.

A lovely young girl stood before the gates of Heaven, requesting admission. St. Peter opened the gates and, before allowing her in, asked the usual question: "Are you a virgin?"

"Why, of course!" she answered with confidence. For verification, the venerable saint asked an angel doctor to examine her. After the check-up, the good doctor submitted a report on the results thereof. In brief, the report recommended that she be allowed entry into the portals of Heaven. An asterisk, however was marked on the entry because, although she was a virgin, there were seven slight dents on her maidenhead.

Using his discretion, St. Peter allowed her to enter. Writing in the Registry Book, he asked her for her name.

"Snow White," she replied with a curtsy.

During lunch hour, Lorna entered the doctor's clinic on the second floor of the same building where she worked. She was met by a good-looking man in a white uniform. She told him about her ailment.

"I have a pain in my right shoulder for several days now. Will you please look at it?"

"Certainly," he said. "Now, lie down on this table and we'll see if a little massage will relieve you of the pain."

After restless moments, the lovely patient complained: "Doctor, that is not my shoulder you're massaging!"

The young man smiled: "Oh, no? Well, I'm not a doctor either!"

⚑

It was a childless marriage of many years for a lovely Chinese lady, and she was most concerned about having progeny. So she went to the medical center for consultation and treatment seeking the services of a well-known gynecologist.

"Now take off your clothes and lie down on that table," the medical expert told her.

The woman looked at him and frowned. "But doctor, you must understand," explained the lovely lady, "I want a Chinese baby!"

⚑

Mang Tonio, a widower for many years, met a young and pretty woman. After a whirlwind courtship, he decided to marry her.

"Papa," advised his eldest son, "since you are far ahead of her in years, I think you should check with your doctor for the state of your health and virility."

After the medical examination, Mang Tonio told him the good news.

"Well, hijo," said Mang Tonio, "the doctor told me that I was healthy for a man my age and that the marriage with this young woman would do me good, especially since I will have somebody to look after me in my declining years. By the way, hijo, how many times a week is semi-annually?"

⚑

Famous last words of women before saying goodbye to their virginity:

"I thought you would be different."
"My mother would die if she ever found out."
"Please, darling, I'm afraid I might get pregnant!"
"If we do it, you'll surely hate me."
"I'll hate myself in the morning."
"What sort of girl do you think I am?"
"What if I get pregnant? What will we do?"
"My mother will kill me if she learns about this."

"My husband would not like it."

"What if my husband finds out about us?"

"And you call yourself his best friend!"

"I'm only doing this because I love you very much."

"I surely will never see you after this."

"Oh, please don't! You know very well it's a sin!"

"I'm married and you're married, and never the twain shall meet!"

"What have I done to you to deserve this?"

"I can only give myself to a man in marriage."

"Please be gentle. This is my first time."

"I am reserving this only for my husband."

"If I give myself to you, what will happen to my future?"

"Ay, bahala na ang Dios!"

One early morning, Titong and Chito staggered out of a cocktail lounge in Ermita district, fully loaded with spirits when they saw a dog licking his genitals with gusto.

"Gosh," remarked Titong, "I wish I could do that!"

"Oh, well," said Chito, "I guess you'd better pet him first so he won't bite you."

Jose was courting Clarita by the book. Every evening, well almost anyway, he would visit her and they would spend some hours after dinner in the sala of her house, to the consternation of her father. He was trying to reduce the electric bills with some frustration.

Having reached the limits of his patience, he yelled down to his daughter one night.

"Is that man still there? It's past bedtime. What's going on there?"

"Yes, papa, Jose is still here," replied Clarita. "He is telling me everything that's in his heart!"

"Well, next time," instructed the old man, "tell him to tell you what's in his head. Maybe he can go home earlier!"

A dramatic actor, noted for the size of his pubic weapon, was invited by an admirer to her home. Once in the privacy of the bedroom, she unbuttoned his trousers and held the huge tool in her hand and started to fondle it.

"My, how lovely!" she sighed. "No wonder you call him Caesar. How regal he is in his dimensions. How imposing is his stature. How majestic! How erect! Such tremendous character! Such...."

"Stop! Stop!" explained the actor, interrupting her. "I came to bury Caesar, not to praise him!"

The executive vice-president of a large corporation, young, married and good-looking, was trying hard to score with his new, young lovely secretary for the past several weeks, but in vain. Finally, as his birthday was fast approaching, he made a desperate pitch. He asked her to celebrate his birthday with him at some secluded place. She said she would think about it.

The following day, she consented, but only if the celebration would be at her apartment. He was terribly delighted. After all, her apartment would be an ideal rendezvous.

Thus, on the night of his birthday, at her apartment, they had cocktails, appetizers, dinner by candlelight, and some drinks. They danced rather closely to soft music. After a while, she broke away from him to go to her bedroom to prepare herself for him, telling him to come into the room in ten minutes.

In no time, the young executive took off his clothes and in his birthday suit, knocked on the bedroom door, eager and excited. At last, his mind was savoring the moment he would make his conquest!

A sweet voice from behind the door told him to enter. A twist of the knob and the door swung open. The room was in total darkness. As he entered, naked, calling her name, the lights suddenly opened. The entire office force began to sing: "Happy Birthday to you!"

A lovely matron with unusual caprices had her inner thighs tattooed with Reagan and Gorbachev images, respectively, looking up. Two weeks after the tattoo operation, she removed the bandages before a mirror to see the result. To her consternation, the faces embossed on her thighs bore no resemblance to the international figures.

She rushed to the tattoo clinic in a rage, demanding her money back. To resolve the conflict, he proposed a neutral arbiter for a third opinion. They both agreed to ask a renowned painter for a verdict.

Opening her thighs and showing her tattoos, the matron asked, "Does the face on the right side look like Reagan?"

"Hard to tell," said the inebriated painter, concentrating on the right thigh.

"What about the left side?" asked the lady, "Does the image look like Gorbachev?"

"It's rather difficult to say," said the spirited artist, gazing intently at her left thigh. "But that fellow in the middle with the black beard and bad breath is most surely Fidel Castro!"

⚑

A Filipino doctor invented a miracle drug that is so powerful that you have to be in perfect health to use it.

⚑

A gay friend attended a religious service and donated a huge amount in the collection plate. When the Pastor found out, he made an announcement to thank my friend for his generous donation. "For your generosity, we will let you select three Hymns," the Pastor said. The gay *caballero* immediately stood up and pointed to three good looking men and said, "Him, Him, and Him."

⚑

When Speaker Manny Villar spoke before the Makati Rotarians, he had the audience open-mouthed — they all yawned at the same time.

⚑

A woman politician smiled a lot when she guested on a TV program — she has nice even teeth; 1, 3, 5 and 7 are missing.

⚑

Resist the Mind's Aging Process

The main ingredient found in this formulation is: GINGKO BILOBA. The therapeutic use of gingko biloba goes back centuries and is described in the traditional Chinese pharmacopoeia. In France and Germany, extracts of gingko are administered orally and intravenously and are among the most commonly prescribed pharmaceutical drugs. A recent report in the Lancet indicated, "The various compounds of gingko extract may have a role in different stages in the decline of intellectual function via several mechanisms of action.

The effectiveness of gingko biloba may be explained by several mechanisms including increased blood flow, improved cerebral metabolism, protection of the brain against hypoxic damage, and perhaps most importantly, the ability to reduce free-radical activity. Other key ingredients which also enhance brain function are: Lecithin, Vitamin B-12, Folic Acid, Acetyl-L-carnitine, Phospatidylserine, and Aged Garlic Extract.

Maintain brain health and enjoy a healthier, happier life.

Dietary Supplement

KYOLIC

Neuro·Logic ™

Improves Memory & Mental Acuity*

120 capsules formulated by David Perlmutter, M.D.

Board Certified Neurologist

36

Home is a place where a man is free to say anything he wants because no one pays any attention to him.

Behind every successful man is a very loyal wife and a surprised mother-in-law.

The way prices are going up, they ought to call those big stores "supermarkups"

There is a new shampoo made out of low calories — it's especially made for fatheads.

One senator does not know the meaning of the word "fear", he does not know the meaning of the word "corrupt", he does not know the meaning of the word "autonomy". There are many words he doesn't know the meaning of.

Senator Jaworski says that speeches are like babies — easy to conceive, hard to deliver.

You know a man is a success when the newspapers start to quote him on subjects he knows nothing about.

One candidate vying for the UP presidency is a very intelligent man. Ang tatay niya summa cum laude sa Ateneo. Ang nanay niya summa cum laude sa CEU, ang kapatid niya summa cum laude sa FEU, ang asawa niya sumama sa iba.

One senator I know is just like a blister, he doesn't show up until the work is all done.

The manager of a five-star hotel was informed that a man was trapped in an elevator between the fourth and fifth floors. He rushed under the stalled elevator car and yelled out to the passenger: "Keep cool sir, we'll have you out soon. We already called the elevator mechanic." There was a brief pause, then a tense voice answered, "I *am* the elevator mechanic."

Do you know why there's no life on other planets? Because their scientists were a little more advanced than ours.

Today, when you break a mirror, it means good luck. It means you'll be around for another seven years.

Manila's two top businessmen, Bert Lina and Pabling Calma, were comparing notes. "I just collected P100,000 from my insurance firm for fire damage," said Pabling. "Same here," Bert Lina said. "I just collected a half-million-peso insurance for flood damage." There was a long, thoughtful pause. Then Pabling asked, "Tell me, Bert, how do you start a flood?"

I asked Senator Orly Mercado what business ethics means. "Well, it's like this..." Orly said, citing an example. "A man comes into a store and buys something. He gives me a crisp new one hundred peso bill which is just the right amount. As I turn to the cash register, I discover it is not one but two one hundred peso bills seemingly stuck together. Now comes the business ethics: Should I tell my partner?"

Rotarian Tony Marco is having trouble with his car. It won't start and the payments won't stop.

With the spate of killings in our country, our cemeteries are getting overcrowded. Now where you get buried, it's standing room only.

Rotarian Tony Ortigas comes from a broken home. His kids broke everything inside his house.

The average man has probably thought twice about running away from home, once as a child and once as a husband.

The Real Boss: Gary with the power
behind the Lina Group of Companies

Morning with Evening

Television best acting is done by stars who lost congratulating the Star Award winners.

Economists claim that women's hemlines go up when prices rise. This is a trend that bears watching.

All Soul's Day Tidbit — A man was caught trying to steal a car in front of the Loyola Memorial Cemetery. When questioned by the police why he took the car, he said, "I thought the owner was dead."

At the cemetery, a boy asked me what RIP means. Everybody knows that. It means "Return if Possible."

Now Erap Estrada is careful about his speeches. The only time he has trouble with his English is when he mixes it with Scotch.

A Board of Directors is a group of individuals who, as individuals, can do nothing, but who as a board, can decide that nothing can be done.

Chinese Problem — Me no come, wife no come, baby comes — How come?

Most of the people favoring birth control have already been born.

True to Life — An old man collapsed on a crowded street in Quiapo and immediately a large crowd gathered. "Give the man a drink of Ginebra," a little old lady suggested. "Give him some air," said the little old lady. "Call a doctor," someone suggested. "Give him a drink of Ginebra," repeated the old lady. The argument continued until suddenly the victim sat up and said, "Will you all shut up and listen to the little old lady?"

Reincarnation is true. Did you ever notice how many dead people come to life everyday at five in the afternoon? Check your office.

Court Scene

WITNESS: Pagkatapos namin kinuha ang pera niya, naghiwa-hiwalay na kami.

INTERPRETER: After we took his money, we sepa-separated.

The favorite pastime of criminals is taking a nap — carnap, kidnap, shipnap.

Ninety percent of them don't get caught because our lawmen are always caught napping.

We now have a mini skirt budget. Everytime they talk about it, it goes higher.

Filipinas are experts in family planning. The day after they get married, half her family moves in with her husband and the other half is planning to.

Tony Portillo is substituting candy for smoking. You can tell how hard he tries because everytime he throws the candy wrapper he steps on it and grinds it with his foot.

A teacher at Don Bosco always wears dark glasses when she teaches her class because her students are too bright.

Any girl who says "No" is badly disappointed if you don't hold her for further questioning.

Musical disaster: when you are on your favorite piece and your organ gives out.

Who is the real Gary Lising?

The Big J with the Small G

What's small and gray and screws in the wall? A mouse.

Anyone who says man was born free never paid an obstetrician's bill.

Marriage is the occupation that pays the highest wages for unskilled labor.

What do you get when you cross an elephant with a prostitute? A 2000 pound hooker who will do it for peanuts and remember you forever.

This petting without going all the way can have serious consequences — a man can get rubbed off.

Things sure have changed — in ancient times, a Trojan meant "warrior".

Adultery: The wrong man in the right place.

There's a new game called "Fertility Roulette." You shake up five aspirins and a birth control pill in a hat and let your girlfriend pick one.

Do you know the difference between a mosquito and a fly? You can't sew a zipper on a mosquito.

The Boss

When the Baby was first made all the parts wanted to be Boss. The Brain said, "Since I control everything and do all the thinking I should be Boss."

The Feet said, "Since I carry man where he wants to go and get him into position to do what the Brain wants I should be Boss."

The Hands said, "Since I must do all the work and earn all the money to keep the rest of you going, I should be Boss."

The Eyes said, "Since I must look out for all of you and tell you where danger lurks, I should be Boss."

And so it went, the Heart, the Ears, the Lungs, and finally the Asshole spoke and demanded to be Boss.

All the other parts laughed and laughed at the idea of an Asshole being Boss.

The Asshole was so angered that he blocked himself off and refused to function.

Soon the Brain was feverish, the Eyes crossed and ached, the Feet were too weak to walk, the Hands hung limply at the sides, the Heart and Lungs struggled to keep going.

All pleaded with the Brain to repent and let the Asshole be Boss, and so it happened.

All the other parts did all the work and the Asshole just bossed and passed out a lot of shit.

Moral: You do not have to be a BRAIN to be the BOSS, just an ASSHOLE.

(Author Unknown)

'Twas the night before Christmas
and all through the house
everyone felt shitty
even the mouse.
Mom on the toilet,
Dad smoking grass,
I had just settled down
for a nice piece of ass.

When out on the roof
I heard such a clatter
I sprung from my piece
to see what was the matter.
Out on the roof
I saw some old prick
I knew in a moment
it must be Saint Nick.

He came down the chimney
like a bat out of hell.
I knew in a second
the fucker had fell.
He filled all the stockings
with whiskey and beer,
and a big rubber dick
for my brother, the queer.

He rose up the chimney
with a thundering fart.
The son of a bitch
blew my chimney apart
he swore and he cussed
as he rose out of sight.

Piss on you all—
It's been a hell of a night!

The Tale of Robin Hood

Have you heard the tale of Robin Hood
And how he did the poor people good?
But there is more to this famous story
Of Sherwood Forest's pride and glory.

At night when all the robbing was done
His merry men would have some fun.
In fact it would be fair to say
You merry men were rather gay.

As Little John starts to unwind
Robin takes him from behind,
And as they frolic in the grass
Robin rams it up his arse.

One night when they were all at play
A gorgeous rider came their way.
She sauntered up to Friar Tuck
And said, "I'm Marion, want a fuck?"

The Friar couldn't believe his ears
She was offering sex to us old queers.
Whilst Tuck recovered from the shock,
Robin presented her with his cock.

The three old men all had a bash
As Marion's clothes went in a flash.
For Marion mumbled, "This is sheer bliss,"
As they filled her every orifice.

When all was done, she gave a whine,
"Thank you boys, for a lovely time,
But for your pleasure you must pay
I've got the Clap, so have a nice day."

"Now listen here," said Friar Tuck
"We couldn't really give a fuck."
And laughing loud, says, "You silly cow,
We've all got AIDS, so who's fucked now?"

49

The difference between looking into the eyes of a horse and looking into the eyes of a woman is you have to get off the horse.

Do you know the difference between a snow woman and a snow man? Snow balls.

He's a super salesman — he keeps talking about sex until you wind up doing something about it.

Queersville: the home of mixed nuts.

Girls, a perfect husband is like parking space — somebody always beats you to him.

Would you call a rooster with a sore throat a hoarse cock?

Having a bee crawl under your pants leg makes you feel like a new bride — you know you're going to get it, you just don't know when.

He was a queer burglar — he blew the safe, then went down on the elevator.

Your wife doesn't love you any more when you begin to find strange pants buttons around the house.

I call my girlfriend Bedbug — she spends all her time on the mattress.

Semi-dog style is the same as regular, but without the preliminary sniffing.

Eve was the first carpenter in history — she made Adam's banana stand.

I don't mind having my mother-in-law live with us, but I do wish she'd wait until we get married.

Would you call an ex-husband a stalemate?

What is slippery, wet and greasy; when it's in, it moves so easy; when it's out, it flops about? Obvious — a fish.

One thing about the battle of the sexes — it will never turn into a cold war.

I know a secretary who lost her job because of a mistake she refused to make.

QUESTION :   What part of the man's anatomy becomes 12 times its normal size during periods of excitement?
ANSWER   :   The pupil of his eyes. Check it out.

Pornography per se is not a crime. Showing ugly bodies cavorting is a crime.

Rep. Ace Barbers while browsing confiscated smut materials, volunteered to study anti-pornography further. He brought all the evidence at home for further study. Let's hope he won't have a stiff neck after examining them.

A mayoralty candidate was asked how many supporters he has. He replied that he has no supporters at all because he is not an athlete.

The election was orderly. Most of the candidates ordered their goons all around town.

One candidate was always smiling; you never see him frown. He's the only candidate in town who has sunburned teeth.

A candidate didn't get many applauses with his speeches but his smiles are deafening.

I wonder what Tremist are like before they become Extremist.

War in Beirut, war in Nicaragua, war in Ireland, war in Korea, war in Mindanao — makes you think that war is a way of teaching us Geography.

For those of you who don't know the date of Mother's day — It's nine months after Father's night.

I have four consultants when I write about religion. They are Matthew, Mark, Luke and John.

53

LINA GROUP OF COMPANIES

 LINAHEIM PROPERTIES, INC.

 2100 CUSTOMS BROKERS, INC.

 INTEGRATED WASTE MANAGEMENT, INC.

 Agua de Laguna PURE DRINKING WATER

 LAGUNA LAKERS, INC.

 ASSURANCE INTEGRATED MANAGEMENT CONSULTANTS, INCORPORATED

 LINA FARM & FOOD SERVICES CORP.

 MINDANAO EXPRESS CORPORATE AIR, INC.

 Airfreight 2100 Inc.
Licensee of Federal Express Corporation

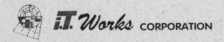 CORPORATION

 U-OCEAN, INC

 U-FREIGHT, INC.

54

So many actors and actresses are running for public office. After the elections, most of the defeated candidates will try their luck at showbiz.

Rotarian Reli Reyes of horseracing fame has very few supporters but he has lots and lots of jockeys.

Many candidates are like heart transplants. They always get rejected.

A councilor received a total of three votes. "Now I know for sure you are keeping another woman," his wife said.

A mayoralty candidate representing the urban poor says he is running because he wants to be urban rich.

The U.S. Secretary of State came here with a dog that looks like a terrier. He says it's actually a police dog. It only looks like a terrier because it is in the secret service.

There are now three groups of people in the Philippines today — the have beens, the are nows and the may bes.

I was very lucky yesterday, I bought P500 worth of instant sweepstakes and I finally won P20.

Sixteen outstanding fathers were honored during the Father's Day Ceremony. One of them is a bachelor.

There is so much pollution now in Metro Manila. I put air in my car tires and they cough.

Mayor Lito Atienza is standing pat on his decision to impose curfew in Ermita. This is to prevent the increasing number of teenage prostitutes. The hobbits are exempt from the curfew.

Most of the bullets used by soldiers on both sides were marked with these words: "To whom it may concern."

The security of our country is very insecure.

The new cabinet members appeared on T.V. with make-up on. That just proves that the Cabinet revamp is purely cosmetics.

Many say that Erap is looking more and more like a raisin everyday. A raisin is a worried grape.

Outlaws may be a menace to our society but in-laws are worse.

It's odd that men take up crime when there are so many legal ways to be dishonest.

Advice to old politicians: Two things are bad for the heart — running up stairs and running down people.

Many critics are always criticizing our government. A critic is a legless man who teaches running.

An Ambassador is an honest man sent abroad to lie for his country.

Imagination makes a politician think he's a statesman.

Filipinos have mastered the art of being prosperous even though they are broke.

The two best live shows in the Philippines today are the Senate and the Congress.

I went to a cheese festival wherein all they served was imported cheese. They tasted like they were deported.

Our politicians never make the same mistake twice. Every session they find some new mistake to make.

A woman always asks her husband's opinion after she's made up her mind.

Advice: Don't lend money to friends. It gives them amnesia.

Two guys met at the Peninsula Lobby:

"You must be from Ateneo," said the first man.

"How did you know?" the second man replied.

"Well, it's the way you talk and the way you handle yourself in general," the first man said.

"And you're from La Salle," the second man said.

"How did you know?" the first man asked. "Is it something about my clothes or talk and the way I handle myself?"

"No," the second man replied. "I read it off your school ring when you were picking your nose."

The Tarlac Governor says there's oil in Tarlac. He's right. They have an oversupply of Johnson's Baby Oil.

The reliable weatherman, Ernie Baron, is right eighty percent of the time. It's the weather that's wrong.

The strikers are still willing to do an honest day's work. The trouble is that they want a week's pay for it.

Everytime I lend a book to Pocholo Borromeo he doesn't return it. He's a professional bookkeeper.

Did you know that many Filipino wives' favorite book is their husband's checkbook?

Golf is having the most fun without taking your clothes off.
— General Willy Florendo, PAF

A student took a bus home after school but his mother made him take it back.

Advice to business establishments who accept checks: Don't count your checks before they're cashed.

Pabling Calma's son tells me that his Daddy hasn't been home ever since his mother caught Santa Claus kissing the maid.

It took a lot of will power, but finally I've given up trying to give up smoking.

In the present stock market conditions, people are neither bulls nor bears. They are chicken.

Many Filipina girls are being beatified everyday by Cardinal Fanny Serrano, Cardinal Pitoy Moreno and Cardinal Goulee Gorospe.

Don't ever drink liquor that's marked with the picture of Rip Van Winkle. It will make you sleep indefinitely. At least you won't have a hangover.

Up to now, we still don't know who killed Ninoy. Japanese journalist Wakamiya, one of the witnesses, is Wamasabi.

A husband is like an egg — if kept continually in hot water, he becomes hardboiled.

Mass production cheapens everything — even laws.

Edu Manzano used to take my advice and now that he's so successful, I take his.

Someone wrote me and said that I am a unique person. I was very flattered although she spelled unique as E-U-N-U-C-H.

There is a new liquor that has flouride as its main ingredient so it won't drive holes into your teeth, just your liver.

One of the first things a child learns when he goes to school is that other kids get bigger allowances than he does.

63

In the Philippines, things are happening so fast. History books are adding a new chapter a week.

On age — Sixty is when the biological urge slowly turns into an occasional nudge.

A lot of men in their sixties are heir-minded but very few are heir-conditioned.

I found out that many employees are nonviolent — they even refuse to punch a time clock.

Investing politicians: they fly now, we pay later.

About the Post Office handling the mail: A woman sent her boy a bible by parcel post. By the time it got to him, seven of the Ten Commandments were broken.

A politician was so shook up after saying that if he is lying, may the Lord strike him blind. Then the blackout happened.

MEMORANDUM

TO : ALL STAFF

FROM : M. DIRECTOR

SUBJECT : SPECIAL HIGH INTENSITY TRAINING PROGRAMME

In order to ensure that we continue to provide the highest quality technical skills, we are undertaking a new employee training programme. It is our intention to keep all employees adequately trained through our programme of "Special High Intensity Training" (from now on to be referred to as SHIT). We are proud of the fact that our company is giving employees more SHIT than any other company in the country.

If you feel that you are not receiving your share of SHIT on the job, please tell your supervisor. You can then be placed on top of the SHIT list for special attention.

Supervisors are highly trained and qualified to provide you with all the SHIT you can handle while on the job.

If you consider yourself adequately trained at present, you may be interested in helping train others, your name can then be added to our "Basic Understanding Lecture List-Special High Intensity Training" (BULL-SHIT).

Our programme also needs a volunteer to serve as the "Special High Intensity Training-Head of Enouragement and Development." If you would like to be the office SHIT-HEAD, just notify your Supervisor, you may already be qualified.

If you have further questions, please direct them to the "Head of Training" (HOT SHIT) programme.

Lastly, you may be sure that your supervisor will treat you as if you are Frank, Understanding, Loyal, Listening and Open for the Special High Intensity Training (FULL OF SHIT).

You will be hearing more about SHIT in the future.

Thank you,

Boss In General, Special High Intensity Training,
Supervisor (BIG SHIT)

P.S. With the abilities and personalities that some employees display, they could easily be selected to be Director of Intensity Programming—Special High Intensity Training (DIPSHIT).

WORK RULES

1. SICKNESS: No excuses will be acceptable. We will no longer accept your doctor's statement as proof of illness as we believe that if you are able to go to the doctor, you are able to come to work.

2. LEAVE OF ABSENCE FOR AN OPERATION: We are no longer allowing this practice. We wish to discourage any thoughts that you may not need all of whatever you have, and you should not consider having anything removed. We hired you as you are, and to have anything removed certainly makes you less than we bargained for.

3. DEATH, OTHER THAN YOUR OWN: This is no excuse. If you can arrange for funeral services to be held late in the afternoon, however, we can let you off an hour early, provided all of your work is up to date.

4. DEATH, YOUR OWN: This will be accepted as an excuse, but we would like at least two weeks notice, as we feel it is your duty to teach someone else your job.

5. PERSONAL HYGIENE: Entirely too much time is being spent in the washrooms. In the future, you will follow the practice of going in alphabetical order, for instance, those surnames beginning with "A" will be allowed to go from 9-9:05, and so on. If you are unable to go at your appointed time, it will be necessary to wait until the next day when your time comes around again.

6. QUANTITY OF WORK: No matter how much you do, you'll never do enough.

66

7. QUALITY OF WORK: The minimum acceptable level is perfection.

8. ADVICE FROM OWNER: Eat a live toad the first thing in the morning and nothing worse will happen to you the rest of the day.

9. THE BOSS IS ALWAYS RIGHT.

10. WHEN THE BOSS IS WRONG, REFER TO RULE (NUMBER 9)

Many Colonels are slated for promotion — Colonel Sanders is not one of them. Maybe because he's chicken.

Jose Cuisia was approached by the NPA asking him to join their ranks — they offered him the Rank of Commander — Commander Liwanag.

A writer known for her angry columns was described as somebody who woke up on the wrong side of somebody else's bed.

VAT is a bloodsucking type of Tax. CARP is a fish that Reforms Land.

I'm looking for a rich girl who's too proud to have her husband work.

Sex is the formula by which one and one makes three.

🚩

People who play the stock market are often led astray by false profits.

🚩

So many people have been badly burned in the stock market by picking up a hot tip.

🚩

Advice to the investors: To make a thousand pesos in the Stock Market, start with five thousand and quit when you've lost four.

🚩

I don't know what's happening to prices. Even meat prices are too high. I just bought two kilos of pork on the installment plan. For P150, you don't get pork chops, you get pork *chips*.

🚩

Times have changed. Years ago you gambled with your money or put it in the bank, now you can gamble with your money by putting it in a bank.

🚩

My friend named his newborn son "HALLOWED." He says, HALLOWED is the name of God the Father in the Bible — "Our Father who are in heaven, HALLOWED be thy name…"

A woman was caught shoplifting at the lingerie department of Rustan's. Mr. Jun Lopez, the General Manager, let the woman go because it was her first slip.

I could tell that Baby Arenas is the loyal type. Once she reached the age she liked, she stuck to it.

In the last elections, many persons received Doctorate degrees — for doctoring the elections.

The people in Muntinlupa are not satisfied with one thing — they want Totings.

Catholics in the US split on the matter of abortion although the Vatican is against it. Czeckoslovakia Abortion Law has been passed. They refer to abortion as a cancelled Czech.

The polls are places where you stand in line for a chance to decide who will spend your money.

I think the most gifted politician is Senator Kit Tatad. He is the only one I know who can give you an answer that makes you completely forget the question.

70

I asked a candidate what he thinks of early marriages — he said he doesn't know because he has always been married in the afternoon.

No wonder they call the Huey helicopters "choppers". All the crash victims were mangled and chopped up.

The downfall of three great men in history were caused by the letter "W" Napoleon's downfall was Waterloo, former U.S. President Nixon's downfall was Watergate. Ferdinand Marcos's downfall was Wife.

Sec. Titus Pardo says that an optimist is a man who earns P500 a week and buys P4,000 suits on credit. A pessimist is the guy who sells them.

A politician complained of a headache and had many doctors examine his head. Unfortunately the doctors can't find anything.

Good Manners: never add cream and sugar to your coffee after it is in the saucer.

Marriage is nothing but an attempt to change a night owl into a homing pigeon.

Today a billion pesos is just a drop in the budget.

Four armed men and women held up a rural bank in Parañaque. The holduppers were very polite and told the bank personnel that this is the first time they tried to hold up a bank. They claimed that the only possession they have are the guns in their hands. The rural bank took pity on them and gave them the money.

Statistics show that ninety percent of the people afflicted with AIDS are incurable romantics.

A peace negotiator says that, "There should be no more bloodshed and violence." He was addressing this to his wife.

Many ex-politicians who are itching to run for office are sure to be scratched at the polls.

Marriage is the only union that permits a woman to work unlimited overtime without pay.

The cheerleader of the San Miguel Brewery basketball team is very unique. She cheers the players one by one.

Many of the Nestlé employees belong to five unions just so they'll always be on strike.

The Finance Secretary says that "Running in debt isn't too bad." It's running after creditors that hurts.

Paqui Ortega is a pessimistic businessman because he complains about the noise when opportunity knocks.

Boss' Lament — many secretaries can't type too well but most of them can erase 50 words a minute.

They now have a stock market doll, you wind it up and it drops to the bottom.

They call a broker a "broker" because often when you see him you are.

I knew a businessman who was very generous with his girlfriend that he finally married her for his money.

I

With food prices soaring, I think it could be better to eat the money.

I

Wars in the Philippines are like a TV series — they always end with "To be continued."

I

The owner of Eppie's, the lingerie manufacturer, is known as the king of the undie world.

I

Ninety-nine percent of our senators are millionaires. Before the elections, they were billionaires.

I

I know a very rich family and they're all in panic because the son and only heir of their fortune is dating one of the servants. There's nothing wrong with that, really. The thing is, he's dating the driver.

I

Don Jaime Zobel de Ayala says that the stomach comes first. Art and culture is the second priority. I guess it's because Don Jaime knows a lot of cultural artists who are starving.

Senator proposing a bill: "All those who are in favor say 'aye', all those who are against say 'I resign.' The bill was passed unopposed.

The Majority Floor Leader introduced a bill. Sen. Cayetano said, "I second the motion." Another senator said, "I third it."

Most people would like to throw money in gambling, drinking and painting the town red with wild women but they can't because they got a government to support.

The Metro Manila crime wave is getting out of hand. It's getting so bad even the holduppers travel in pairs.

In a free enterprise, our businessmen are partners with the government. When they make a profit, the government shares with them; when they lose money, they shoulder it themselves, and the government does not share in the losses. Ergo, everybody wants to be in the government.

I saw a pig riding in a Mercedes. This is the first time I saw pork and Benz.

A telephone is very polite. It only speaks when spoken to.

Isn't TV wonderful? To be able to sit in the comforts of your own home, drink beer, eat potato chips and all night long watch your wife's favorite programs.

Virginia Doe, a 24-year-old waitress from Manila, reported to the Western Police District that she was raped three times last month by a Saudi Arabian. When questioned by the police why she reported the crime only after a month, she said that it was only now that she found out the check bounced.

I asked U-Freight Chairman Bert Lina who his wife is voting for. He said his wife is voting whoever he is voting for. I asked him who he is voting for and he said, his wife has not decided yet.

A sultan says he has one thousand heirs in Sabah. "To Heir is Human, to Forget is Divine."

Linda Lovelace of *Deep Throat* fame is slated to come to Manila to lecture against pornography. One of the sponsors considered is Swift's hotdog.

There is an IBM typewriter that is selling like hot cakes in Pampanga. The machine costs only about P500. Its only defect is that it has no "H."

In his speech in Congress, Sec. Orly Mercado was saying that he needs men with diligence. One solon immediately stood up and said, "'Yan na naman kayo, delihensiya na naman."

In the Holyfield-Lennox fight, a Filipino, Jose Santos, wanted to see the fight but had no money to pay for the admission ticket. He climbed up the flagpole so he cold watch the fight for free. He was so touched when the audience rose to their feet and said, "Jose, can you see?"

Executive Order No. 29 is a bill granting total privileges to the blind. They may now use the mail for free as long as its not in Braille.

To solve the problem in Mindanao, experts suggested an Autonomous Body. The Tadtad movement will appoint the head.

A Philippine Ambassador went to Africa and was immediately invited to a state dinner by the African President. While they were dining, the African President casually asked our Ambassador how he like Patrick Lumamba, the Prime Minister of Africa. Our Ambassador tactfully said, "Patrick Lumamba? Oh, I like him very much." The African President passing a plate replied, "Good, have some more of him."

Sec. Rivera and Joey Stevens with walter

Singing in the rain

The Secretary of Labor never said he's anti-labor. He was just misquoted. He said his auntie was in labor.

Abdul Wahid Bidin is the first Muslim in the Supreme Court. Now he can make a law legalizing Mecca-wayan as a pilgrimage site for poor Muslims who cannot afford to go to Mecca.

Article VI of the Draft Constitution states that "No person shall be a senator unless he is a natural-born citizen of the Philippines." That means all those who were born Caesarean are not eligible.

The importation of frozen fish was approved by the Bureau of Fisheries and Aquatic Resources — that is according to Ed Espiritu. He said he paid for the frozen fish in cold cash.

At the recent Ateneo alumni homecoming, I saw so many old faces and new teeth.

Filipino boxing great Pancho Villa was inducted into Boxing's Hall of Fame. Erap will also be inducted into the Political Hole of Fame.

There is a restaurant in Ongpin that specializes in noodles with American flavor. It is called Mami Vice.

The Land Transportation Commission wages war on smoke belchers. Riding in a smoking car is hazardous to your health. Smoking a car is even more dangerous.

The shuffling of cabinet members is similar to Meralco's power adjustment — it's electrifying.

The lucrative tobacco industry in the Ilocos Region is drying up because of lack of credit, mainly due to the foreclosure of rural banks. This is one industry that is going up in smoke.

Political plums are not raised by the seed. It is done by expert grafting.

Public interest — a term used by every politician to support his ideas.

A relative of Vince Carlos was so depressed he tried to commit suicide by cutting his throat with an electric razor.

Food for thought: Imagination is something that sits up with a woman when her husband comes home late.

Bert Nievera is one of our top singers. He's good; as a matter of fact, I know that with diligence and hard work, in five years he'll be as good as his son Martin.

Hollywood trivia: American actor Red Buttons changed his name to Blue Zipper.

Jeweller Tony Marco got a new job — he teaches nervous people how to eat jello.

The Moro Islamic Liberation Front Islammed the door on the ongoing ceasefire talks.

The Secretary of Labor is a kind of man who really works for the people. Once when his son asked him to tell a bedtime story, the Secretary started, "Once upon a time and a half."

Here's a tip to women: you *can* stay young forever. If you live modestly, get lots of sleep, work hard, jog daily, and lie constantly about your age.

A woman mixed her birth control pills with saccharine. She now has the sweetest body in the world.

The movie *King Kong II* was a huge success — who says there is no money in monkey business?

The peace talks are deadlocked. Many Filipinos are dead and many are locked up while the talks are going on.

Twelve thousand lepers are roaming Metro Manila. Lend them an ear, a finger, a nose, an eye...

My father was a leper; he lep my mother a long time ago.

The Marines said they only fired in the air; 12 flying voters were shot down.

A drunk was rolling on the ground in front of the bust of Marcos in Naguilian. "I'll never drink again," he said. "Why do you say that?" asked his friend. "Because I can see two of them," he wailed.

I play golf in the low eighties. If it gets hotter than that, I won't play.
— Sec. Vicente Rivera, DOTC

I was invited to entertain guests at the opening of a new place to tell a few jokes. The other speaker was Manny Villar who opened the festivities with a long speech on the Philippines' economic achievements. "The Department of Environment and Natural Resources is breaking its production targets. It is rapidly advancing toward complete mechanism and our natural resources will soon rank among the strongest in Asia," he said. I leaned over his shoulder and said, "Manny who's supposed to be telling jokes — you or me?"

The Malayan Insurance Co. is very good — If you bump your head they pay you a lump sum.

At the casino, a man walked up to his wife and said, "Give me the money I told you not to give me."

I went to my girlfriend's house yesterday to find her crying because her dog ate the steak she cooked for me. "Don't cry," I told her, "I'll buy you another dog."

A government official volunteered to go to the wilderness of Mindanao to negotiate a ceasefire agreement with a Japanese straggler.

The laws of the Philippines allow a man only one wife — this is known as monotony.

A noted golfer accidentally shot Juan Santos, his caddy, in the golf course. He made a hole in Juan.

A Chinese brought food to the cemetery. A Filipino asked the Chinese what time he expects his dead to eat his food. "The same time your dead comes to smell the flowers you brought," he replied.

A politician was seen campaigning in the cemetery. He says it's force of habit.

Funeraria Nacional is offering a unique package: Die now and pay later.

Favorite song of Christine Jorgensen, the first man who had a sex change: "Bye Bye Birdie".

Blessed are those who have gall bladder problems for they shall be known as pismakers.

(Anecdote of Meralco boss Manolo Lopez) A man who was condemned to die in the electric chair was offered a last cigarette. "No thanks," he said, "I'm trying to quit."

According to Paqui Ortigas, honesty is a golfer's chief handicap.

A Pope dies and was miraculously brought back to life after a week. The conclave at the Vatican were asking all sorts of questions about God. "How does He look like? Does He have a beard? Does He look like any of the paintings we have of Him?" The Pope answered them, "Well, to begin with," he says, "she's black."

Currently showing in Metro Manila is the movie *The Fly*, the unique story of a zipper in a man's pants.

Do you know what one fly said to the other? Hey, your man is open.

Dodie Peñalosa's motto: it's better to give than to receive.

Most Manghuhulas come from Hawaii.

Famous radio announcement by Joe Taruc: Isang malaking sakuna ang nangyari kanina sa gitna ng Padre Faura at Taft Avenue. Nabaril ako.

A premature baby is one who's born before its parents are married.

I'm writing a new book about how to eat everything you want, stay out as late as you like, drink all you can and go out with as many women you could care to. The title of my book is *How to Die at Thirty-Five*.

Confucius says, "Man who urinates on ground spreads piss on earth."

The difference between an unwritten and a written law is that the unwritten law is often enforced.

If you don't believe in God, you don't have an invisible means of support.

I have a lot in common with Ramon Jacinto. My parents are also in the iron and steel business. My mother irons and my father steals.

I'd like to vote for the best man but he isn't running this year.

One senatorial hopeful is so hungry for publicity he carried a card in his wallet which reads "I am a candidate. In case of accident, call a press conference."

Have you ever wondered how hard it is for a giraffe to have a sore throat or a centipede to have ingrown toenails?

It doesn't matter if you're born poor and you die poor as long as you're rich in between.

John "The Beast" Mugabi is a tough boxer. He is half-Filipino. He is distantly related to Mugabi Concepcion.

The Igorot tribal leaders met with the President. Since the meeting was formal, they wore black tie and white G-strings.

Rotarian Antero Sison, Jr. wrote a book on atheism and then prayed that it becomes a best seller.

Have you ever considered where people in hell tell each other to go?

A young starlet told her father that she was made pregnant by a rich businessman. The father confronted the rich man with gun in hand. "Don't be upset," he said. "If it's a boy, I'll give you ₱ 100,000 and if it's a girl, I'll give you P200,000." The old man thought for a long time. "And if it's a miscarriage," he asked, "does she get another chance?"

You can't get ulcers from what you eat. You get ulcers from what's eating you.

Jun Urbano, noted television director and my mentor, was inside a booth at the Peninsula's men's room and found there was no tissue paper. He noticed a pair of feet in the next booth. He knocked on the wall and asked, "Do you have any Kleenex?" "Sorry, I don't have any Kleenex." After a moment of silence, he knocked on the wall again and said, "Do you have two fives for a ten?"

Did you ever notice that at Christmas people keep their radios on all hours of the morning playing *Silent Night?*

A big businessman, known for thriftiness is so tight; whenever he winks, his kneecaps move.

Ms. Saigon and Mr. Ongpin

MakaBoots, MakaGary and MakaRonnie

Fr. James Reuter once asked me if I have parents. I said yes. He said, "Bring them to me and I'll marry them."

The PLDT announced that there will be 32,000 phones about to be installed all over the Philippines — that means we will have 32,000 more wrong numbers.

My businessman-friend Tony Portillo came back from abroad because his business was not doing well. He was selling PX goods in the U.S.

A golfer was so used to cheating that when he hit a hole in one, he put down a zero on his scorecard.

Dr. Eusebio of the Makati Medical Center asked me to be a blood donor: How can I be one? I am not even a blood owner!

According to Louie Ocampo, the only time most wives stop talking is when their mothers start.

What is the poorest country in the world? Poortugal.

A soldier escaped from his NPA captors and related his ordeal to his CO. "First, they burned my body with cigarettes, then they pulled my nails out, then they whipped me and slapped me, then they opened my wounds and put salt in them." The CO asked him, "And then what happened?" "And then," he said trembling, "and then they tortured me."

Some of us are called to do more than the others. Me, I have been called to do less.

At the Makati Medical Center, when you are scheduled to have an operation, they give you two anesthetics — one to put you to sleep, the other when you see the bill.

According to statistics, a woman gives birth in the Philippines every five minutes. I'd like to meet that woman.

Sen. Robert Jaworski was so nervous when he was scheduled to deliver a speech that he had to go to the comfort room to get a hold of himself.

Sixteen thousand farmers received their certificates of land transfer from the Department of Agrarian Reform. Now that's a lot of crop.

In Scotland, 200 people who drowned were proclaimed the winners of the contest on who could hold their breath under water the longest.

If an athlete has athlete's foot, what does an astronaut have? A missiletoe.

New York-based Filipino artists Raul Sunico and Rene Dalandan teamed up for a two-piano concierto at the Met. They have a piano that has yellow ivory keys. They said that the yellow ivory keys were taken from an elephant who smoked a lot.

The Post Office raised their rates again. Now, when you begin a letter with "Dear" — you mean it.

My friend Don Jaime Zobel is so rich that when he tried to cash a check one day, the bank bounced.

Why does everybody want to be Adolf Hitler's secretary? Because he was a great dictator.

Richard Gomez says that he and his wife resolved not to go to sleep mad. As of now they've been awake for 3 weeks.

I met a girl who has everything a man desires — muscles and a beard.

Rotarian Pabling Calma says that he is at an age now that whenever he goes out with a girl he can't take yes for an answer.

Sen. Blas Ople has young blood but he keeps it in an old container.

A funny thing happened to Speaker Villar — he opened his mouth and a foot fell out.

Rep. Ermita is said to be very supportive of athletes. He is an honest-to-goodness athletic supporter.

In Japan, Mrs. Marcos is known as a shoegun.

Who is the real Paul Anka?

The three Wise Men

97

A Philippine cat fish was named after the Emperor of Japan — Hirohito.

Sen. Juan Flavier showed me a picture of a cheese that looks like the real thing, even the smell. He tested it by putting the picture of the lifelike portrait of the cheese as bait in his mousetrap. The next morning, he found a lifelike picture of a mouse caught in the mousetrap.

The penalty for bigamy is two mothers-in-law.

In Brazil, body organs can be bought. The donors sell an eye or kidney or a lung to relieve their tight financial situation. The body organs on sale are cheap. You can get a cornea for $5,000, or a lung for $4,000. Here in the Philippines, there are donors, too. Erap Estrada once tried to donate his brain for P10,000,000. It was expensive because it has never been used.

Everybody is expecting the Rev. James D. Souza of Bombay, India, to conduct a series of charismatic sessions at St. Paul's College. I hope he won't make Indian.

Always cover your mouth when you sneeze to keep your teeth from falling out.

My father used to be an old newspaperman. He sold old newspapers.

I sent my picture to the lonely hearts club. They sent it back saying they were not *that* lonely.

The best way to double your money is to fold it and put it back in your pocket.

One thousand female sex workers underwent tests for AIDS under a program funded by the World Health Organization. This is a first in Philippine medical history. All of them passed the test with flying colors. Do you know why sex workers used to be called "hospitality girls"? One date with them and you land in the hospital.

The PCGG must love poor people — it created so many of them.

The ceasefire talks must really be effective — the government has ceased firing government employees.

Jorgen Smith, an anthropologist, uncovered a mummy with a tampon stuck to it. He is puzzled because he doesn't know what period it came from.

According to studies, women are capable of reversing the theory of evolution. They can make monkeys out of men.

⚑

Did you know that Nene Pimentel married his childhood sweetheart? He married her when he was in his second childhood.

⚑

The Philippine postal service announced the printing of a postage stamp commemorating prostitution in the Philippines. It costs 2 pesos, but it will cost 20 pesos if you lick it.

⚑

The Philippines is now a great country again, where anybody can be president — that's the risk it has to take.

⚑

Warren Curtis of Massachusetts bit the ear of a dog and won a $100 bet. He now faces a 6-year jail term. He is planning to immigrate here where dog-biting and dog-eating are legal.

⚑

Joe Concepcion's private joy is raising orchids. He even talks to them. He once tried talking to one of his orchids in Chinese, and the orchids turned yellow.

⚑

Amelie Kischner, 62, and Michael Koppel, 23, got married in Metz, France. Their best man was Amelie's son Stefan, 48. Stefan's son, 28, was the ring bearer. Friends advised him to take it easy. He says, "if she dies, she dies."

The first blackout happened during a PBA game last season. It occurred when Norman Black was thrown out of the game.

Raffy Recto is a delight to watch on TV talk shows. I like the straightforward way he dodges all the issues.

Ernie Maceda went rowing in the Pasig River and he accidentally fell over and was on the point of drowning. At the last moment, a man jumped in and rescued him. Only after he had pulled the half-drowned Senator to the riverbank did he become aware of his identity. In order to show his gratitude, Ernie asked him what he wanted in return. "I only want one thing," the rescuer answered. "Please don't tell anybody that it was me who pulled you out."

QUESTION :   Is it true that Erap collects political jokes?
ANSWER   :   No, but he collects people who tell him.

Sadam Hussein dies and ascends to heaven. St. Peter refuses his entry and sends him to hell. The next day, St. Peter is awakened by loud noises outside his window. Looking out, he sees a huge crowd of devils all demanding political asylum.

QUESTION :   Why did Turing Tolentino take his oath of office at the driveway
             of the Manila Hotel?
ANSWER   :   So it would be faster to get away.

QUESTION :   What general said these famous words: "I shall return"?
ANSWER   :   General Ver.

Three inmates were talking at the Bicutan.
"What are you in for?" asked the first.
"I spoke badly of General Dumpit in 1960, what about you?"
"I spoke well of General Dumpit in 1985."
"And what about you?" he said, turning to the third man.
The third man replied, "I am General Dumpit."

At the Makati Medical Center, the nurses wake you up at 4 in the morning to give
you a sleeping pill.

Erap to TOYM Awardees: Don't rest on your laurels. Rest it on your Aquinos,
Enriles, Ramoses, Mitras and Macedas.

The Clairvoyant Society of the Philippines postponed their meeting yesterday due
to unforeseen circumstances.

Gabby Lopez says that the Luzon blackout made him realize the importance of electricity. "Imagine," he says, "if there was no electricity, we would all be watching TV by candlelight."

An old ConCom delegate who is a confirmed homosexual does not deny his relationship with a 16-year-old boy. According to him, AIDS does not matter.

"I am a Rotarian, not a Communist," says Vince Carlos. When the Reds heard this, they breathed a sigh of relief.

Vic-Vic Villavicencio and Tito Eduque of Saisaki say that the key to enjoy Japanese food is sushi.

Why do they always criticize John Osmeña? People who know him say that he has a sunny disposition. He has that usual something that brightens up a room whenever he leaves it.

Erap Estrada is really a man of labor. He is responsible for putting more women into labor than any man in the Philippines.

During the early days of Ferdinand Marcos' tenure, a group of disgruntled cabinet men were leaving his office. "You know," said one, "sometimes I wish he was the Pope instead of the President." "Why?" asked another in the group. "Because," he said, "then we would only have to kiss his ring."

The Transportation Secretary gave PLDT 30 days to improve their work. It will take him that long just to contact them.

Did you ever stop to think that wrong numbers are never busy?

Danding Cojuangco is a very humble man and he's got a lot to be humble about. He has a lot of talent but it's in his wife's name.

Don Jaime Zobel worked hard all his life and before he was 3 years old, he was already a millionaire.

Miriam to Ronnie Puno: I hope you jump into a bicycle and discover that it has no seat.

Erap Estrada was asked what his opinions are regarding sex on TV. "Very uncomfortable," he says.

Try not to confuse NP with PMP. Both parties are already confused.

If you want to come out of the casino as a millionaire, go in as a billionaire.

When our politicians make a joke, it's a law. When they make a law, it's a joke.

Judge Ocampo died a Catholic because he was shot in the temple.

Lydia de Vega agreed to tie the matrimonial knot with Engineer Paolo Mercado on one condition: he has to catch her first.

A man was found floating in the Pasig River with his hands tied behind his back. His body was riddled with bullets and knife wounds and his tongue was cut off. The police suspect foul play.

A gem from Erap: "A man who points an accusing finger should remember that he has three fingers pointing at himself."

Erap is a very generous person. Enrile can attest to that. He gave him ulcers, nausea, diarrhea, migraines, etc.

Chief Justice Davide is a man who cannot be swayed into anything. When he makes up his mind, he is full of indecisions.

Meet the Press will soon be reviewed on TV. There will also be a television show about butchers. It will be called *Press the Meat*.

Ace Barbers met a friend on the street. "Where are you going?" "To a Congress meeting." "Didn't you go to a Congress meeting last night?" "Yes," he said. "Can we meet for a drink tomorrow night then?" "Sorry, I have to go to another Congress meeting." "You sure are so busy. How do you manage to sleep?" "At the Congress meetings," Ace said.

"Everything I Have Is Yours" — today's most sequestered song.

AND NOW THE NEWS

The United States today announced that the World can be destroyed in one minute and twenty-one seconds. The Lord's Prayer was shortened accordingly by Jaime Cardinal Sin.

Avant garde film maker Peque Gallaga today shocked the entire film world with his newest movie *Init Pero Malamig* which features a love scene between two fully-clothed people. In its defense, Gallaga said the clothed scene was done in excellent taste and it will only be shown in foreign markets.

Tragic news from Metro Manila — Dora Naza, a well known authority in gourmet dishes, today fell into a vat of boiling cheese and was fondued to death. Mourners are invited to the East Ocean at 3:00 p.m. tomorrow where they can view the leftovers.

Update on China — the Communist world has its classes too. The upper class are those who can afford Coca-Cola. Sex is also finding its place all over. Their fortune cookies now come out with a centerfold. A friend of mine who just came from there tells me that he found a real bargain. He ran across an all-you-can-eat restaurant in Canton. Only one drawback — they give you only one chopstick.

Dacuycuy, a rich elderly millionaire lay on his deathbed. He had no friends or relatives so he summoned his doctor, Dr. Fores; his lawyer, Joker Arroyo; and Cardinal Sin. "They say you can't take it with you but I am going to show you that I can," he gasped. "I have 3 million pesos in cash under my bed. It is in 3 boxes of one million each. I want each one of you to take a box now and just before they bury me, you throw the boxes in."

The three attended the funeral and each threw in his box. On the way home from the funeral, Cardinal Sin said, "Gentlemen, I want to confess. I needed P400,000 for a new church building so I took out P400,000 and threw in only P600,000." "I have to tell the truth too," said Dr. Fores. "I'm building a new hospital so I took P500,000 and threw in only P500,000." "Me," Joker said, "I threw in my check for one million pesos."

Ernie Maceda was an incurable romantic until penicillin came along.

The triumphant return of President Cory was greeted with a wildly cheering crowd during her ticker tape parade. But the Metro Aides were seen crying — it's not true that they were overcome by emotion. They were crying because they had to clean up after.

A Texas pilot flew to Paris entirely on alcohol. Both pilot and plane were high and instead landed in London. The name of the Texas pilot is Johnny Walker. He's black.

Speaking of aviation, Dong Puno is an aviation lawyer — he has plenty of flying experience. He used to fly a kite.

One of the Big J's ancestors is Alexander Graham Jaworski of Poland. He was acclaimed the first telephone pole.

The PBA locker is where you can experience the thrill of victory and the agony of the smell of feet.

Alaska lost its first game. Meron nang tumalo sa Alaska.

A major in the Philippine Army was seen inside the Peninsula comfort room talking to his privates.

The popular game *sungka* is back. Everybody is playing it with cars using the street potholes as the sungka.

Most politicians now belong to the NP – No Party.

Sportsman Vic-Vic Villavicencio of Saisaki almost dislocated his shoulders describing the fish he caught.

I attended a wedding of a friend who married Nanette Inventor's cousin. The bride was much bigger than Nanette that when they walked down the aisle, they had to walk single file.

Imelda loves everything about America — the people of America, the songs of America, the Bank of America.

A two-headed snake was discovered in the ricefields in Japan's Chiba Prefecture. Two-headed snakes are very rare in Japan. Here in the Philippines, we have plenty of them.

If golf is a rich man's game, how come there are so many poor players?
— Bert Lina of FedEx

There are now four kinds of milk in the country: powdered, condensed, evaporated, and contaminated.

Tony Portillo, an enterprising businessman, is opening up a furniture business that will distribute only expensive outdoor benches made of wood from Germany. He guarantees that his benches will give class to your patio and backyard. It will be called Mercedes Bench.

Golfer Bert Lina says that golf is not necessarily a rich man's game. He knows so many poor players.

Dr. Peny Reloza recommended that I try the mud pack treatment at Sweeney's Beauty Parlor located on Pasay Road. I tried it and for three days I looked good... then the mud fell off.

What do you call a man who stops smoking Hope cigarettes? Hopeless.

Seen at the gate of the Loyola Memorial Park Cemetery is a poster of Marlboro Cigarettes saying "Welcome to Marlboro Country."

An economist is a man who knows more about money than people who have it.

A Chinese bridegroom killed his wife with a long passionate kiss in the neck. Doctors said that the intensity caused heart palpitations that killed the bride. They found the bride and groom unconscious. I don't know why the groom was also out cold. The police put his neck back in his pants and rushed him to the hospital.

This story gave inspiration to many Filipinos who are unhappy with their marriage. So ladies, if your husband is feeling amorous all of a sudden and tries to kiss you in the neck, you'll know what he's up to.

What a crazy world! A 70-year-old farmer was sentenced to life imprisonment for raping a 10-year-old girl. Aside from the rape, he was also charged with assault with a dead weapon.

A judge dismissed the rape case against one acting Mayor. The judge finds the claim of a nightclub dancer incredible. He says that a girl with skirts up can run faster than a man with pants down.

Success is relative — the more success you have, the more relatives you have.

The World Whores Congress opened recently in Brussels. The delegates from the Philippines did not elect to go because of their fear of the dreaded herpes and AIDS. The Philippine spokesman, Lyn Calubaquib said that if they go and attend the Congress, their Brussels might sprout.

I saw a rich woman who had her face lifted at the Makati Medical Center. The rest of her body still drops.

Rey Langit, the dynamic announcer, is one guy who works only for the love of mike.

Double names seemed to be popular in the 1960s. Former Pres. Marcos named his son Bongbong, Pres. Kennedy named his son John John, Pres. Ngo Din Diem named his son Ngo Ngo, Pres. Wee of Singapore named his son...oh, you know that already.

Manuel Conde named all his five sons after him — Manuel Urbano, Jr., Manuel Urbano III, Manuel Urbano IV, Manuel Urbano V. His only daughter is named Manuela.

Filipinos who go to the States also change their names once they get there. Restituto Fruto changed his name to Tutti Frutti. Maximo Factora changed his name to Max Factor. Miguel Joson changed his name to Michael Jackson. Ignacio Quizon changed his name to Ignition Key.

My uncle has twins — one girl and one boy. He named the girl Denise and named the boy Denephew.

My friend Procopia Cubeta was so ashamed of her name that she spent a fortune just to let a judge legally change it. Now she is happy. Her name has been changed to Rosemary Cubeta.

A fashion show is in the works to showcase the different kinds of winter clothes. It will be produced by Eloys.

An independent poll was made to find out what men do after sex. According to the survey, 10 percent go to the bathroom, 10 percent smoke a cigarette, the other 80 percent go back to their wives.

What our country needs is fewer people telling us what our country needs.

The Philippines is the only country in the world where businessmen get together over a P5,000-steak dinner and discuss hard times.

Manolo Lopez of Meralco says that the only one who is happy when there is a brownout is the man who is about to sit on the electric chair.

30 leading industrialists from West Germany are here to look into investment possibilities. Dr. Lutz Stevenhagen, Germany's Minister of State, heads the delegation. Assigned to show them around are Reli German and German Moreno.

⚑

Erap Estrada is giving a speech about the Virtues of Work. "Look at me," he says. "I'm a self-made man." A voice from somewhere in the crowd calls out, "And when are you going to finish the job?"

⚑

There is a new credit card exclusively for wives. It self-destructs after P5,000.00.

⚑

Two Ateneans met at the alumni homecoming and talked about the good old days. "Almost all our friends are gone," said Sonny, "but the one I miss most is Tito." "Why Tito?" his friend asked. "Because," Sonny said, "I married his widow."

⚑

I asked my dentist, Doctor Bololong Erana, to put in a tooth to match my other teeth. So he put in a tooth with four cavities.

⚑

A new year's resolution is one that goes out in one year and out the other.

⚑

Idi Amin comes from Uganda but he's upangit.

I asked Ato Magdia the big boss of Zuellig and also a very good finance man, what a balance sheet is. He said, a balance sheet is what you put out after eating a balanced diet.

There are three ways a man can wear his hair: parted, unparted and departed.

Once upon a time, a lion ate a bull. He felt so good, he roared and roared. A hunter heard him and killed him with one shot. Moral of the story: If you're full of bull, keep your mouth shut.

FM's favorite movie is *Take the Money and Run*.

The Vatican reported that the Holy Pontiff's visit to Chile was violently hot.

The KMU is planning to picket the Makati Medical Center. It seems there's a labor problem in the maternity ward.

Advice to husbands: If your wife is making you lead a dog's life, next time you pass a tree, embarrass her.

DEFINITIONS

Marshmallow – a pregnant aspirin
Goldfinger – an expensive gynecologist
Sheep – sanitary napkins for elephants
Jesuit House – a place for unwed fathers
Abortion – heir today, gone tomorrow
Raisin – a worried grape
Homosexual – a man who gets a nosebleed every 28 days
Bisexual – a man who gets out and buys sex
Kidnap – a child sleeping

Imelda is also up to her neck in showbusiness. She is reportedly auditioning for a part in the revival of the musical *How to Marry a Millionaire*.

Senator Nene Pimentel cheated death when his plane landed on its belly. The pilot developed landing gear problems and while they were circling, the pilot put on his parachute and said, "Don't worry, Senator, I'll go and get help." It's a good thing Nene did not let him go.

Three friends — Tony a Filipino, Marco an Italian and Gop an Indian — were bragging about their endurance. They decided to put this to a test. They got a stinking goat and put the goat inside the tent. The one who stayed in the tent the longest would win the endurance test. Tony went in first. After five minutes he came out holding his nose. Next, Marco the Italian went in. After 15 minutes he also came out saying he couldn't stand the smell. It was Gop the Indian's turn. He went in. Ten minutes passed, then 15, then 20, he was still inside the tent with the goat. Another 15 minutes passed and the goat came out.

Most of our ambassadors-at-large are given the title of Ambassador Extra Pleni-Impotent-iary.

A man from Tondo died from eating fish with formalin. He was embalmed while he was still alive. May he rest in fish.

A man was caught dumping a dead body at Arlegui Street in Quiapo. The authorities charged him with littering.

A columnist is in hot water again for calling the CA an idiot. He is not charged with libel or slander but for revealing a state secret.

A Philippine Air Force cargo plane suffered a flat tire while in the air. According to the pilot, the flat tire was caused by rocky air pockets.

A Philippine Air Force parachutist was reassured by his officer that all the Philippine Air Force parachutes are safe. The officer guaranteed him that if his chute won't open, he can always exchange it. The parachutist then jumped to conclusion.

Comedians par excellence

Three Men and a Baby

Cardinal Sin during his visit to China met with Chinese leader Zhao Ziyang. After the meeting, both are singing an old tune, "I also have a yellow bird."

Most politicians are born with a silver spoon in their mouths but they speak with forked tongues.

A lady politician was born with a silver spoon in her mouth. She was all right after the doctor took the spoon out of her mouth but she has never stopped talking since.

Cause-oriented groups are diminishing while cash-oriented groups are increasing.

A monologue is a conversation between you and Nikki Coseteng.

In the Philippines today, there are three kinds of people — the leftists, the rightists and the underhanded.

My uncle and aunt asked my nephew what he wanted for Christmas. My nephew said, "I wanna watch." So they let him.

Everytime the stock market goes down, another class graduates from the school of experience.

The pet peeve of Ramon Mitra is people who talk while he is interrupting.

Rumor mongering is the spies of life.

Cardinal Sin's visit to China was not authorized by the Pope. Cardinal Sin's excuse is that he just went to trace his roots — the root of all sins.

Did you ever notice that there are more fights held at peace rallies than at the boxing at the park?

Now a part of the marriage vows is "Till debt do us part."

The trouble with having a husband who works like a horse is that all he wants to do in the evenings is to hit the hay.

Rotarian Tony Pastelero is also a police reporter — once a month he reports to the police.

A criminal is a person with predatory instincts who has no sufficient capital to form a corporation.

I call my umbrella "Adam" because one of its ribs is missing.

Orly Mercado once asked a soldier, "What were you in civilian life?" "Very happy, sir," the soldier replied.

In the United States, they have falling leaves. In the Philippines, we have falling planes.

We joke about the Post Office but there's one thing working for them — You will never get a busy signal from a mailbox.

Having a sense of humor is the ability to laugh at something that's not happening to you.

125

Most of our intelligence agents are not.

Sen. Ramon Revilla, after his heart bypass, was made chairman of the Senate Committee on Health.

The Americans are shrewd businessmen. They are now trying to sell the government choppers that are slightly imperfect. They have only one defect. The blades stay stationary while the bodies turn.

Three vigilantes were killed by still unknown assailants. Their comrades held a vigil at their wake.

The government is planning to split the ownership of Meralco. 50 percent will go to A.C. and 50 percent will go to D.C.

Survey shows that among all the Philippine presidents, President Cory has the best legs.

President Erap has plans to back some independent candidates in the elections. Those independents are very dependent on him.

Misuari and Abbas are bonafide members of the Mindanao Allowance.

Stevie Wonder, Ray Charles and Jose Feliciano will do a concert together — it promises to be out of sight.

The casino is a high class place, you have to wear a tie to lose your shirt.

Cardinal Sin is set to go after the casinos. He plans to press the President to close government casinos that recently opened nationwide. He says that the casinos are in direct competition with his bingo socials. As the old saying goes — *You no play da game, you no make a da rules.*

Norma Jean Almadaver is a prostitute who is a candidate for Lieutenant Governor of California. Most of her supporters are her former customers. She says she is running because she will not allow California to be prostituted.

Akil Akil is a Lebanese who owns the Basha Restaurant in Mabini. There you can sample Lebanese delicacies and witness the true art form of belly dancing. Belly dancing is a new kind of dancing wherein beautiful girls are made to lie on the floor and you can dance on their bellies. Akil Akil is a common name in Lebanon. People over there keep shouting the name all the time.

Pete Lacaba is a guy who sticks his No's into other people's business.

Rotarian Tony Ortega's only racket is tennis. He is an avid tennis player. He regularly plays tennis at King's Court.

A group of concerned citizens are sponsoring a walkathon for the benefit of "Tahanang Walang Hagdan" for disabled soldiers. Asked to head the walkathon are Art Borjal, Noli Agcaoili and Nonoy Zuñiga.

All Christian Monsod's friends affectionately call him Boy. But his wife Solita calls him Hoy.

I wrote a letter to the Postmaster General on how to improve the service at the Post Office, but the letter got lost.

Josie Lichauco is an asset to the Department of Transportation. This dynamic lady is a hardworking woman who is known for her tolerance. "Be tolerant of

A golfer I know was so used to cheating that
when he shot a hole in one, he wrote zero on his score card.
—Paeng Buenaventura

someone who disagrees with you, after all he has a right to his stupid opinions," she says.

🚩

The Board of Censors sent agents to review a play called *How Do I Love Thee, Let Me Count the Ways*. The agents saw the play, counted the ways and arrested the whole cast.

🚩

A twenty-year-old woman gave birth to triplets. They were named Tim, Tom and Tat. The mother and the boys are doing fine except when it comes to feeding time. The mother does not have a tit for Tat.

🚩

It was discussed that the latest China hydrogen bomb test was a hoax. Our insiders told us that this was accomplished by ten million Chinese shouting "BANG" simultaneously.

🚩

A businessman made a killing at the stock market. He shot his broker.

🚩

What do you call a man who goes inside a restaurant, orders and leaves without paying? Policeman.

🚩

Japan has just invented a low cost car that runs entirely on electricity. It costs only about P10,000. Very cheap. The only hitch is that it needs an extension cord costing about P950,000, depending on how far you want to go.

Why are they criticizing Jun Magsaysay? He has not done anything.

New graduates' lament: They work hard, study hard and try harder to improve their skills and end up without a job because they are overqualified.

A reporter asked a board director of San Miguel what he does as a director. "Nothing," the board of director said. Turning to Bono Adaza, the reporter asked, "What about you? What do you do?" "I help him," Bono replied.

Rotarian Ato Magadia, takes so many different colored pills, that he dreams in technicolor.

Rotarian Tony Ortigas, was so touched by the pleas of an orphanage official asking for help that he donated an orphan.

Playing poker with the politicians is a no-win situation unless you take out the joker first.

The three kings followed the star until it stopped above a cave. The first and second kings went in; the third king was about to enter when he tripped and exclaimed, "Jesus Christ!" The Blessed Virgin heard this and said, "You know, Joseph, that's a better name than Irving."

A businessman accumulated wealth very fast — he borrowed money from everybody.

A girl swallowed a pin when she was six years old and she didn't feel a prick until she was sixteen.

Life is like a game of golf, as soon as a man gets out of one hole he starts looking for another.

The government is planning a new program to combat juvenile delinquency. It's called "War on Puberty".

Japan's Mitsubishi looks at possible investment in the country. They couldn't do it before because Mitsu was Bishi.

Uranus is the only planet named after a part of the human anatomy.

Jojo Binay was so busy fighting the Comelec about registrations, he forgot to register.

Did you know that the law allows a man 16 wives, if he can afford it, four better, four richer, and four poorer.

Filipino men can be classified into three categories: the handsome, the intellectual and the great majority.

I can always depend on my friends; they can't stand to see me starve, so whenever they speak to me, they close their eyes.

Did you ever notice that narrow-minded people are almost always thick-headed?

To tell the difference between a male and female chromosome, you have to pull down their genes.

*If you can't find happiness along the way,
you won't find it at the end of the road.*

food for thought from
JOSE MARIE CHAN

*Jose Marie Chan's albums
in CDs and cassettes:*

A Golden Collection

Constant Change

Christmas in Our Heart

Thank You, Love

*Strictly Commercial
(The Jingles Collection)*

*Souvenirs
(The Standards-Retro Collection)*

Pacqui Ortigas says that a successful executive can delegate all the responsibilities, shift all the blame and appropriate all the credit.

⚑

Was Adam the first man? The creationists are having doubts because Eve was very friendly with an ape before Adam knew what it was all about.

⚑

Butz Aquino is just right for the role of roving ambassador. He is an impeccable dresser. All his suits are made by YSL — yari sa Laguna.

⚑

A former General succumbed early this morning. Reports say that while he was singing a Frankie Laine ditty, "Granada," it exploded.

⚑

Japan's Seiko Watch Co. and France's Patek Philippe are on the verge of merging. It will be called Seiko-Patek.

⚑

A photographer friend of mine is making a lot of money. He takes pictures of politicians after office hours and they pay him P50,000 to destroy the negatives.

⚑

During the registration for the Alcoholic Anonymous Convention, a Senator obviously drunk, staggered in front of the Registration Desk. "Did you come to register?" asked the clerk. "No," the Senator replied, "I came to resign."

135

Ten Cabinet members surrounding the President were also chosen in the Political TOYM – Ten Outstanding Yes Men.

Magdira Dimaampao was nominated by President Aquino as the new member of the Comelec. Four years from now, Magdira ang Matibay.

Five men posing as medical students robbed the BPI Family Bank of one million pesos. The robbers made a clean getaway. Immediately after the robbery, twenty policemen guarded the bank.

Anatomy of Married life: The first year, wife stands at the door and kisses husband when he leaves the office. His dog barks. Twenty years later husband leaves for office, wife still stands at the door and barks at him while dog kisses him.

The population of gays around the world is growing, proving the adage that women are really the stronger sex.

According to Mayor Mathay, the sun danced because he won.

Edwin Andrews is a firm believer in reincarnation. He told his lawyer to prepare his will leaving everything to himself.

⚑

A noted fashion designer told me that in his opinion there are two major problems in the world today: Death and AIDS. So far he has avoided one of them.

⚑

Bishops air views on Marriage Bill. Here are guys who like to give views on something that they have not experienced.

⚑

When the President visited China, all the Reds there were very alert.

⚑

Foreign Affairs Secretary Domingo Siazon assured the DFA employees that there will be no mass dismissal – as long as they go to mass.

⚑

There is no truth to the rumor that the show of Julio Iglesias was sponsored by the Iglesia Ni Kristo.

⚑

Chinese Philosopher Interview

REPORTER :   Ladies and Gentlemen, in honor of tonight's affair and since it
                is the Year of the Monkey, we have invited a philosopher who

is the direct descendant of Confucius. The resemblance is uncanny because our guest always looks like he is confused. He is a man of many talents. He studied philosophy at the Kuang Chi University in Ongpin, took his masters in politics at the London School of Economics in Taipei. He has been the adviser of the great men in China like Mao Tse Tung, Chou En Lai, Chang Kai Shek and Dewey Dee. He is also a man blessed with uncanny talent in promotions. He is here tonight to impart some of his knowledge to us. So without further ado, please give a warm welcome to our guest.

(ENTER GARY)

REP.   :   Good evening, Muhammed Wat Chua.

GARY   :   Good evening.

REP.   :   Muhammed Wat Chua, are you Chinese?

GARY   :   No, I'm half-breed.

REP.   :   What do you mean?

GARY   :   I breed only through one nostril. Actually I'm half-Chinese and half-Filipino. My full name is Muhammed Mong Puet Mo Chua. Mong Puet Mo is the family name of my mother. Her first name is Paquita.

REP.   :   Paquita Mong Puet Mo?

GARY   :   Later, there are so many people here.

REP.   :   Sir, people have been saying that you are two-faced. Is that true?

GARY   :   That's a lie! If I have two faces, do you think I will use this one?

REP.   :   I heard you also have a Ph.D.

GARY   :   Yes, not only Ph.D., I also have an M.A., LLB, BS, BSBA and an A.B. The only thing I don't have is a JOB.

REP.   :   Have you ever been married, Sir?

GARY   :   Thrice. But all my wives died. Two of them died of poisoned mushrooms and the other died of strangulation.

REP.   :   How come?

GARY   :   She did not want to eat the poisoned mushrooms.

REP.   :   What is your means of livelihood?

GARY   :   I am a marriage counselor.

REP.   :   Do you have any degrees to back up your profession?

GARY   :   Yes, my first degree was given to me by Harvard, my second degree was given to me by Yale and I was recently given a third degree by the police.

REP.   :   I see. I heard you are also an advocate on sex education.

138

GARY	:	That's true.
REP.	:	Do you mind if I ask you a few more questions?
GARY	:	Go ahead.
REP.	:	What is your stand on bisexuals?
GARY	:	There is nothing wrong with that, as a matter of fact, I am a bisexual.
REP.	:	Really?
GARY	:	Yes, everytime I see sex, I buy it.
REP.	:	Do you think sex education is good for the students?
GARY	:	Yes, especially if there is homework.
REP.	:	You are also known as an expert on detecting people who are in love.
GARY	:	Yes, very easy to detect.
REP.	:	How do you know if a man is in love?
GARY	:	By the bulge in his pants.
REP.	:	I see, what about a woman?
GARY	:	A woman is really in love because of her tears.
REP.	:	Tears?
GARY	:	The tears running down her legs.
REP.	:	They say that it's very lucky to have a baby in the Year of the Monkey. How true is that?
GARY	:	That's very true, if you are a woman. Very hard for a man to give birth.
REP.	:	You seem to be very well-versed with the Chinese customs, are there any particular Chinese customs you think we should know?
GARY	:	Yes, for instance, why don't the Chinese use this finger? (shows pinky) Can you tell us why they don't use this finger?
REP.	:	You got me there, why don't they use this finger?
GARY	:	Because this finger is mine.
REP.	:	I heard you are also a world traveler.
GARY	:	Yes, I have been everywhere.
REP.	:	Have you been to India?
GARY	:	Of course, several times.
REP.	:	Have you seen the Taj Mahal?
GARY	:	Seen the Taj Mahal? Ha! I know him personally.
REP.	:	Have you been to Greece?
GARY	:	Yes, several times.
REP.	:	What part of Greece?
GARY	:	Greece Park.
REP.	:	I heard you are also a linguist.
GARY	:	Yes, I speak all languages except Greek.
REP.	:	Do you mind if I test you?

GARY	:	Go ahead.
REP.	:	*Parlez vous Francais?*
GARY	:	That's Greek to me.
REP.	:	Do you have anything to say before you go?
GARY	:	Yes, to our wives and sweethearts, may they never meet.
REP.	:	Thank you, Mr. Chua.

An optimist is a man who gets married at the age of 80 and starts looking for a house close to a school.

I was born six months after my mother left college. That's why I'm smart. I stayed three months in college.

A baby is the interest on a nine-month deposit.

If you don't go to bed early on Christmas eve, Santa will never come.

My wife just ran off with my best friend — whoever he is.

What did the male octopus say to the female octopus? I want to hold your hand, hand, hand, hand...

140

Martin, Kuh and Kuhlang

Senator Revilla with his anting-anting

The couple who takes a bath just before they go to bed are about to come clean.

Married life with an old man is like pulling a car uphill with a rope.

There is a minor difference between a good girl and a swell girl. The good girl goes out, goes home, goes to bed. A swell girl goes out, goes to bed, goes home.

Then there was a butcher who fell into the sausage grinder and went home half-cocked.

My sister married her husband for life and later discovered he didn't have any.

A senator I know always blows his nose — that's his way of ventilating his brains.

A friend of mine bumped his car into a lamppost and lost all his teeth except one — the one with the toothache.

Many politicians are so cheap, they don't even pay attention.

To prevent a cold in the head from going to your chest, just tie a knot around your neck.

Tito Eduque of Saisaki says that liquor may shorten your life but you'll see twice as much in half the time.

Somebody suggested I should follow Ramon Tulfo's style of writing. I can't because it's against my religion. I'm a Devout Coward.

I met a girl with a very nice ponytail. The fact that she looks like a horse has nothing to do with it.

Beggars are sprouting all over the country. A beggar went to my house asking for food. I asked him if he likes yesterday's leftovers. He said yes, so I told him to come back tomorrow.

Prima Ballerina Maniya Barredo is one of the many Filipinos who have achieved international fame. She is scheduled to do the ballet version of *Romeo & Juliet*. Because of the budget limitations she will do the balcony scene in the orchestra.

My gynecologist friend says his being deaf is no problem because he reads lips very well.

Mixed Emotions: When you see your mother-in-law backing off a ravine in your brand new Mercedes Benz.

Pete Lacaba is known by movie producers as Julius Scissors.

We are never too old to learn new ways to be stupid.

The base of Satanism in the Philippines was pinpointed to be in an American school in Baguio. I didn't know devils like cold climates.

In the last elections, entertainers go on TV and kid politicians, and the politicians go on TV and kid the people.

Golf is a game where you yell fore, shoot a six and write down five.
— Peter Favila of Allied Bank

Gus Lagman's computer is so old, it has lost its memory.

A winning senator rushed home and excitedly told his wife, "Sweetheart I've been proclaimed, I won!" "Honestly?" said the wife. "Why bring that up?" the senator replied.

A senator nominated to be senate president said that he was so surprised by the nomination that his acceptance speech fell off his pocket.

My uncle, a taxi driver, quit his job because so many people talk behind his back.

The House Committee on Revision of Laws has decided to revive the death term. It was dead for sometime.

Most of our flyovers have zippers.

Former Executive Secretary Joker Arroyo has tact. Tact is juggling a hot potato long enough for it to become a cold issue.

146

In Congress, many things are opened by mistake but none so frequently as one's mouth.

⚑

The search for UP president is on. Candidates should look like the Oblation.

⚑

An NGO reports that a Filipina maid has filed rape charges against her Egyptian employer. As a result of the rape, the Filipina maid is now an Egyptian mummy.

⚑

Tony Portillo started to smoke cigarettes again because he is trying to quit his habit of chewing gum.

⚑

A Congressman was accused of being a leftist by his wife. She accused him of making "kaliwa".

⚑

Among all the strikes going on around the country, Paeng Nepomuceno's strike is most welcome.

⚑

Why can't Saddam be circumcised? Because there is no end to that prick.

⚑

I went to Saudi and wrote love letters in the sand. I almost married a camel.

Sen. Greg Honasan is the most wanted man today — by women.

The market is being flooded by fake Minoxidil, the wonder stimulator for hair growth. Bembol Roco is still complaining. The stimulator promised to grow heavy hair. Bembol now has a strand of hair but it weighs 25 kilos.

The real Minoxidil really works wonders on men with thinning hair, if you follow instructions correctly. A man misread the label and drank the lotion. He now has a very hairy tongue.

The Labor Secretary says that labor unrest has magnified to alarming proportions. Labor matters are already pregnant with problems, and because of this, the Secretary is experiencing labor pains.

Public opinion is just private opinion that makes noise enough to attract converts.

Liquor kills more people than bullets. Well, I'd rather be full of liquor than full of bullets.

Former National Security Commissioner Emmanuel Soriano is always on TV making announcements involving security. He says he knows of a secret way to keep peace in the country. Well, he sure knows how to keep a secret.

A lady politician thinks she's a siren but she looks more like a false alarm.

A politician who was named as the chairman of Domestic Affairs was chosen among a field of experts. He was selected because all of his affairs are domestic. He has no foreign affairs.

The AFP and NPA encounters produce at least ten deaths a day. The funeral business is booming. Their "hanapbuhay" is "hanap patay".

Pak Awang Syed, an 84-year-old Malay traditional medicine man has been married eighty times. It takes guts to have 80 mothers-in-law.

Death Penalty is restored by Congress. Debt Penalty is also restored by the BIR.

Dog Trivia: the Dachshund is a German Shepherd after taxes.

Leadership Is Our Driving Force

A Soldier's Soldier

General Angelo T Reyes
Chief of Staff
Armed Forces of the Philippines

Intelligent, courageous and innovative leadership
shall be the heart and soul of the AFP.
Effective leadership and management of the
human factor still remain as the basic elements behind
mission accomplishment. The driving force behind
all progressive military and human endeavors
is still leadership —
Enlightened, Dynamic and Courageous.

An expert is a man who creates confusion out of simplicity. It's no wonder there are so many experts in Congress.

Real courage is marrying a three-time widowed woman.

A man sent a ₱10,000 check to TV Patrol's "Lingkod Bayan" but didn't sign it. He wanted to remain anonymous.

The only bad thing about being a good sport is you have to lose to be one.

Here are some unforgettable lines from our Politicians:
"That's just the tip of the ice cube."
"I second the movement."
"Those who have no stone cast the first sin."

The first thing people pray for when going to church is parking space.

Gringo started out as an unwanted child, but he overcame that handicap. Now he is wanted in all parts of the Philippines.

151

You can avoid criticism by saying nothing, doing nothing and being nothing.

Early to bed and early to rise makes a man healthy and socially dead.

A socialite had her appendix removed. The doctor wanted to give her a local anaesthetic, but she insisted on something imported.

The Secretary of Public Works and Highways was being interviewed on the radio. "You're on the air, Mr. Secretary." The Secretary replied, "That's all right. You can take out the air."

Last week was National Press Week. Many *plantsadoras* celebrated it.

The Manila Police jailed a man for making big money. It was one inch too big.

Peace is a period set aside between wars to enable the generals to write their books.

Catholic schools to teach sex: Now the teachers can learn from the students.

Church urged to oppose mail-order marriages, most especially for priests and nuns.

The Manila Police found an Ilocano dead inside his room with 14 bumps on his head. The authorities say he tried to hang himself with a giant rubber band.

Julio Iglesias came and left. He just came here to have a Visita de Iglesias.

According to the Agrarian Reform experts, CARP is not pronounced as CRAP.

A Congressman says that the CARP problem is an open wound. To quote him, *"Sugat sa kalingkingan ay nararamdaman ng buong katawan"* or is it *"Sugat ng buong katawan nararamdaman sa kalingkingan"*?

After Julio Iglesias, Stevie Wonder is scheduled to have a two day concert at the Ultra. He will sing hit songs like "For Your Eyes Only", "I Only Have Eyes for You", and "I'll Be Seeing You".

Why is Stevie Wonder always yawning? Because he is always experiencing 24-hour nights.

Why does Stevie Wonder always wear dark glasses? Because he wants to look like Randy Santiago.

Nowadays women dress to express themselves. Of course, some of them have very little to say.

What do you call a man who marries another man? A priest.

Dieting is a system of starving yourself to death just so you can live a little longer.

There are two periods when to address a golf ball — before and after swinging.

More golf games have been won with pencils than with putters or drivers.

The Tasadays were taken out of the *Encyclopaedia Britannica* records. This prompted Congress to summon them to the House so they will be questioned. Some of the Tasadays have relatives in Congress. The Tasadays also want to know who's representing them in Congress. No, Jojo Binay does not represent them.

Never argue with a doctor. He has inside information.

The current trend is to have shorter honeymoons — but more of them.

Sunshine Cruz is one bold actress who made it to the top because her clothes didn't.

Most of our policemen never hit a man when he's down — they kick him.

I went to a wedding where the bride was so ugly, everybody kissed the groom.

The Senate Committee on Education decided to implement free education for public high schools. That's good news. Now some politicians can try to finish their studies.

Buttman and Robin

Bugsy: Papa, are you a
self-made man?
Gary: Yes, son. Why do you
ask?
Bugsy: Why did you make
yourself to look like that?

Politics — where candidates pat you on the back so they will know where to plant the knife.

I was deeply touched by the gesture the Makati West Rotarians gave me during my talk at their fellowship meeting last week. I was really touched especially when they asked me to pay for my lunch.

Trivia: The limbo dance was invented by a Puerto Rican trying to get inside a pay toilet.

The US Ambassador and the Japanese Ambassador met for the first time. "Ohio," the Japanese Ambassador said. The US Ambassador caught unawares answered, "New York".

Thousands of homosexual couples staged a mass wedding in Washington, D.C. Leave it to the Americans to come up with a solution to the population explosion.

A movie producer is planning to make a movie about the life of Sen. Franklin Drilon tentatively titled *A Man Called House*.

Businessman Tony Portillo is offering ₱ 20,000 to any man who will take care of his problem. I immediately applied for the job. I asked him how I will get paid. He said that that was my first problem.

In Seoul, South Korea, Park Son Do sliced off the ear of a man who owed him money and refused to pay him. He lent him an ear instead. The victim's name is Van Gogh Choi.

The Justice Department at last filed murder charges against Victoriano Tutuan and an inmate Jose Obosa. They are charged with killing Secretary Jaime Ferrer. Now Tutuan and his tutas will feel the whole wrath of the law.

Rotarian Poch Borromeo loves to play golf at night. He says he doesn't have any problem with his game because he uses night clubs.

True or False? When Jojo Binay was born, the doctor who delivered him did not use forceps. He used tweezers.

In the coming Olympics, the Philippines is going to introduce an event in which it excels. The special event is called the Bank Run.

The talented band entertaining the Kamayan habitues nightly is composed of blind but highly talented musicians. Their band is called Love. I guess it's because love is blind.

A congressman was nicknamed Crime by his constituents because whenever they go out and eat, Crime does not pay.

Defense Secretary Orly Mercado has a very unusual piggery. His boars are named after popular personalities such as Cabauatan, Abadilla, Enrile, Honasan, etc. They are VIPs — Very Important Pigs.

Do you know what happened to the ugly duckling in China? It became a Peking Duck.

The principal advantage of being a defeated politician is that you don't have to explain why you didn't keep your campaign promises.

PLDT – Perennially Lost Dial Tone or Puro Lang Dial Tone. PLDT is a new means of transportation. It can bring you home on the telephone.

Executive Secretary Zamora says that the Philippine budget would be pruned. But how can you prune a raisin?

Sources say that the corporal involved in the tanknapping was really a mechanic. He staged a mechanicoup.

The proliferation of smut publications and films in the country prompted two women lawmakers, Senators Miriam Defensor Santiago and Nikki Coseteng, to support a bill putting more teeth into the existing anti-obscenity laws. Wags say it's better obscene than heard.

New meaning of PAL – Pinagbibili Aeroplanong Luma.

Batasan Bombed! Witnesses say the bomb was only a big firecracker. The Batasan was nabawasan.

Religious story — The good cardinal died the day the driver of a Saulog bus died. Both went to heaven. God gave the cardinal a small room and gave the Saulog driver a big suite. Naturally the cardinal complained to God about the discrepancy. God explained. He told the cardinal while he was on earth his sermon put many people to sleep while in the case of the Saulog bus driver, whenever he drove his bus, everybody prayed.

Blessed are the peacemakers for they shall never be out of work.

I once hit two balls in one stroke. That's because I stepped on a rake.
— Sen. Sonny Jaworski

Never argue with a fool, onlookers may not know who is who.

If Jose Rizal were alive today, he would be very, very old.

Most of the defeated candidates are poor losers. If you lose, you are automatically become poor.

I don't know why my pet bulldog is always making faces at me.

Study shows that alcohol and cocaine kill brain cells. That doesn't bother the addicts and the alcoholics. They are brainless people.

The PCGG aborted a new bid to smuggle out cattle. The smugglers were caught trying to pass off the cattle as big goats.

Contrary to the fact that the Philippines enjoys a high literacy rate, survey shows that about 5.8 million of the 56 million Filipinos still cannot rid or rite.

In Poland, all shoes made in Poland have the initials T.G.I.F. meaning Toes Go In First.

The Philippines will finally have an honest to goodness saint. This was announced by Cardinal Sin, after his talk with the Pope. It took a Sin to announce a Saint.

Channel 4 was bombed. This time the violence was outside the boob tube.

Definition of a clever politician — a man who can talk for an hour without saying anything, serve six years without accomplishing anything and get reelected without doing anything.

Most politicians start out to do well and they usually end up well-to-do.

One congresswoman was bragging about her upbringing. She says, she was born with a silver platter in her mouth. That explains her big mouth.

A solon dining with his constituents asked a fellow solon to please pass the rice. He said "Rice, please." The solon whom he was addressing immediately stood up.

The Comelec Chairman says that his job is a thankless job. I've got news for him. If he resigns, everybody will be thanking him.

One congressman is truly a man with compassion. Every Christmas he goes to the slums of Tondo just to visit his parents.

Maria Benitez Olivera of San Juan, Argentina gave birth to her 32nd child. She says that child will be her last because her husband has finally bought a television set.

Why is the Statue of Liberty bowlegged? You would be bowlegged too if you gave birth to a nation.

Businessman Tony Portillo is contemplating on investing in the meat-packing business — he plans to manufacture girdles.

Ed Espiritu says the stock market is creating a whole new class in the Philippines — the nouveau poor.

I met a woman whose face was so wrinkled that when she wore long earrings she looked like a venetian blind.

One of life's great tribulations — every time I meet a girl who can cook like my mother, she looks like my father.

Bomb explodes in Fort Santiago. Fifth Santiago is next.

The Thomas Jefferson Library was also bombed. Nobody heard the explosion — maybe it's because the library has a "silence please" sign.

What's the similarity between an ass and Elizabeth Barrett Browning? Both are poets.

Malacañang is like Spain, it also has a Coryda de Toros. It is composed mostly of many bullheaded people.

Japanese Trivia: Who is chicken tereyaki? He is the oldest living kamikaze pilot.

166

Endangered crocodiles find Palawan sanctuary; some of them found sanctuary in Congress.

One of the women in Congress looks a lot like Helen of Destroy, the woman who launched a thousand sheep.

Divorce is now recognized here as long as you do it abroad. Divorce is what results when the bonds of matrimony no long bear interest.

My neighbor couldn't afford a divorce so he shot his wife.

A friend of mine says his wife won't give him a divorce. She says that she's lived with him for 20 years, so why should she make him happy now?

President Erap told his Cabinet members to stay clean. Four of them immediately took a bath.

Deodorant commercials are really doing their job for togetherness — the family that sprays together, stays together.

A deodorant salesman is known as an odor-to-odor salesman.

The Philippine Air Force ordered jet fighters from Italy. It's easy to recognize Italian jets. They have hair under the wings.

Good News: Senator Cayetano announces that henceforth, *pandesal*, the Philippine staple bread will become much bigger. It will also become much lighter.

Nowadays, a girl with a lot of hidden talent usually wears clothes that reveal it.

A movie actress who likes to take milk baths was hurt while taking a bath. The cow slipped and fell on her head.

When delivering privilege speeches, many politicians get carried away by the sound of their mouths.

Food for thought: A man gets weak when a woman tells him how strong he is.

Doctors who practice without a license are called quacks or ducktors.

One spectator at the coup saw his friend there. *"Ano'ng ginagawa mo rito?"* he asked. His friend replied, *"Nanonood ng shooting."*

The coup made so many cigarette vendors richer.

I know one cabinet member who's got the only office in the Philipines that has wall-to-wall relatives.

Dodie Peñalosa was knocked out. The fight was televised and it was full of his Family Rubbing Alcohol commercials. After the fight he was still endorsing the product. *"Ito ang gamit ng mga* ex-champion *katulad ko."* Now, there's the rub.

Many good soldiers did not die in the war — they were killed by vintage World War II planes that malfunctioned.

My neighbor's pig gave birth to a piglet with five heads — unbeliebaboy!

Up to now Larry Henares believes that I am an abortion that lived. He must have known that I was once the poster child for birth control.

Scientists have definitely proved that smoking one cigarette diminishes your life by one minute. A friend of mine read this article two weeks ago and immediately stopped smoking. Unfortunately, he passed away soon after he decided to stop his vice. He got run over by a truck.

Our Congress doesn't have a bonafide clown. And so as not to deprive the Filipino people, the congressmen take turn at it in every session.

Cabinet Revamp Suggestions

Secretary of National Defense — Miriam Defensor Santiago
Comelec Chairman — Jojo Binay
Secretary of Finance — Reli German
Secretary of Foreign Affairs — Joey Cuisia
AFP Chief of Staff — General Lim
Secretary of Trade and Industry — Raul Concepcion
Secretary of Health — Jovy Salonga
Secretary of Labor — Romy Jalosjos
Secretary of Agriculture — Mang Pandoy
Presidential Spokesman — Bono Adaza
Plain Secretary — Dawn Zulueta

It's difficult to get a man to understand something when his salary depends upon his not understanding it.

Man is a creature of superior intelligence who elects creatures of inferior intelligence to govern him.

Bigamy — Two rites that make a wrong.

Two NCAA coed athletes were accused of prostitution on campus. The NCAA authorities state that these two athletes might lose their amateur standing.

Those 50 alleged communists in the government are well-educated and well red.

Congressman Butz Aquino's favorite sports is water polo, but he had to give it up because he kept on drowning so many horses.

One congresswoman has a pretty little head. For a head, it's pretty little.

GIVE: an agreement between two golfers who can't putt.
— J.V. Eejercito

We should not complain when we watch TV. We are free to watch any program we choose. We are very lucky. In the communist countries, the TV watches you.

Ike Gutierrez is a technocrat par excellence. He is a man of rare gifts. I know because I never got one from him.

The hobbits of Malate went on a shopping spree. All they bought were shorts.

A bank is an institution that lends you an umbrella and then wants it back when it begins to rain.

Our congressmen and congresswomen pass bills left and right. Very few pass bills to the center.

Cardinal Sin says that only in the spirit of sharing can we shape a solution to the unsolvable and perennial crisis in the country. If you don't share, you become a spirit.

Rotarian Poch Borromeo recently bought an air conditioner worth ₱60,000. I asked him how come it cost so much. "Because," he said, "it's colored."

The difference between an amateur and a professional athlete is that the latter is paid by check.

Cosmetics are a woman's way of keeping a man from reading between the lines.

The weakness of public opinion is that so many people express it privately.

Advice to Presidentiables: The trouble with stretching the truth is that it's likely to snap back.

Cure — what a doctor does to a disease while killing the patient.

Our politicians try to drink from the fountain of knowledge. Most of them, though, just gargle.

A woman gave birth to triplets. One of the triplets died. So now, she only has twins.

What term is used for:

the killing of a priest? Paricide
the killing of a Swiss national? Swisside
the killing of a Chinese? Intsikticide
the killing of somebody inside his residence? Homicide
the killing of somebody who bugs you? Pesticide
the killing of somebody at the Boulevard? Baycide
the killing of somebody named Geno? Genocide
the killing of somebody at sea? Seacide
the killing of somebody outdoors? Outcide
the killing of somebody indoors? Incide

The ASEAN Summit is over. The delegates were here for a total of three days. The total time of the meetings was one hour and forty-five minutes. That's the sum of it.

Senator Franklin Drilon had no platform because his form is round.

Amado Dulnuan is a very talented foot painter. Just go to him and he will paint your foot.

The House of Congress approved the granting of ₱50,000 death insurance for every soldier. The insurance company who is insuring the soldiers will go bankrupt in one year.

A very rich man who was destitute ordered his driver to drive over the cliff because he wanted to commit suicide.

Ladies, don't wait too long for love. I know a girl who waited so long for her ship to come in, her pier collapsed.

A first time politician attended a cocktail party and was too excited about the experience. When the waiter asked him, "Cocktails, sir?" he answered, "Yes." "What kind?" the waiter asked. "Shrimp," he replied.

The illegal abortion clinics in Manila are so crowded. There is a three-year waiting list for patients.

To be is to do — Socrates
To do is to be — Descartes
Do be do be do — Frank Sinatra

A good executive is the man who believes in sharing the credits with the one who did the work.

The reason why so many congressmen work so hard is because they are too nervous to steal.

The man who brags about sitting on top of the world might remember that the world turns every 24 hours.

I performed for the prisoners of the Muntinlupa State Prison. They were a very captive audience.

Rico Puno and Ronnie Poe have their own followers in Quezon City. Rico's followers are called Macapuno and Ronnie's followers are called Macaronnie.

Most of the AFP officers say they will never be caught "under the bed." But they don't mind being "under the saya."

Natwar Singh is not related to Gary Lising. Gary is not an Indian — he keeps his appointments.

Among the governors, Joey Lina has the most relatives — Carolina, Rosalina, Rizalina, Pualina, Marilina, Magdalina. With his relatives alone, how can he miss?

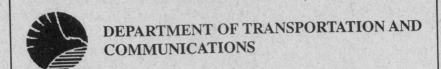

DEPARTMENT OF TRANSPORTATION AND COMMUNICATIONS

FULL *SWING* INTO THE YEAR 2000

OUR VISION

Free access to basic services; Integrated national network of facilities; Policy environment fostering, competition, public-private partnership, a balance between economic efficiency and national or social integration; networks conforming to international and industry standards.

MAJOR PROJECTS

Woossh!! Straight across the nation's tough developmental course, the modernization efforts of the Department of Transportation and Communication is in full swing. With powerful strokes, DOTC is transforming the landscape of the Philippine transportation and communications industry into a potent force--- strengthening and sustaining our nation's growth. Equipped with DOTC's very own cache of full range development projects, we are pursuing major infrastructures that will nurture and safeguard the lives, livelihood and future of our people, as we forge full swing into the new century.

Ninoy Aquino International Airport (Terminal 2) Development Project
Ninoy Aquino International Airport (Terminal 3) Development Project
Davao International Airport Development Project
Nationwide Air Navigation Facilities Modernization Project Phase III
Modernization of the National Civil Aviation System
LRT LINE I Rehabilitation Project Phase (I, 2, 3)
M M Strategic Mass Rail Transit Development (Line 2) Project
EDSA LRT System (LRT 3), PhaseI
Batangas port Development Project
Fishing Port Project Package II
General Santos (TAMBLER)Fishing Port
Upgrading of Mactan International Airport Airfield Lighting System
Maritime Safety Improvement Project -B
Social Reform Related Feeder Ports Development Project
Rgn'l Telecommunications Development Project Regions I&2 Phase C,
National Telephone Program Tranche I-2. Rest of the Tranche
National Telephonde Program. Tranche I-2. Rest of the Tranch. Stage 2.
Phil. German Advisory Assistance in the Field of Telecommunications
Postal Mechanization and modernization Program , PH. III
Global Maritime Distress and Safety Systems (GMDSS)
Acquisition of Search and Rescue (SAR) Vessels
LRTA – Automated Fare Collection System Project
LTO Database infrastructure and Information Tecnology System

Most of our politicians are like some gamblers — they don't have enough sense to quit while they are ahead.

A woman wears a padded bra to accentuate the positive and a girdle to eliminate the negative.

At the fishing towns around the Philippines, boat-buying is legal.

How many times does a cock crow in one minute? It depends on how strong the cock is.

A Muslim warrior embraced the Catholic religion by embracing a Catholic nun. The drama started when the Muslim warrior and the Catholic nun tried convincing each other to join their respective religion. It really worked. Now the Muslim warrior is a priest and the Catholic nun is now a Muslim.

I was a teacher's pet. That's because she couldn't afford a dog.

A noted singer once licked his microphone and said, "Tasting, tasting, one two three tasting."

⚑

Advice — Be true to your teeth and they will never be false to you.

⚑

Youth governor Joey Lina took part in a blood compact with the Laguna youths to symbolize youth support for him. The ritual was a re-enactment of the 16th century blood compact between Rajah Humabon and Miguel Lopez de Legazpi. Joey Lina's first words after the bloodtaking was, *"Aray"*.

⚑

Speaking of nuclear weapons, the hydrogen bomb has made one contribution to democracy — with it, all men are cremated equal.

⚑

The biggest job of Congress is how to get the money from the taxpayer without upsetting the voter.

⚑

During the snap elections, a farmer was questioned about vote buying. "Did you sell your vote?" the prosecutor asked. "No, sir, I voted for Marcos because I like him." "We have evidence that he gave you ₱500," the prosecutor barked. The farmer said, "Well, when a fellow gives you ₱500, you will naturally like him."

⚑

Politicians are like tea bags; they don't know their own strengths until they get into hot water.

Joe Con's campaign for "Light a Candle" worked. When everybody lit their candles, Joe Con sang, "Happy Birthday".

New political party — Latang Pilipino. Yes, the Pilipino can.

HUSBAND	:	Sweetheart, if I die, will you remarry?
WIFE	:	I suppose so.
HUSBAND	:	Will you and he sleep on the same bed?
WIFE	:	I guess so.
HUSBAND	:	Will you make love to him?
WIFE	:	I think I will.
HUSBAND	:	Will you give him my golf clubs?
WIFE	:	No, he's left-handed.

On their wedding night, the young groom started to get undressed. He takes off his pants and she notices that his knees are full of holes and are scarred. The wife says, "What happened to you?" The man said, "Well, when I was young, I had the Kneesels." He then took off his socks and his wife saw his toes deformed. "What happened to your feet?" "Well, when I was young I had Toelio," he said. He then took off his shorts. His wife says, "You had Smallcox, too?"

What is the best thing to come out of a penis when you stroke it? The wrinkles.

"Just try to relax, Miss. Haven't you been examined like this before?" he asked. "Yes," she said, "but not by a doctor."

"""

Husband and wife were fighting about their sex life. "You never even tell me when you're having an orgasm!" the man yelled. "How can I?" she said, "you're never here."

"""

A congressman's wife was telling her friend that since she and her husband had gotten twin beds, her sex life had improved tremendously. "How can that be?" asked the friend. "Well," she said, "my bed is in Makati and his bed is in Quezon City."

"""

As he lay in his deathbed the man said to his wife, "I can't die without telling you the truth. I cheated on you. All those nights when I told you I was working late I was with other women." His wife looked at him calmly and said, "I know. Why do you think I poisoned you?"

"""

Wrist Band — Something you wear on your wrist so you'll know the right from the left.

"""

Sign in front of Sabater Pascual Optical:

"Eyes examined while you wait. If you don't see what you want, this is the right place to come to."

Dr. Joseph to patient: "Now," he said indicating the large eye chart on the wall, "What's the smallest line of letters you can read on the chart?" The patient looked at the wall carefully and said, "What chart?"

Little boy   :   Mommy, where do babies come from?
Mommy   :   From the stork.
Little boy   :   I know, but who fucks the stork?

What are the three words you don't want to hear when making love? "Honey, I'm home!"

A nymphomaniac's dilemma — Meeting a guy with AIDS and a huge penis.

How does a coward commit suicide? He shoots himself at the back.

Boyong, a 40-year-old Ilocano tailor, was still unmarried. He believed there was something wrong with his hormones. Women didn't find him attractive. "Why don't you go to Dr. Akiko? She's an acupuncturist, she can help you," a friend advised. So Boyong went to Dr. Akiko. She told him to take off his clothes and bend over and hold his ankles. Dr. Akiko examined Boyong carefully and announced, "You have Exockery Disease." "Doc, what is that?" Boyong asked. "Your ass rooks exockery like your face!" the doctor exclaimed.

Why is masturbation better than intercourse?
1. Because you know who you are dealing with.
2. Because you know when you've had enough.
3. Because you don't have to be polite afterwards.
4. Because it's free.

Do you know how to keep an asshole in suspense? I'll tell you tomorrow.

Pabling told Chet that the girl he picked up last night was a minor. "Was she inexperienced?" Chet asked. "No, she gives a great blowjob. The trouble is when I woke up this morning, my penis was full of bubble gum."

Recommended book for aging men: *How to Tell the Difference Between an Orgasm and a Heart Attack.*

How can you tell if you're having a wild orgasm? Your wife wakes up.

A father went to his dentist and asked him to put braces on his daughter's teeth. "She has beautiful teeth," said the dentist, "why do you want to put braces on her?" "To keep the guys from asking her for blowjobs," replied the father.

Why do farts smell? So deaf people can enjoy them too.

A farmer talking to his cow: "Just because I pulled your tits several times doesn't mean I love you."

Edwin met a gorgeous girl at the Pen lobby. "You really have a gorgeous figure," Edwin said. "I'd give you ₱10,000 just to hug you for a minute if …if only… ." The girl smiled and said, "Don't be bashful, Edwin, if only what?" "If only you'd give me a free blowjob afterwards," Edwin said.

Donnie met a girl at a party and he checked her in a Pasig motel. They were locked passionately in an embrace when the girl said, "What I'm doing is strictly against doctor's orders." "Are you sick?" Donnie asked. "No, I'm married to a doctor."

People who tend towards Government — Rightist
People who tend to oppose the Government — Leftist
People who tend in the middle — Middle Ist

I know a baseball player who is so honest he refuses to steal first base.

Rotarian Leo Caguioa went to a massage parlor in Makati. *"Ano ba mayroon kayo rito?"* he asked. *"Mayroon ho kaming* Sauna Bath, Turkish Bath, at Swedish Bath," an attendant replied. *"Ano pa?"* Leo asked. *"Tebath,"* she replied. Leo took all four.

Federation Express is different from the Enrile Express. The Enrile Express only goes to Cagayan.

How do the Chinese get their names? By throwing pots and pans in the wall and get the names from the sound the pots and pans produce e.g. Chiong, Chang, Ling, Tan, etc...

A beautiful Polish tourist confronted a man and asked him why he was always staring at her. "Because," the man replied, "I am a poll watcher."

Many senatorial bets ran under the Lakas ng Loob Party and Lakas Talo.

Alvarez adopted as son of Bicol — at last, he now has parents.

A handicapped golfer is a man playing golf with his boss.
— Sec. Domingo Siazon, DFA

Advice: Everytime you attend a political dinner, do not sit next to a senator or congressman — they never pass anything.

One worried Presidential candidate: "I am apprehensive about my winning. When the people wave at me, they do it with only one finger."

They are now selling toilet paper with the pictures of Presidential candidates so the assholes can see who they are voting for.

DOCTOR   : You are the father of triplets.
POLITICIAN : Impossible! I demand a recount!

Erap Estrada to his speechwriter: "Don't use big words in my speeches. I want to know what I'm talking about."

Surveys say that about 80 percent of our politicians are bottlefed babies. Just goes to show you that even their mothers didn't trust them.

A LAMP Senator seeking votes spoke on the platform. When he was in the middle of his speech, he was heckled, "I'd rather vote for the Devil!" "Suppose your friend doesn't run," said the Senator, "may I count on your support?"

A group of congressmen were in a conference. One said, "We have two billion appropriations to spend. What are we going to do with it?" "Why don't we bridge our Pasig River lengthwise?"

A senator woke up sweating profusely. He said he had a terrible dream. He dreamt that all the money he was spending in the election was his own.

Young Boy	:	Daddy, what is a traitor in politics?
LAMP Politician	:	A traitor is a man who leaves the LAMP and goes over to the other one.
Young Boy	:	Then what is a man who leaves the LAKAS and comes over to the LAMP?
LAMP Politician	:	A convert, my son!

| EDWIN | : | I don't want to vote for any of the candidates. I don't know any of them. |
| CHET | : | I don't know what to do either. I know all of them. |

Today we can rent anything — rent a house, rent a TV, rent a place, rent a trip. The only thing you cannot rent is a politician. You still have to buy them.

John Osmeña is overwhelmingly confident. On his last birthday, he sent his parents a telegram of congratulations.

Man confessing to Cardinal Sin:
Bless me Father for I have sinned. Yesterday I killed two Erap supporters.
Cardinal Sin: I'm not interested in your politics, just tell me your sins.

A friend of mine was asked why he lost in the election. He said that they didn't re-elect him because of his youth. I said, "How can that be, you're over 50 years old and your youth has been spent." "I know," he said, "they found out how I spent it."

Miriam Defensor Santiago approached a voter and said, "I've come to ask you to support me." The voter said, "I'm sorry ma'am, I'm already married."

Why is the camel called the ship of the desert? Because it is filled with Arab semen.

What is a birth control pill? The other thing a woman can put in her mouth to keep her from being pregnant.

What did the sanitary napkin say to the condom? "If you break, we will both be unemployed."

Homocide: Crime you commit if you kill a homosexual.

What is a virgin in the province? A girl who can outrun her brothers.

Why doesn't Saddam get hemorrhoids? Because he's a perfect asshole.

How did Captain Hook die? He became disoriented and wiped with the wrong hand.

If lovers celebrate Valentine's Day, what do lonely men celebrate? Palm Sunday.

What do husbands have in their pants that their wives do not want in their faces? Wrinkles.

What is the difference between a pregnant woman and a light bulb? A light bulb can be unscrewed.

Golfer Interview

SCENE – GOLF COURSE

Interviewer: Good evening, this is Fed Tailon your sportscaster bringing you the latest development in the golfing world. Mr. Gary Casius Miñoza Lising, the only Filipino who won all the foreign golf tournaments after beating such golfing greats as Tiger Woods, David Duval, and other noted golfers in the game of chess. He is also responsible for the training of Gerald Rosales in his preparation for the Asian Games, unfortunately he taught him how to play bowling. And now for the first time, ladies and gentlemen, it gives me great pleasure to present the great Gary Casius Miñoza Lising.

(Enter Gary in full golfing outfit)

Int: Congratulations, Mr. Lising, for winning the All-Filipino Open.
Gary: Thank you, I won that in a play-off.
Int: In that tournament, who was your opponent?
Gary: My opponent was the rich golfer Akihito Nakagucci.
Int: Nakagucci? But I thought it was an All-Filipino Open.
Gary: Yes, but he was naturalized before the tournament.
Int: You sure look great. You are known for your sartorial elegance especially golfing outfits.
Gary: Yes, even my socks are like a golf course.
Int: Golf course? Why?
Gary: My socks also have 18 holes.
Int: How did you do on your first day on the course?
Gary: I shot a 68.
Int: 68? Wow!
Gary: Tomorrow I start on the second hole.
Int: I see. Mr. Lising, all in all, how many tournaments have you won?
Gary: (Counts fingers up to ten) Two.
Int: I heard you shot a hole in one on the first hole.
Gary: Yes.
Int: Why are you sad?
Gary: Because on the second hole, I shot 182. But last week I was really lucky.
Int: Why?

Gary: Because, I shot a birdie, an eagle and a duck.

Int: Sir, does golf give you problems?

Gary: Yes, my wife says she'll leave me if I don't stop playing golf.

Int: That's terrible.

Gary: Yes, I'm going to miss her.

Int: Are there any sad experiences you had while playing golf?

Gary: Yes, I once played with my brother-in-law Rolly, and on the 4th green he just dropped dead.

Int: What did you do?

Gary: For the rest of the day, I hit the ball, dragged Rolly, hit the ball, dragged Rolly… it was very tiring.

Int: In your club, sir, I noticed that the golfers have big wrists, big hands, big shoulders and big thighs.

Gary: You should see the men, they are bigger.

Int: Sir, can you give us some helpful tips on the game of golf?

Gary: Sure — first we concentrate on the driver, it's very important.

Int: Why is the driver important?

Gary: How can you go home without him?

Int: How far do you usually drive?

Gary: The farthest was when I went to Baguio.

Int: No, I meant with your clubs.

Gary: Oh, I'm sorry, the farthest I've hit the ball was 350 yards.

Int: 350 yards? Wow, that's very, very good.

Gary: Yes, but I'm not satisfied.

Int: Why?

Gary: Because I also putt the same way — 350 yards.

Int: Have you ever hit a perfect ball?

Gary: Yes, as a matter of fact, I hit two perfectly good balls yesterday.

Int: Two balls at once? How?

Gary: I stepped on a rake.

Int: How do you avoid a bogey?

Gary: Simple, by dancing the waltz.

Int: No, I mean in golf.

Gary: I'm sorry, to avoid a bogey, you just subtract your real score, so you can put par.

Int: I see, now, how do you get out of a sand trap?

Gary: By not playing in Saudi Arabia.

Int: I heard your favorite is the iron. Why?

Gary: The iron? Yes, I use that to press my clothes.

Int: Sir, do you have any advice to give to your fellow golfers before we sign off?

Gary: Yes, when playing golf, always wear two pairs of pants.

Int: Why?

Gary: In case you get a hole in one.

In Africa, native tribes beat the ground with clubs and utter bloodcurdling screams. Anthropologists call it the release of primitive expression. Here, we call it golf.

Nonong Runes of Immuvit ran to the clubhouse and called his doctor. "My child swallowed two of my tees," he cried, "What will I do?" The doctor replied, "Practice your putting."

According to Richard Gomez, golf is very much like life. You're constantly working and driving hard only to end up in the hole.

While playing golf with Brother Benedict of La Salle he kept on staring at me until the ninth hole. "Is there anything wrong, Father?" I asked. "Nothing," he said, "I was just wondering if your parents are first cousins."

Former Executive Secretary Ruben Torres was asked by Ramon Jacinto, while playing on the golf course at South Woods, if he had heard the latest political jokes. "Hear them?" he said, "I work with them."

While watching the masters golf classic on television, John Lesaca told Jon Cuenco to turn the volume up. "SSSH," John said, "not while Couples is putting."

Ronnie Henares walked up to the grounds manager of Santa Elena. "I'm sorry but I'm afraid I made an accident in the third hole." "An accident?" the grounds manager said. "Yes, yes I... I... couldn't help it. I had to move my bowels," Ronnie replied. "Don't worry," the ground manager said. "It will only take a moment to clean it up." "I'm afraid it will take longer than a moment!" Ronnie said. "You see, I followed thru."

Col. Rico Javier of RPGA was playing golf at the Rivera Country Club with Nelson Cheng, a businessman from China. Their conversation turned to politics. "In China, we also have elections," Chen said. "When was your last election?" Col. Javier asked. "Just befo blekfast," Chen replied.

A golfer's wife goes shopping for shoes but forgot to wear her underwear. She sits down and the shoe salesman looks up her dress and says, "Wow! I'd like to fill that up with ice cream and eat it all up." The golfer's wife is offended and says, "I'm going home to tell my husband." When she got home, she tells her husband, "Sweetheart, I went shopping for shoes with no underwear on and the shoe salesman looked up my dress and said that he'd like to fill it up with ice cream and eat it all up. What are you going to do about it?" Her husband says, "There are three things I want to tell you. First, what are you doing shopping for shoes? You have more shoes than Imelda Marcos. Second, what are you doing shopping with no panties on and third, I'm not going to fight with a man who can eat all that ice cream!"

Golfer Jimmy Fabregas went to the BIR to pay his taxes with a smile. But the BIR wanted cash.

Golf Ball — A small dimpled object which remains on the tee while perspiring human fans it vigorously with a golf club.

Grade School Teacher: Bugsy, do you know what happens to boys who curse and use bad language when they're playing marbles?
Bugsy: Yes Ma'm, they grow up and become golfers.

Backswing: A menacing gesture, usually harmless.

Caddy: A man who stands behind a golfer and did not see the ball, too.

"John cheats at golf," Anjo said, as he entered the clubhouse. "He lost his ball in the rough and played another ball without losing a stroke." "How do you know he didn't find his ball?" Noel asked. "Because I picked it up and put it in my pocket," Anjo replied.

Golfer's Dream: A wife who will kiss his balls every morning to make his putter rise.

Paeng Nepumuceno says one of the advantages Bowling has over Golf is you never lose a Bowling Ball.

Ruben Torres said he played a round of golf with President Ramos. When they got to the 18th hole, a lady fan of the President asked, "Why does the President have two caddies?"

While playing in the Cavalier Cup, I hit a Toyota car that was to be awarded to the player in the tournament who shot a Hole in One. General Garcia approached me and said, "You have to hit the hole not my car."

Poch Borromeo thought Tiger Woods is a Golf Course.

Cardinal Sin: There are two things you can do with your head down — Play Golf and Pray.

Two clean-living golfers, Conrado and Jaime, were talking on the way to the 18th green. "Conrado," Jaime said, "if anyone of us dies first and goes to heaven, we should make it a point to let the other know how the golf courses in heaven are." "That's a good idea," Conrado replied. Sure enough, after a month, Jaime died. After a week Conrado was awakened by a voice in the middle of the night. It was Jaime's voice. "Conrado," the voice said, "the golf courses here in heaven are superb, I have been playing here everyday since I arrived and I always score under par. As a matter of fact we will have a tournament tomorrow." "I wish I can join you," replied Conrado. Jaime's voice said, "Of course you are joining! Your tee-off is at seven a.m. tomorrow."

Tony Verzosa, an Ilocano golfer, once joined Bert Nievera, Dave Brodett and Gary Lising for a round of golf. Tony requested for a caddy that can easily find golf balls. A burly caddy volunteered and said that he is an expert in finding golf balls. "Okay," Tony said, *"maghanap ka na nang bola para makaumpisa na ako."*

Amanda Page once asked me what those bulges in my pocket were. I said they're golf balls. "Oh," she said, "are they like tennis elbows?"

While playing in Sta. Elena Golf Course I was confronted by a big "Jabong" *"Anong gagamitin ko?"* I asked my caddy. My caddy said, *"lumang bola,* sir."

The difference between learning to play golf and learning to drive a car is that in golf, you never hit anything.

Gen. Angie Reyes once said to me, "Gary, you look very nice. Your golf shirt is very stylish, your pants are very smart, your golf bag is pure leather and your irons and woods are the most expensive in the world. It's such a shame you have to spoil it all by playing golf."

The secert to missing a tree when playing golf is to aim straight at it.
— General Angelo T. Reyes, Chief of Staff, AFP

Golfer's Wife: I tried to share his interest but his golf bag was too heavy for me.

Joey Stevens thinks that golf is a game where you yell fore, shoot a six, then write five.

When Executive Secretary Ruben Torres played with mega businessman Ramon Jacinto, Ramon noticed his caddy always looking at his watch. After Sec. Torres hit a shot that hooked, he notice his caddy looking at his watch. Ramon Jacinto was curious and asked Ruben's caddy why he was always looking at his watch. The caddy said it wasn't a watch he's looking at, it's a compass.

In most major tournaments, Toyota's Bobby Yupangco always donates a Toyota car for a hole in one. He always picks a par five hole that has a forced dog leg.

Pres. Ramos was playing with a couple of big businessmen. On the third hole, the President asked, *"Saan ba 'yung bola 'ko?"* One of the businessmen, who was obviously asking for a favor, replied, *"Nasa green na, sir!"* Pres. Ramos answered, *"Paano nangyari yon? Hindi pa ako tumira."*

Golfer Jaime Fabregas once hit an approach shot that hit the rake on the sand and landed on the fringe of the green. According to him that shot was one of his fringe benefits.

While playing with Rico Puno, I saw him hit a drive that hooked. His ball hit a tree then cut across the fairway, hit a post and sailed straight to the sand trap. His ball hit a rake and landed six inches to the hole, nearly making a hole in one. *"Sayang,"* Rico said, *"sana nilakasan ko."*

A golfer friend of mine was complaining that his sex life is hopeless because of his short putts.

Subas Herrero complains that if he puts the ball where he could see it, he couldn't hit it, and if he puts it where he could hit it, he couldn't see it.

There is a lady golfer who is so fat that when she stands on the fairway she looks like a golf ball.

Anjo Yllana and John Estrada were sitting on the 19th tee at Camp John Hay during the 6th Goma Cup, telling each other about the dreams they had the night before. John said, "I dreamt I was on a beautiful golf course. The weather was perfect, no winds, no waiting and every shot I took landed on the green. I had a wonderful time." Anjo said, "I dreamt I was on a beautiful island with Brooke Shields and Dawn Zulueta and we were having so much fun running around and skinny dipping." John looked at Anjo and said, "You had two beautiful women in your dream and you didn't call me? What kind of best friend are you?" "I called you," Anjo said, "but Janice said you were out golfing!"

Little boy: Sir, why does Secretary Seriles have very big nose holes?
Erap: Because his fingers are very fat.

Erap invited me to go to the casino in Las Vegas. But he became thirsty so we went to the vendo machine near the casino. Erap dropped a coin and a Coke can came out. He let me hold the Coke can. He dropped another coin and he let me hold the can again. This went on until I had an armload of Coke in cans. I said, "Sir, *ang dami na nito. Alis na tayo.*" "*Sandali lang,*" Erap said. "*Nananalo ako, eh.*"

A die-hard golfer always has two caddies whenever he plays golf. When I asked him why he needs two caddies, he replied that his wife asked him to do it. His wife feels he doesn't spend enough time with his two kids.

Q: What's the difference between a painter and a golfer when they are making love?
A: The painter make many strokes while the golfer wants to get in the hole in fast strokes as possible.

Cassius Casas tied Elkington after four rounds in the Bangkok Open. When he arrived at the first playoff hole, a reporter asked him, "How long have you been playing golf?" Casius looked at the reporter and said, "just finished."

Anjo Yllana arrived at South Woods and asked the caddy, "How much are six, five and four?" "Ten," said the caddy. Anjo said, *"Okey ka, sige, ikaw na lang ang mag-caddy sa akin."*

Erap keeps fit by swimming in his pool everyday. Sometimes there is water in the pool.

Erap was swimming in his pool with an effeminate senator, when a condom suddenly floated. Erap looked at the Senator and said, *"Umutot ka ano?"*

After playing 18 holes at the Orchard Golf Course with Rene Cayetano, we ordered lunch at the coffee shop. Since I lost the game, I was the one paying. When I asked for the bill, Rene said, "Please give a big tip to the waitress, she has three kids and one of them is mine."

Three senior golfers — one is 60 years old, the second one is 70 years old and the third one is 80 years old — were on their way to the second hole. The 60-year-old golfer said, "I wish I could take a healthy piss again." The 70-year-old then said, "I wish I could take a healthy crap again." The 80-year-old responds, "Every morning around 9:30 a.m. I take a healthy piss, around 11:00 a.m. I take a healthy crap. I just wish I could wake up before noon!"

A sex survey found that 50 percent of golfers have sex four to five times a week. The survey numbers dropped to 10 percent when the phrase "with partner" was added.

A golfer I knew died in bed with an 18-year-old. He was 68 years old. He came and went at the same time.

GIVE — an agreement between two losers who can putt.

Noel Trinidad's PRO keeps his head down so Noel can't see him laughing.

When ex-Pres. Ramos saw me swing my driver, he said I hit like Tigerger Woods ("*tigerger*" means "trembling" in Ilocano).

The first time President Erap played golf, he was so nervous. He drank a bottle of Johnny Walker Blue before he teed off. He shot the happiest 132 of his life.

Monry Mapa says that whoever designed the Sta. Elena Golf Course must have loved dogs. There are many dog legs — even the comfort room has a dog leg.

I asked Frankie Miñoza's advice how I can get more distance with my drive. He told me to hit the ball hard and then run backwards.

Richard Gomez says that whenever Noel Trinidad, Subas Herrero, Jaime Fabregas and Gary Lising play, the safest place to stay is in the fairway.

PLDT boss Tony Cojuangco, playing at Southwoods, hit his ball on the rough. He asks his caddie to look for his ball. The caddie put down his bag and looked for the ball. He found the ball but lost the bag.

Ramon Jacinto was once asked why he married twice. He says he took a mulligan.

Jennifer Rosales, the Philippines' pride, is a very good golfer. When she plays well, she wins, when she plays badly, she finishes second, when she plays terribly, she finishes third.

Tiger Woods: "You da man!"
Jimmy Fabregas: "You da puta!"

On a flight to Cebu for a golf tournament, I asked the flight attendant why I had to put my head between my legs in crash landings. "So you can kiss your ass goodbye," she replied.

On a recent KGB Tournament, Dick Ildefonso was asked what his score was. He said, three under. One under a tree, one under a bush and one under the water.

Cardinal Sin said most of our politicians are so corrupt. They always break 11 of the 10 commandments.

An aging golfer rejuvenated his sex life by taking three Viagra pills. After a week of sexual bliss, he died of overdose. The personnel at the funeral parlor had a hard time closing the coffin.

Do's and Dont's for golfers 60 and above on taking Viagra

1. Swallow the pill immediately; you might get a stiff neck.
2. Do not eat it like candy because it might harden your tongue.
3. After swallowing the pill, tie your sex organ with a strong string around your waist in order not to show the bulge.
4. Do not use Viagra when having sex with yourself.
5. Do not let your wife or girlfriend use it, because you will experience the sensation of trying to put an oyster inside a very stiff vagina.

The real spelling of the wonder pill is V-I-A-G-R-A not B-A-Y-A-G-R-A.

Erap banned Viagra in Subic, kasi tumitigas daw ang ulo ni Dick.

Agot, Sharon, Dieter and Gary:
One of these is an alien

DOTC Sec. Jun Rivera with a Pothole

Compañero Rene Cayetano was having a drink at the Ayala Alabang Club when he was approached by a man with dark glasses and a cane and introduced himself as a golf champion. "I am the champion of the Blind Golfers Association and as one champion to another, I would like to challenge you to a match that could be a fundraiser for the blind." He said to Rene that to make it more interesting, he challenged him to play at ₱5,000 a hole. Rene tried to avoid the challenge but the blind man was insistent. Rene finally agreed. "Okay, when will we play?" Rene asked. The blind man replied, "Any night, any night at all."

Richard was taking so much care before driving from the fifth tee that Anjo asked him, "Why the concentration?" "I want to make this shot a good one," said Richard. "My mother-in-law is in the club house watching me." "Impossible," said Anjo, "You could never hit her from this distance!"

Erap: Pare, ang ganda ng jeans mo.
Orly: Salamat, sir.
Erap: Anong brand 'yan?
Orly: Guess.
Erap: Levi's?

Erap dialed the phone. He wanted to talk to the UP President.
Erap: Hello? UP Diliman?
Operator: I'm sorry, sir, you got the wrong number. This is Padre Faura.
Erap: Oh, I'm sorry, Father.

According to Noel Trinidad, the secret of missing a tree while playing golf is to aim straight at it.

While playing a round of golf with Gen. Willy Florendo, he told me that my golf game is improving because I am missing the ball much closer than I used to.

According to Subas Herrero, golf is a game where the ball lies poorly and the players well.

According to Ronnie Henares, Mulligan is invented by a man who wanted to hit one more twenty-yard grounder.

In the third Goma Cup, pregnant Nadia Montenegro made a birdie putt from the fringe. She said, "That putt was so good, I could feel the baby applauding."

Cardinal Sin: Honor thy caddie, for he knoweth your real score.

According to Dick Villalon, "I have only one problem when I play golf. I stand too close to the ball after I've hit it."

Ana Puno went to the management of South Woods to complain that she had been stung by a bee. The manager looked very concerned. "Where?" he asked. "Between the first and second hole," Ana said. "Wow, you must have a wide stance," the manager replied.

The club officials at Sta. Elena were called to the 6th tee where three men were fighting. A fourth lay dead in a bunker. When the three men were pacified, they got an explanation. "That's my partner there on the bunker," said one man. "He had a stroke and these two shitheads want to add it to my score."

President Erap says real golfers don't cry when they line up their fourth putt.

DOTC Sec. Juan Rivera advises golfers: "It's good sportsmanship not to pick up lost golf balls while they are still rolling."

Poch Borromeo is really a consummate golfer. He even yells "fore" when he putts.

According to Jimmy Dichaves, a handicapped golfer is a man who plays with his boss.

Golfer Richard Steele, the international referee who officiated the Mira-Pacquiao fight arrived. He immediately went to the gym. He approached Manny's manager and said, "What is your fighter's name son?" "Pacquiao," the manager said. Richard Steele looked at him and said, "Pack you, too."

Congratulations to Sec. Jun Rivera for handling the very successful first Erap Golf Tournament. The proceeds will go to the poor kids who will be taught how to play golf.

Lawyer Estelito Mendoza, counsel to Mrs. Imelda Marcos, reacting to insinuations that her acquittal was due to more than the "normal course of justice," says he should not get credit. Why? Well, he says, Imelda paid him in cash.

Meralco Bossman Manolo Lopez says that the difference betwene electricity and lighting is that you don't pay for lighting.

All survivors of the Orient Pearl tragedy will be awarded free roundtrip tickets to a destination of their choice — courtesy of Sulpicio Lines.

The Supreme Court upheld the conviction of Leo Echegaray. He will be the first Filipino to die by lethal injection. When Echegaray protested and said he was afraid of needles, the prison doctors assured him that the injection would be painless.

After taking Viagra, Harold Smith, 60, keeled over and died. One newspaper claimed that he died from a lethal erection.

The efficiency expert developed a system that got all the men in the Senate on their toes — he raised the urinals by six inches.

President Erap vows to curb kidnappings in three months but the kidnappers have appealed for an extension.

There is a restaurant in the South called "Cooking Ng Ina Mo." Across the street is another restaurant called "Cooking Ng Ina Mo Rin." Further down the road is yet another restaurant called "Cooking Ng Ina Niyong Lahat."

Erap was on an official tour in France when one of the guides pointed out the statue of Joan of Arc. "She is one of our greatest French heroines," said the guide. Erap exclaimed, "Oh yes, I even know her husband, Noah!"

Erap was busy working in his office at his Greenhills residence. The maid knocked on the door and asked, "Sir, busy *ba kayo?*" Erap replied, *"Hindi ka ba nagbabasa ng dyaryo? Presidente na ako, hindi Bise!"*

Bold star Criselda Volks says that when she reaches super stardom status, she will change her name to Criselda Benz.

Foreign Affairs Secretary Domingo "Jun" Siazon is the ultimate, urbane diplomat. He always thinks twice before saying nothing.

A blind man walked into Rustan's Department Store with his seeing eye dog. He lifted the dog up by its tail and swung the dog round and round. The manager rushed up to the blind man and exclaimed, "What do you think you're doing?" The blind man replied, "Oh, just looking around!"

Erap was frantic. He just had to contact his son Jinggoy.
Beeper operator: Message please.
Erap: Jinggoy, you left your beeper with me.

Erap talking to one of the Asian beauties.
Erap: Miss Japan, what country are you from?

Dateline Iloilo — Ramon Catacutan, a blind masseur shot and killed Alberto Alon Chavez, also a blind man. According to the police, they had a violent quarrel over a blind date.

There is no truth to the rumor that Congressman Romy Jalosjos will be appointed as Chairman of Bantay Bata Foundation.

What's the difference between a condom and a parachute? If a parachute has a hole you die. If a condom has a hole, you live!

President Erap is contemplating on settling the PAL strike by buying the airlines himself. He will name the airline ERAPLANO, Inc.

According to Mr. Starr and Larry King, Monica Lewinsky is lying. That is not true. She was on her knees.

Did you know that our very own Vice President, Gloria Macapagal was once a classmate of President Clinton? She told me that during their final exams, VP Gloria took the written exams. President Clinton took the orals.

Dr. Benjamin Rigor, a UE Medical School graduate and Chairman of the Department of Anesthesiology, School of Medicine, University of Louisville, Kentucky was invited to a seminar at UST. He delivered his lecture without any feelings.

After his defeat at the presidential polls, Joe De Venecia is now very well rested. He is in the pink of health. He has no more eyebags. They turned into suitcases.

Ruben Pagaspas was accused of killing his mother and father. He asked the court to be lenient to him on the grounds that he is an orphan.

According to PAL Chair Lucio Tan, Mr. Ambrocio Co, a Chinese billionaire is negotiating with him to buy Philippine Airlines. If the deal pushes thru, Mr. Co will name the airline COPAL.

The main reason why Former Secretary of Health Estrella resigned is because he is sick.

SNN Boss Meckoy Quiogue, whose family owns Funeraria Nacional, is a man of habit. He always closes his letters with "Eventually Yours".

With the advent of bad movies, MTRCB Chair Armida Siguion Reyna plans to put an "O" rating in the movies which means "Not Suitable for Anyone".

Far East Bank's President, Obie Espiritu's advice: Don't ever tell a secret inside a bank because there are so many tellers.

Vic Lim of Robinson's Bank offered his services to President Estrada as a Chinese Interpreter. Vic knows Mandarin. He checks in there all the time.

Former Senator Jovito Salonga is a fellow who is always seen smiling. He smiles a lot because his teeth are the only things that are not wrinkled.

An official of the DOTC died and at his funeral, his co-worker approached Sec. Jun Rivera and asked if he could have the dead man's place. "I have no objection," the Secretary said, "if the undertaker is willing."

Redentor Romero, the Philippines' first and only international conductor, is writing his memoirs to help other Filipino musicians in his line of work. He taught my uncle in conducting. Now he is working as a conductor at the California Bus Lines.

Marilou Reyes Bloomquist manages an antique shop in Greenhills. Aga Muhlach, an antique collector, goes there every week to ask if there's anything new.

A fashion show called "Disenyo—Alay Para Sa Mahirap" was conceived by the

Mare foundation of the First Lady, Dr. Luisa Ejercito Estrada. Fortune Aleta is the overall chairperson. The models are politicians, movie actors and socialites. All designs cost a fortune.

Ombudsman Aniano Desierto has proven that he is a very fair man. The Desierto ruling not only cleared the brothers of Imelda, he also cleared the brother of Ferdinand. He is clearing all Marcos cronies. Yasay wants to be a Marcos crony.

Big fish eluded Lacson's men. They caught all the small fries.

US public to hear Monica Lewinsky's voice on internet. This time her mouth will have no obstruction.

Typhoon Loleng batters Bicol. The residents are panic stricken. President Estrada calmed them down. "Be cool," he said.

SBMA Chief Tong Payumo sells "Estradanomics" abroad. In Subic, "Payumonomics" will replace "Gordonomics". Both plans are comical.

The truth is out—Thomas Jefferson, the third President of the United States and author of the Declaration of Independence fathered a child by one of his slaves.

There is no truth to the rumor that President Clinton is a descendant of that union.

San Agustin Church organ rises again after 22 years. They reinforced this organ with several hundreds of Viagra pills.

A 9 mm bullet shattered the teeth of PO1 Efren Haringa fired by PO1 Rogelio Cuento. The bullet pierced his tongue and exited through the jaw. PO1 Haringa tried to bite the bullet but failed. He now has a tongue in cheek.

Q1:   What is a Dogma?
Ans.:   Mother of a puppy.

Did you know that there are over 50 million laws worldwide just to enforce the Ten Commandments?

The PCGG is wondering where President Marcos kept most of his money. Why don't they try looking at the 3,000 empty shoe boxes?

I never knew that Dong Puno was short. I noticed it only when I saw him at an ABS-CBN party dancing with sexy actress Joyce Jimenez. He looked like he had three heads.

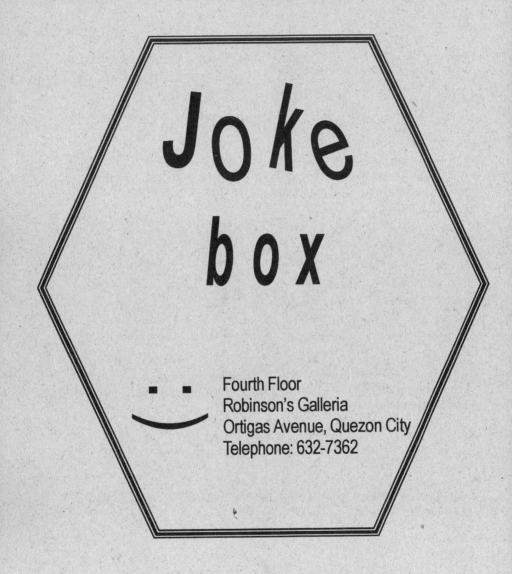

Jo*k*e

box

Fourth Floor
Robinson's Galleria
Ortigas Avenue, Quezon City
Telephone: 632-7362

Walter Bucaycay, a Filipino residing in California, was arrested for using food stamps to mail a watermelon.

At the Makati Medical Center, I met an Asian with German measles and a German with Asian flu.

Freddie Garcia of ABS-CBN is a very efficient executive. He has three secretaries: a tall girl for long hand, a short girl for shorthand and a midget for footnotes.

Former Speaker Ramon Mitra says that the only time a woman is justified to spit on a man's face is when his beard is on fire.

Poetic justice: A Frenchman who had his penis amputated in a sex change operation has since realized his mistake and wants to return to being a man. He was raped by the man who got his transplanted penis.

Father Tito Calauag celebrated his 40th birthday recently. The party was like an Ateneo homecoming. I am grateful to him because he was the one who convinced me to go back to my religious duties. Now I go to mass everyday except Sunday.

The new ABS-CBN sitcom starring lovebirds Richard Gomez and Lucy Torres is sure to rate in the charts. The title of the sitcom is *Richard Loves Lucy*. Wilma doesn't.

🚩

A group of hardened criminals raided the warehouse of Mercury Drug and carted off 50 million pesos worth of the anti-impotence pill Viagra. Gen. Ping Lacson promised to catch the hardened criminals and give them a very stiff sentence.

🚩

An exhibitionist identified as Alexander Capuli was arrested by cops for allegedly showing his shortcomings to victim Mary Jane Dalupang along Scout Fernandez Street. The suspect is devoid of shame. Capuli is not even natuli.

🚩

Presidential pal Atong Ang sued the *Inquirer* for having carried a paid announcement about his death. The publication of his obituary caused anxiety among his relatives and friends. The *Inquirer* rectified this faux pas by printing his birth announcement after his obituary.

🚩

Ruth Abacita, an optometrist from La Union, was raped and killed in San Fabian town. The police suspect one of her pupils.

🚩

Maalikaya suit against Mayor Mathay is dismissed. The court's decision caused a sensation.

In the MBA, the Pampanga Dragons won mainly because of Ato Agustin, known as Puff, the magic dragon. During the finals the Negros Slashers wanted to get a superhero to offset Agustin. They wanted Batman but they got Bat-og.

A big hit among jailbirds of the Quezon City Jail is a band called The No-Bail Band composed of inmates convicted of crimes that are not bailable. They are a big hit; most of the convicts in the audience always request for the song, "Please Release Me."

The Nevada Boxing Commission reinstated the boxing license of former heavyweight champ Mike Tyson on the condition that all his opponents wear steel earmuffs.

Rep. Alfred Romualdez is being sued by his former wife for millions of pesos. Kring- Kring Gonzales, the present wife of the congressman says she will help defray the expenses. They will not spend their honeymoon in Brunei. Till debt do us part.

Do you know why they built fences around the cemetery? Because people are dying to get in.

An inmate at the mental hospital escaped and raped a housemaid in Mandaluyong. Nut bolts and screws.

⚑

President Erap's defense of his friend Anwar Ibrahim affected 800,000 Filipino workers in Malaysia. Many Filipinos there say, "Malisia."

⚑

One of my favorite bombshell Glydel Mercado is finishing her movie titled *Sidhi*; her leading man is actor extra ordinaire Albert Martinez. Also starring in this movie is superstar Nora Aunor. She will have no dialogue. She will play the part of Pilar, a *pipi*.

⚑

There is a pharmacy in Pasig owned by Olga Dacuycoy Ivanovich, a Filipina who is married to a Russian national. The name of the pharmacy is Farmacia With Love.

⚑

Good news for ladies, there is now a foolproof birth control pill. Just hold it between your knees and don't let it drop.

⚑

President Estrada is one of the major sponsors in the wedding of Rep. Albert Romualdez and Kring Kring Gonzales. Because of the presence of the President at his wedding, Rep. Romualdez will stand erect.

⚑

VP Gloria Macapagal urged an end to female gender bias. On the contrary, women are always bias. Bias this, bias that.

An Italian tourist Frank Bogli was charged for bringing pornographic materials into the country. He complained to the police that he shouldn't be charged with pornography when he doesn't even own a pornograph.

Eight Iloilo police chiefs were sacked over jueteng. The Ilonggos are jueteng for them to be tried.

There is no truth to the rumor that Goma's wife Lucy Torres is related to the former Executive Secretary Ruben Torres.

The Vatican sanctions the use of Viagra pills. The church definitely believes in resurrection.

The Oval Office at the White House will be known officially as the Oral Office.

Italian priest Luciano Benedetti's abductors cut their ransom demand after the priest lessened their penance.

An American advertising man created a product that sells ideas. He writes his ideas into a piece of paper and puts them inside a tin can. It's called canned thoughts.

Rustom Padilla and Jake Roxas will do a torrid kissing scene in a new movie. Asked to comment on this love scene, Jake and Rustom cannot say anything; they were both tongue-tied.

Dionisio Alibudbud, a tricycle driver won an all-expense paid trip to Hong Kong in a raffle. This is his first trip abroad. When he arrived in Hong Kong his guide asked him where he wanted to go first. Albudbud said, "Chinatown."

Cardinal Sin was released from the Cardinal Santos Memorial Hospital. Now the hospital is sinless. Praise God.

Nereo Alfaro, a jobless patient at the Tondo Medical Center being treated for a recurring intestinal disease killed himself. Autopsy revealed that he is cured of his illness.

A mayor had officially opened a one-man art show. He was startled to see a nude painting of his wife reclining on a couch. Enraged, he confronted and accused the artist of making his wife pose nude in his studio. The artist denied this. He said he painted it from memory.

Rotarian Poch Borromeo on Egos:
Three words that can inflate an ego — "I love you"
Three words that can deflate an ego — "Is it in?"

Rep. Mike Defensor is a handsome, charming young man. He could be the first politician ever to turn into an actor.

President Erap's climb to the presidency is mainly due to the tireless campaign of his bosom buddy, Fernando Poe Jr.. Ronnie did this with no strings attached. All the President could say to his friend is, "Salamat Poe."

Jose Go, president of Orient Bank, has been banned for life. Jose Go is going. He will undergo orientation.

I am very lucky to have a very diligent lavandera. She washes my underwear even when I'm still wearing them.

Rep. Nani Perez of Batangas is into orchid crossbreeding. He is fond of crossbreeding. He once crossbred a monkey with a politician. He got a blooming idiot.

Parañaque City Councilor Anjo Yllana's very first bill was unanimously approved. His bill requires motorists to wear seatbelts whether the car is moving or parked.

Elizabeth Oropesa agreed to pose nude for eight of the country's noted artists for a book to be published by the Department of Tourism. Her nude session will be different from Ara Mina's. The artists will also be in the nude.

The honorable Henrietta De Villa, Ambassador of the Philippines to the Vatican, presented a bottle of Tanduay Rhum to Pope John Paul II. The Pope tasted the rhum and he felt like he was Steven Seagal.

Ara Mina is venturing into singing. She has all the equipment for singing: nice face, nice voice and very nice lungs.

Chowking drops Philander Rodman, the brother of NBA's superstar Dennis Rodman, from its basketball team. Philander, like his famous brother, also has colored hair which he also changes everyday. Trouble is, he hides it under his shorts.

President Erap did a wonderful job in Singapore. His three days in Singapore is better than his first 100 days.

Ambuklao Dam, Angat Dam and Linga Dam are overflowing. Claude Van Damme has nothing to do with it.

Salvador Baka, a rancher, opened a steak house in Glorietta. The prices of steaks are reasonable. A T-bone steak costs ₱75, with meat, ₱600.

Floods caused by typhoon Iliang devastated the streets of Manila. The traffic watch turned into baywatch.

AIDS is now widespread in the Philippines — acute income deficiency syndrome.

Some of the President's men are members of the KGB — Kung Gabi Bakla.

A general who was assigned to the task force asked President Erap for a transfer. He was transferred to Jolo. Now he has a tankless job.

A retired bold actress recently gave birth to a baby boy. The baby had ten fingers just like any normal baby. Seven on one hand, three on the other.

Gov. Lito Lapid assigned Col. Calinisan to do the clean-up of the debris left by super typhoon Iliang.

Gloria Macapagal's Chief of Staff Willie Villarama says drinking liquor makes him feel like a child. After every drinking session, he always crawls back home.

Airborne traffic formally launched by DOTC Secretary Vicente Rivera. The only problem is how to put traffic signs up in the air.

Noe Lopez, son of Rustan's Supermarket's big boss Jun Lopez, is behind the success of Starbucks. He learned the coffee business after taking so many coffee breaks.

Many Singaporean tourists are now here buying Filipino paintings. They bring them back home where they frame and hang them.

According to Dr. Margie Holmes, when you go to sleep with a sex problem, you wake up with a solution in hand.

Ara Mina's ideal man: tall, dark and vasectomized.

Bold star Aya Medel says that diabetes is hereditary. She inherited her diabetes from her sugar daddy.

Erap sees stronger ties in Singapore. I hope it's not a rope.

Rannie Tuason is a dentist who always takes an oath before pulling a tooth. "I promise to pull the tooth, the whole tooth and nothing but the tooth. So help me God."

Q: What is the similarity between Michael Jordan and a Christmas tree?
Ans.:   They both have colored balls.

Pedro Tubigan, a fire eater at the carnival in Cubao, got a standing ovation for eating firecrackers. For an encore, he tried to smoke a stick of dynamite. He was eventually fired by the carnival's owner.

Poch Borromeo of GNC is a very superstitious man. He walks around with a rabbit's foot. His other foot is normal.

Col. Rodolfo Caisip of Valenzuela said that there are no kidnappings under his jurisdiction. What about the Chiong case? Before making a decision, he should think about it first. He made this statement after paying a ransom.

Six top jockeys at the San Lazaro Racetrack were suspended for not wearing briefs.

National Security adviser, Alexander Aguirre belittled reports that Vice President Gloria Macapagal is planning to lead a military takeover during the President's absence. Palace says that RP is safe while Erap is away. Remember, while the cat is away, the mouse will play.

Mayor Fred Lim has been a dedicated law enforcer and public servant for years. Now he can continue his crusade for peace and justice through his new TV show entitled *Katapat: Mayor Fred Lim*. The show will not include Chinese nationals.

Yellow water is coming out of faucets in Manila exclusively for Chinese citizens. This water is different. You drink it yellow and it comes out clear.

Be careful! Vegetables with Formalin are in the market. Sonia Alibudbud, a vendor said that she sells these vegetables to funeral parlors where they in turn feed the vegetables to the cadavers in order to preserve them.

"I HATE IT WHEN THEY TAKE UP A SPORT TO BE NEAR YOU
AND TURN OUT TO BE GOOD AT IT."

Claude Van Damme, a martial arts expert, was recently here on a visit. Monsour Del Rosario was asked what he thinks of Jean Claude. Monsour said, "Frankly, my dear, I don't give a Van Damme."

Ruffa Gutierrez vehemently denied that Internet nude photo of herself. She assigned an internet expert to examine the photograph. She is right. The findings showed that the face is real but the body is that of Edu Manzano.

The official National Bird of the United States is the Bald Eagle. By act of Congress the Bald Eagle will now be replaced by the Spread Eagle.

The latest craze in the fashion world today is the Pitoy Moreno designer jeans. The zipper is at the back.

TB among public school teachers rising. TB or not TB, that is the question.

Q: Why do Indian women have red sports on their foreheads?
Ans.: So you will know if she's bola-bola or asado.

In a every short time Tong Payumo has become a household word. Garbage is also a household word.

Jose Go is a successful banker of an unsuccessful bank.

Our advice to Finance Secretary Ed Espiritu: the only way to balance the Philippine budget is to tilt the country.

Quote of the day: I have so many problems, if anything happens today, it will be two weeks before I can worry about it.—Erap Estrada

Executive Secretary Ronnie Zamora is also a man of honor. If you want to make him laugh on Wednesday, tell him a joke on Monday.

Erap's drinking diet: it does not do anything to the rest of your body, but it makes your head lighter.

On my recent trip to Malacañang, I asked the President if I could tell a political joke. "You don't have to Gary, there are too many of them around," he replied.

Have you heard about Cardinal Sin's accident? He was taking his usual walk when a motor boat hit him.

Did you know that Ronaldo Valdez is a hypochondriac? He even left instructions that when he dies he wants to be buried next to a doctor.

Ara Mina is planning to run for Congress in the next elections. She is the most ideal person to run for office because she has nothing to hide.

Brownouts are again being scheduled. But why? The counting of votes is already over.

Princess Punzalan, speaking on behalf of the KAPP, says that nudity in itself is a crime, not against the laws of men but against the laws of God. This means that whenever we take a bath we commit a crime.

Secretary Puno says that he expects one million new jobs in 2000. He promised jobs but not salaries.

Tourism Boss Gemma Cruz Araneta and ex-tourism head Mina Gabor are engaged in a Senate word war. The verbal tussle is a tourist attraction.

House Speaker Manny Villar vows job security to all security guards.

An aging actor asked his doctor for something that would enhance his manhood in preparation for his date in the evening. The doctor gave him a Viagra pill. The next morning, the actor went back to the doctor to ask something to soothe his arms. The doctor asked why. The actor said his date did not show up.

Presidential Spokesman Jerry Barican says that President Joseph Estrada is not interested in a second term. He will just wait for the third term.

According to the *Inquirer*, the scientific name of "Pikon" is JOSEPHUS EJERCITOS ESTRADAMUS.

The Cherry Hills tragedy will soon be made into a movie. It will star Cherie Gil; Gil Portes will direct.

The scientific name of coffee mug: MASLOG.

Puno to Santiago: DILG (Don't Interfere Let Go)

If you fight with Sen. Juan Flavier you should protect your kneecaps.

Michael Jackson started life as a black man. Now he's a white girl.

Arnold Schwarzenegger looks like a cocoon full of walnuts.

Q: Cardinal Sin, do you pray for the senators?
Cardinal Sin: No, I look at the senators and pray for the country.

I know a donkey who has an I.Q. of 135. He's a smart ass.

What is the opposite of Saklolo? Lick Lola.

I still remember the first time I had sex. I was so scared because I was all alone. — Gary Lising

An athlete in the SEA Games came home prematurely because he said that he had cancer of the toenails. The next day his nails died.

Q. What is your stand on Euthanasia?
Erap: Same as the youth of America.

Q. What would you do if you're in a room with Saddam Hussein, Khaddafi and the editor of the *Inquirer* and you have a gun that has only two bullets?
Erap: Shoot the editor twice.

The Erap political principle: if two wrongs don't make a right, they three.

Whenever Erap plays golf, he always has 3 caddies, one for the right in case he hooks, one for the left in case he slides, and the third one is for the fairway. The third caddy does nothing.

Erap: Golf was invented so that even the man who isn't in politics will have something to lie about.

There is a prostitute in Makati that has a degree in Psychology — she can blow your mind.

How do you know that President Erap just used the computer? Because of the streaks of white correction fluid on the computer screen.

When do Filipinos stop masturbating? When their wives die.

What does a one-legged ballet dancer wear? A one-one.

Bombshell starlet Aya Medel was the special guest in the TV comedy show *Bubble Gang*. She showed her bubbles.

In the movie, *Pahiram Kahit Sandali*, Ara Mina has a love scene with Christopher where both of them are covered with black forest cake and they lick each other off. The black forest of Ara tasted much better than Christopher's.

An old matinee idol was looking at his eighth child intently when he decided to confront his wife. "Sweetheart," he said, *"Bakit ang gaganda ng pitong anak natin pero 'yung bunso, ang pangit? Sabihin mo ang totoo, hindi ako magagalit. Patatawarin kita. Kinaliwa mo ako ano?"* The guilt-laden wife decided to tell the truth. "Sweetheart," she said, *"hindi na kaya ng konsensiya ko. Sasabihin ko na ang totoo. Walo ang anak natin, 'yung bunso lang ang tunay mong anak."*

Parimpunan Harahap, an Indonesian, confessed to raping 203 females: 200 animals and 3 human beings.

Saving Private Ryan starring Tom Hanks is a bonafide blockbuster in the Philippines. Octo Arts boss Orly Ilacad will also do a similar movie locally. Tentative title is *Saving General Ver.*

Ina Raymundo was so excited when her suitor gifted her with a PB diamond. She immediately had it appraised. She was so disappointed when the jeweler said that PB means "puwet ng baso".

Flutist Long Cuenco composed a medley featuring songs with fruits in them. E.G. Watermelon Man, Strawberry Fields, Apple Blossom Time, and the Banana Boat Song. Long named his medley "Flute Salad". Sounds delicious!

DFA Secretary Domingo Siazon says the term "blockade" was not used by the President. He used the word "block". "Blockade" means to surround the area and not let anybody in or out. "Block" means to stop a man from shouting. Block is beautiful.

Controversial consultant Chito Roque quits as consultant to Sen. Nikki Coseteng. Nikki in turn will serve as consultant to Chito Roque.

Comparison of Armed Forces: Philippines and China

	China	Philippines
Personnel	2.93 million	106,500
Reserve	1.2 million	131,000
Army	2.2 million	68,000
Navy	265,000	23,000
Air Force	470,000	15,000
Tanks	9,600	456
	29 submarines	1 Frigate
Ships	1,602 vessels	1.2 million bancas (200 motorized)

David and Goliath — if worse comes to worse we can clobber them in the sea.

Conversation during Erap's state visit to Washington

Erap: Mr. President, I came precisely to ask for your help.

Clinton: What's on your mind, Mr. President?

Erap: Well, my scientists are now building a spaceship that will revolutionize the space age.

Clinton: In what way?

Erap: We will build a spaceship that will land on the sun.

Clinton: Land on the sun? Mr. President, by the time you arrive, your spaceship will be burnt to a crisp!

Erap: We have solved that problem, sir.

Clinton: How?

Erap: We will go at night.

Erap Aide: Sir, *may* message *na kailangang maipadala kaagad kay* Secretary Mercado. *Ano'ng gagawin ko? Ititilex ko ba o ikikibol?*
Erap: *I pac mo.*

President Erap underwent eye surgery successfully. Now he's beginning to see the light.

Reporter: Sir, what do you think of synchronized elections?
Erap: It's all right as long as its not at the same time.

Erap speaking to a crowd in Ali Mall.
Erap: As everybody knows this mall is named after the greatest boxer of all times — Muhammad Mall.

During his heyday, President Erap went to the casino and made a mental bet. He nearly lost his mind.

Presidential spokesman Jerry Barican says he is very loyal to the President. He says he supports Erap when he's right and he keeps quiet 90 percent most of the time.

Wife: *May nagsabi sa akin na nambababae ka raw.*
Husband: *Hindi totoo 'yun. 'Yong babae ang nanlalalake.*

Secretary Rivera and President Erap were playing golf. In the middle of the fairway, Erap asked Secretary Rivera, "*Ano'ng* playing *ka na ba* — three?" Secretary Rivera said, "*Hindi*, two *lang*. Practice swing *lang 'yon*." Erap then replied, "*Bakit ka nagmura pagkatapos ng* practice swing *mo?*"

Meckoy Quiogue, who owns Funeraria Nacional, gave Bata Reyes 10 sets of false teeth as gift for winning at the SEA Games.

Reporter: Sir, what can you say about Cherry Hills tragedy?
Erap: Yes, it's very sad. By the way, can you give my condolences to Rosemarie?

When Erap was in his early twenties, God appeared to him. God explained to Erap about the wonders of heaven. God said that in heaven, one peso is equivalent to 10 million pesos and one minute is equivalent to 10 million years. God asked Erap if he wanted anything. Erap said, "God can you give me one peso?" And God, in all His glory, replied, "Just a minute".

Erap went to the video shop to return a tape he borrowed.
Erap: *Isasauli ko itong* tape.
Video clerk: *Bakit po?*
Erap: *Sira, walang lumalabas na* picture *at wala pang* sound. *Sayang*, suspense thriller *pa naman.*

Video clerk: *Ano po ang* title *ng* tape?
Erap: Head cleaner.

Erap said that if the first born of Beaver and Jackie would be a girl, they will name it Beaverly.

Erap went to a night spot and saw the sign on the door that read "Below 18 not allowed."
Erap to Aide: 17 *lang tayo, tawagin mo yong* driver, *isama natin siya para maging* 18 *tayo.*

Erap describes Senator Juan Flavier as a cool cat — kulang sa sucat.

Gen. Angelo Reyes: Mr. President, I think our troops are overfatigued.
Erap: Over fatigue? Ok, let them wear khaki.

Trivia: Manuel Conde, the legendary actor and director of the immortal film *Siete Infantes de Lara* is the father of noted TV director and the original Mister Shooli, Jun Urbano. He is doing the remake of his father's masterpiece, but in a bolder genre. The title of his film is *Siete ang Panty ni Lara.*

246

Director Tikoy Aguiluz is also doing a sequel of his film *The Boatman*. The sequel will be titled *Boatman & Robin*.

Philippine Board of Advertisers
Model Interview

Interviewer: Good Evening. In honor of tonight's occasion, we have invited one of the top male models in the advertising world. His services are in demand mainly because his physical appearance has revolutionized the thinking of the advertising agencies in the world. He has been all over the world because of his uncanny ability to sell just by using his face. He's here tonight to give some interesting insights on advertising. Please help me welcome our guest.

(Enter Gary)

Int: Good evening, Sir. We're very proud to have you here with us tonight.

Gary: I know that.

Int: May we have your name, sir?

Gary: Why? Are you unhappy with your own?

Int: No, I meant what is your name?

Gary: I'm sorry. Actually, I have two names depending upon the product.

Int: Why do you have two names?

Gary: Well, if the product projects Christianity, then I use my Christian name and if the product deals with the Muslims, then I use my Muslim name.

Int: What is your Christian name?

Gary: Christian Espiritu.

Int: And what is your Muslim name?

Gary: Mohammed De Niro.

Int: Mohammed De Niro?

Gary: Actually, I'm an Italiano. My mother is Ita, and my father is Ilocano.

Int: How should we call you?

Gary: You can call me anytime.

Int: No, what name should we call you?

Gary: Just call me Nick.

Int: Nick?

Gary: Yes, that's my nickname.

Int: I see. I hope you don't mind. May we ask you a few questions about advertising?

Gary: Go ahead.

247

Int: There must be something very special about you to be chosen as a model.

Gary: Well, I was chosen because of my unique quality.

Int: What quality is that?

Gary: I'm the only abortion that lived.

Int: I see. You are a top model even in the United States. Have you ever refused a big contract?

Gary: Yes, once when *Cosmopolitan Magazine* asked me to pose like Burt Reynolds for the centerfold and I refused even if the fee was $ 1 Million.

Int: Why did you refuse?

Gary: Because my hands are too small.

Int: You mentioned that you use your Christian name when you endorse a Christian product. What Christian product have you posed for?

Gary: The Saint Peter condom.

Int: You posed for an ad using a condom?

Gary: No, *I* was the condom.

Int: What product did you pose for using your Muslim name?

Gary: The Rizal Alli Survival Kit. It is now being used by all the people living in Davao. It's all sold out.

Int: What other products have you made popular?

Gary: I popularized the product called Rexona, a very special deodorant for the armpits.

Int: What's so special about it?

Gary: It won't let you down as long as your armpit is down but when it's up, that's a different story.

Int: I heard you also endorsed a product called Sugar Foot.

Gary: Yes. A long time ago but people got mad at me for that.

Int: Why, what happened?

Gary: Whenever I do my thing they always say, "I don't care if they call you Sugar Foot, get your foot out of my Nescafé!"

Int: I understand you have travelled around the world because of the high demand for your services. Have you been to India?

Gary: Of course I've been to India.

Int: What commercial product did you endorse in India?

Gary: Umbrellas.

Int: Have you been to Russia?

Gary: Yes, I promoted a sanitary product.

Int: What product is that?

Gary: It's called the Stallion Sanitary Napkin. It was a big flop in Russia.

Int: Why did it flop?

Gary: Because of its slogan: "It takes the red out."

Int: What was the last place you visited before coming here?

Gary: L.A.

Int: L.A.?

Gary: Yes, Legaspi, Albay.

Int: Who among the Filipino commercial models is at par with you?

Gary: Fernando Poe, Jr. I hate to admit it but I think he is the best. Better that I am.

Int: Why do you say that?

Gary: Because he did his first commercials without doing anything except ride a horse and got paid several millions.

Int: I heard you are doing a commercial with him. Is this true?

Gary: Yes. It is also a beer commercial. I will be the horse.

Int: What other commercials are you presently doing?

Gary: Well, I have been tapped to do the Carlsberg commercial in Denmark. This will be a real test. It will be different.

Int: How will it be different?

Gary: I will do it in Tagalog.

Int: What in your opinion is the basic requirement in order to be a top advertising model like you?

Gary: Actually, there are only two requirements. You have to be very intelligent and very, very handsome.

Int: (Looks at Gary) I'm surprised.

Gary: I'm surprised, too. You see, I'm not intelligent.

My putter is behind the golf bag